THE GIFTS FROM LOSING YOU

FINDING MEANING IN LIFE WHILE LIVING WITH TRAGEDY

SARA GREEN

The Gifts From Losing You
Finding Meaning In Life While Living With Tragedy
Sara Green

ISBN: 978-1-7362413-0-1

Cover Design by Pete White: bywhite.com

For Patrick Michael Green,
our cherished son and much-loved brother.

We will love you forever.

For those who knew and loved Patrick, I hope this memoir gives
you comfort and a place to come to when you are missing him.

For the future generations of our family, while you will never get
the chance to meet Patrick in person, may you feel as if you know
him through the love and words of this tribute to him.

For those who are navigating grief and loss,
may you find hope and inspiration.

CONTENTS

FOREWORD

How do I write a foreword for a book about our deceased son written by my wife? That question had been running around in my head for months. It felt so surreal. This was not something I ever thought I would have to write, but here we were, living a reality we never saw coming.

I've marveled at Sara's dedication since she started this book-writing process. The words have just kept flowing, like lava from a volcano, tens of thousands of words, and while the subject is tragic, her intent has been to help others, not just document the grief we've all experienced.

Since losing Patrick, Sara has used her health coaching skills and intuitive insight to explore and understand her pain and emotional anguish. It has been tough; however, she has found a way to live with her grief; she hasn't let it defeat her or us.

Sara has fiercely protected Patrick's memory and guided our family's grieving. All four of us have taken different paths in this respect, and Sara has ensured none of us has strayed off track or become lost along the way.

Over hundreds and hundreds of hours, Sara has sifted through Patrick's 19 years to preserve the memories, distill the lessons, and share the gifts with us and others. It has been a long and, at times, emotionally draining process for her, but she has loved hearing from so many family, friends, and even total strangers (to us) who were positively impacted by Patrick.

I'm thrilled that our two girls, Annabelle and Matilda, have been able to witness their mother rise up and work tirelessly to create this legacy honoring their much-loved brother. I feel as if each day since the accident has been a personal 1/10, with key dates and random times being 0/10. I'm sure a lot of people experiencing grief feel the same. Hopefully, our story can assist those struggling with loss and help them navigate the way through their own hard times.

Christopher Green,
Patrick's father

INTRODUCTION

Welcome to my heart. What I am about to share with you is an intimate and authentic memoir about losing someone who I deeply and greatly love, my magnificent son, Patrick.

This is a story of personal tragedy, immeasurable love, heartbreak, and sadness, coupled with gratitude, courage, and perseverance. I see my family's experience as an opportunity to serve and help others as our story has meaning in the gifts that it has given us. I feel strongly about this because Patrick's death should not remain senseless. My family cannot lose our son, brother, grandson, nephew, and cousin without there being some blessings to share. Patrick's friends cannot lose their mate without learning from the lessons available to them in his passing.

Shifting our view from devastation to seeing something good is far from an easy task. You may be reading this and thinking, in grief, what could possibly be good? In trying to cope with your own loss, perhaps all you can see is darkness and not a sliver of light. I get it, I really do. Losing Patrick has shaken me to my core; I feel the pain in every cell of my body. The dark moments are all-consuming, and especially in the early days, they felt as if they would last forever. In my healing, I have focused on the gifts we have received to help lift me out of my despair. I acknowledge that this is my experience, which may look and feel vastly different to someone else's. I recognize that there is extreme suffering in the world where there are no blessings to be found. I honor each of your stories, and I offer mine from a place of love.

Perhaps you have lost a child or a loved one. Possibly you're supporting someone close to you who has experienced crushing heartbreak. Loss generates a grief response, and grief looks and feels different for everyone.

You may be able to relate to the waves of sadness that hit you like a tsunami, where you can't get your footing, and you can't take a deep breath; you feel as if you may drown. I hope I can give you a nurturing space to explore your loss and find a way to start living with your grief. I hope you can open your heart and mind to know that you can survive, your life still has meaning, your feelings matter, you can find peace, you are loved, you are enough, your story is powerful, your truth is your anchor, your vulnerability is a strength, and you are not alone. I hope that what I share in these pages can bring even the slimmest shard of light to your darkness. A softening to the raw edges of your pain. A bridge to hope for your days ahead.

Many books have been written about grief and, at first, I doubted whether there needed to be another one. But one day, about four months after losing Patrick, I woke up, and I just knew that I needed to do this. I was called to write. I asked Patrick what he thought. Straight away, I heard a response, "Mum, you have to do it. I will help you. My words will come through you." That was all the confirmation I needed. I let go of the doubt, and I knew that through our tragedy, I could be of service to others.

This memoir follows our lives during the first year after Patrick's death. From the soul-crushing moment when we found out that we had lost him to the days, weeks, and months that followed. I will take you on a journey of love, heartbreak, sorrow, discovery, purpose, healing, self-care, and generosity as my family and I faced all the ever so painful firsts and received the many gifts that we never thought possible. The gifts that have come to us are the light, and they have helped us begin to heal.

Revealing our pain is difficult but telling the tough stories is what connects us. I share our experience from a place of authenticity and love. I am real and honest because I think this helps us remember that we are not that different. We will all suffer a loss of some kind in our lives. Grief is non-discriminatory; it touches all of us regardless of who we are.

The chapters are non-sequential; they are based on themes. I discuss how to look after yourself in grief and ways to find purpose in your life following a tragedy. I share words from Patrick himself, his dad, and his sisters, as well as stories from others about their encounters with him and how he left an everlasting imprint on their hearts. I speak to the lessons Patrick taught us so that we may all be inspired to be better in his memory. I discuss life beyond the physical body and the communication that is possible with our loved ones who have passed. This book serves as a legacy for all of Patrick's goodness that he so willingly shared and gave to others.

This is my family's love story and tribute to Patrick. As you read it, I hope you feel the immense love that is woven through and radiates from the pages. You will experience many emotions as you learn about our beautiful boy. There is a lot of sadness but also immeasurable love and light. Take my hand and allow yourself to feel it all. I hope you smile. Patrick would want you to smile. He would want you to soak up all of the love and the joy that we had in our time with him.

Patrick was, and always will be, deeply loving, fun-seeking, charming, inclusive, loyal, uplifting, inquisitive, magnetic, sensitive, handsome, humble, evolved, and compassionate. These are the reasons why he is now being remembered as someone we and others will never forget.

"When you love a person with every part of you, you are never ready to lose them. It will never be the right time. Ever."

CHAPTER ONE

LOSING YOU

THURSDAY NIGHT

On June 27, 2019, our cherished and deeply loved son and brother, Patrick Michael Green, was ripped away from us in a sudden accident. The shock was indescribable; the pain was even worse. Searing, suffocating, breathtaking pain. How could this be real? Not him, not us. Our hearts instantly shattered. The light around us immediately dimmed. Our close family of five was changed forever.

After being given the utterly life-altering news, I fell to the floor and kept shaking my head no and repeating the words "I can't." It's a moment I'll never forget, but at the same time, it all feels like a blur.

Nothing can prepare you. It's true; you never think it will happen to you and your family. You know it happens to people; it may have happened to someone you know. You just never want to be that someone. However, at some point in our lives, we will all be that someone because we know that death is a part of life. We know we must surrender the need to understand why and be comfortable in not knowing. When you love a person with every part of you, you are never ready to lose them. It will never be the right time. Ever. The Divine Order of Life gets to choose.

Patrick lost his life instantly. He was the passenger on an All-Terrain Vehicle that flipped, and his injuries were fatal. Writing that sentence and seeing it in words fills me with immense despair. This wasn't supposed to be his story.

Losing him was a parent and sibling's worst nightmare. Time stood still. I felt as if I was drowning in my pain. We were desperate to get to Patrick; he was over an hour's drive away. We got in the car and started the horrendous journey to be with his body. It was surreal. "This cannot be happening. Please, someone, tell us that this is not real," screamed the voice in my head.

During the drive, despite our despair and deep shock, we made a family promise that we wouldn't let this break us. This type of trauma can destroy families, even the strong ones. This was a very powerful commitment and a solidifying moment. We were in this together, and we would survive it for one another and for Patrick.

My husband, Chris, started to make phone calls to our family and friends in Australia. Each time he recounted our tragedy, my heart broke a little more. When making my calls, I could barely get the words out. The news spread quickly on social media and via text. Our communities in Cleveland, Melbourne, and Sydney were overcome with shock and sadness. Hearing Patrick's younger sisters, Annabelle (17 years old) and Matilda (13 years old), answer phone calls and respond to messages confirming what no one wanted to learn was true was devastating. They were too young to lose their brother and best friend, who they loved with all their hearts. "Please, I'm begging, someone tell us that this is not real," I kept thinking over and over.

A few hours later, numb and shattered, we returned home. The night was sleepless, although I desperately craved sleep so that I could wake later and realize it was a horrid dream. We were catapult-ed into a reality we would never have chosen. Our existence became divided between life with Patrick in the physical and life without him. Somehow we had to learn to live in the without. We would al-ways be a family of five; it felt so wrong to now have only four people in our house. The energy in our home immediately changed. Losing him left a gaping hole in our hearts and in our lives. This hole felt like a bottomless pit, and on that first night following Patrick's death, I didn't care if that hole swallowed me up. If the hole didn't, then the pain surely would.

THE DAYS THAT FOLLOWED

From the morning after the accident, Chris, myself, and our girls were shown incredible acts of generosity and support from our friends and our local community. We didn't have any family in Cleveland, but we had amazing friends who were like family to us. We were instantly cocooned in love. Relatives and friends traveled from Australia and around the US to be with us as quickly as they could. They were all suffering their own unfathomable grief, having lost their first-born grandson, nephew, and friend. We also felt the deep love and support from those in Australia who could not be here. Theirs was a heavy cross to bear as they mourned the loss of Patrick from afar, wanting so much to be with us.

Life quickly became single focused. All I thought about was Patrick and how to look after Chris, Annabelle, Matilda, and myself so that we could somehow get through this. I knew without a doubt that Patrick did not want us to crumble and fall apart. With his guidance, we began to try to put one foot in front of the other and navigate this unchartered territory that we never imagined we would find ourselves in. We were very fragile and unsteady, but we did it for him and for us. Patrick became an incredible beacon of light, showing us the way. I credit our strength to him.

Our home became the gathering place for people in our community to come and share their grief and seek comfort from one another. Hundreds of people visited. While I greatly appreciated their kindness, if I'm honest, my first instinct was to retreat and be private. However, I realized that I had to surrender to the flood of support, it had a beautiful life of its own, and it came from a place of pure love for Patrick and for us. We had never experienced anything like it. There were lots of tears, hugs, and countless stories shared about Patrick. His friends sat in his bedroom upstairs for hours. There was a constant stream of kids going up and down the stairs, as sitting amongst his belongings provided solace and connection for them, which I understood; I felt the same way.

Deep shock had started to set in. I felt as if I was operating on autopilot as I received visitors; I don't recall many of the conversations or details about those first few days. Brief flickers of moments come to mind, but it's mostly a solemn haze. Our dear friends immediately stepped in and carried us. There was so much to do, but Chris and I were in no state to even know where to start. We felt completely cared for as the necessary funeral plans were made, with our consultation when needed.

My Angels (close friends) dropped everything in their lives to look after me. They scooped me up off the floor, literally, and they made sure I rested and attempted to eat. They stood close by me as I greeted guests watching for any signs that I needed to take a break. They lay with me, held me, massaged my head, wiped my tears, and told me I could survive this. They took over the running of our house, did the dishes, managed the food drop-offs, and even got the fridge repaired when it broke down due to unprecedented use. One or more of them were with me from when I woke up to when I went to bed, they seamlessly worked as a team, and I remember being so grateful for their selflessness and dedication. They were there for me in every sense of the word, without me even having to ask. It was as if they shared their own language between them; they just knew what I needed.

There were also other dear friends doing so much for us behind the scenes that I was aware of. There was magic happening born from a place of true friendship and the desire to do whatever had to be done to ease our load. Reflecting on it now, I am in awe of all of them. I will never forget their devotion and love.

On Saturday morning, two days after the accident, we were jolted into our harsh reality when the doorbell rang; it was the funeral director. I remember thinking to myself, "Please, someone tell him to go away." I didn't want to need him. He was such a lovely man, and he was just doing his job. I suspect he was used to grieving families resisting his presence. Unfortunately for him, he was a glaring reminder of what we had lost, and I admit it, I hated seeing him come through our door. You never imagine yourself having to plan your child's funeral. It's supposed to be the other way around. Yet here we were, facing this nightmare with no way out, no escape. Patrick was our priority, however, and we would do our best for him.

Each decision was so confronting. Having to sign the consent form for your child's cremation is indescribably traumatic. For the funeral, we wanted Patrick's Australian heritage to be represented as our traditions were a little different back home. There wouldn't be a wake held before the service, there wouldn't be a procession into the church, and his casket would be draped with an Australian flag. Our requests were willingly respected, and we were thankful for the care and compassion that was shown to us.

That Saturday afternoon there were lots of people at our house. I was lying down. There was a storm with heavy rain. I remember thinking that it felt cleansing. Friends started calling out to me to come downstairs. I went outside to see the most vibrant double rainbow arching in its glory right over our house. I stood there, soaking up this sign from Patrick. He was already doing amazing things to show us that he was right there with us.

On Sunday morning, we met with Father John, the priest from our local catholic church, where we would celebrate Patrick's life. Again, my resistance was high; it was another situation in which we never expected to find ourselves and another reminder of our heartbreaking reality. More decisions had to be made, and commemorating Patrick continued to be our compass and our guiding light. I was hyper-focused on making sure that we honored Patrick's life in a way that represented him and his age. I wanted every detail, from the readings to the music, to pay tribute to him authentically. It had to represent a 19 year old. Patrick loved music, and I knew that this was a wonderful avenue to connect us all to him. It was likely that Father John had never received such modern song requests, and we were thankful for his flexibility.

Our family arrived from Australia that Sunday night. We were so appreciative that Chris's parents, Rita and Michael, and his four siblings, Richard, Catherine, Matthew, and Sarah, were able to be with us. Making it to Cleveland from Australia within 72 hours of the accident with a distance of almost 24 hours of travel time was a remarkable effort. Having them here gave us the foundation we needed. We moved through the days that followed together as a group of ten, doing our best to carry one another in our immeasurable sadness and pain.

On Monday, we all went to meet Patrick's football team after their morning practice. Patrick's football jerseys and his helmet were displayed on a table, and we all stood in a circle in the locker room. The mood was very somber. Chris addressed the coaches and players. He did an incredible job speaking from his heart about what being a part of this team had meant to Patrick. The friendships, the camaraderie, and all the fun. He shared that he and Patrick often talked about how to raise the energy of a team and how to have a positive impact and contribute as a leader. Patrick's grandfather, Michael, also spoke, which was very special, as did some of the coaches, teammates, and parents. It was deeply moving, and there were lots of tears, but also some laughter.

In the days after losing Patrick, I found it very difficult to be separated from him, knowing that his body was alone. I wanted to protect him. I wanted to be there, right by him. My maternal instincts were so powerful, and I found it hard to contain my longing to be with him. It definitely took me to my edge. This primal tendency to shield Patrick affected me profoundly; it consumed me. I can hardly describe its force in words. As a mother, I felt like a lioness. One of my cubs had been taken from me, and all I wanted to do was break the rules and be with him. I imagined sleeping at the funeral home with him and caring for him because that was what I had always done; protected and looked after him. I was aware enough to know that my idea was not the done thing, nor would I be able to act on it, but my response represented the fierceness and the depth of a mother's love. The only option I had was to surrender and relinquish my instincts. I had to accept and trust the care of strangers and the processes that had to be followed, even though every part of me didn't want to.

I kept re-living the last day of Patrick's life in the physical, over and over in my mind. It was a Thursday. He took our dog, Willow, to his internship that day. The very last photo I took of him was of the two of them sitting together in his car. He texted me throughout his day with sweet updates about how Willow was enjoying her first day in the office with him. One of his co-workers had also brought her dog to work. They walked the dogs a few times together that day and had some very meaningful and deep conversations. They enjoyed it so much that when Patrick left that afternoon, they made plans for him to take Willow again the next week. He got home from work, and we spent our last 30 minutes together, chatting away as we always did as he packed his bag to go away for just one night.

THE FUNERAL

Judging by the number of people who had visited us since the accident, we were expecting a large attendance at Patrick's funeral and afterwards at our house. The day before the service brought a flurry of organization that had again been lovingly planned by our friends. Chris and I had hosted many large gatherings over the years, and it was a strange feeling, not being the organizers. We accepted help as we never had before and felt deep gratitude for all that was being done around us, for us. Meetings were held about the catering, funeral booklet design, flowers, event set-up, and countless other logistics. Tents were assembled. People kept showing up for us, each with their own role to play and desire to help.

The day of Patrick's funeral arrived. I felt sick to the depths of my being, but I was determined to find the courage for him and for our family. What we were about to face made no sense, no sense at all. During the night, it had poured with rain, and heavy winds had raged, and I vaguely recall looking outside to see some of the tents blown over and a power line down across our back deck where people would be congregating in just a few short hours. Again, things were taken care of for us, and it was all sorted out. The communication between our support crew working behind the scenes was on another level.

As I dressed, I stared at myself in the bathroom mirror. I saw my reflection as an empty shell. I heard Patrick's voice say the words he would often say to me, "You look beautiful, Mumma." Every time he said that, my heart would melt with his sincerity. "Thank you, darling," was always my reply.

The time to do the unthinkable came. Together, the ten of us would find the courage, and we would represent Patrick. The car arrived from the funeral home to take us to be with Patrick before we went to the church. The sacredness of our time with him and our time together that morning can only be described as the highest form of love. It was pure love. Love for Patrick and love for one another.

From the funeral home, we began the procession to the church. Patrick was in the car in front of us; his coffin draped with the Australian flag. The cars paused reverently for a few moments at the high school in front of the rock (I will explain the rock in detail later) and also in front of the football field where Patrick played. We appreciated this thoughtful touch. As we neared the church, I saw people walking along the street, obviously on their way to the service. Was this really happening? It all felt as if it was a horrible dream.

We arrived at the church, and the parking lot was already full. We were an hour early; however, a crowd was streaming in. We were told later that people had begun to arrive three hours before the start time. Attendance was estimated at around 1500 people. Some had to stand outside; it was one of the biggest funerals in the church's history. In only six and a half years of living in Cleveland, Patrick had impacted many, many lives.

As we stepped out of the car, I could barely breathe. How do we face this? I had asked Patrick that morning how to do this, and I kept repeating his answer over and over in my mind. We were escorted to a room where we were to wait for instructions about our entrance into the church. In the depths of our despair, we felt the collective energy of our community ready to lift us up to farewell our beloved Patrick.

As we began the procession into the church, the ten of us and two priests, I clung to Chris's arm, unsure whether my body could carry me without it collapsing. Annabelle and Matilda were right behind us, and I heard Matilda say she felt faint. Annabelle reassured her she could do this. Patrick's coffin was already in place. His eight pallbearers, all his close friends, had proceeded in with him earlier; we wanted it that way. As I sat down in the front pew, right next to him, I kept repeating his words to me. I was shattered, yet monumentally proud to be Patrick's mum at this moment. I was present, but I was also caught in another realm of shock and horrendous pain. No parent, sibling, family member, or friend should ever have to endure this suffering, but this was our reality, and we would muster every ounce of our love for Patrick to commemorate him. Our beautiful boy, I could feel him right there, helping all of us get through this.

Chris and I were so proud of our girls; they both gave readings, which was such an incredibly difficult thing for them to do. They wanted to do this for their brother.

My brother-in-law, Rich, was sitting behind me. As I quietly sobbed, his hand did not leave my shoulder. I really appreciated that solid and loving gesture of support.

Chris gave Patrick's eulogy. How do you compose yourself to stand up in front of more than a thousand people and speak about your son who has died so suddenly and so young? Chris has always been an excellent and charismatic speaker, having emceed many events, but this one required immense strength and courage. We listened in awe as he performed what felt like an impossible task. Chris spoke about Patrick and our family. He told stories that made us smile, he used humor, and he captured all the love. It's an undertaking no father ever imagines himself doing, yet Chris did an outstanding job.

Father John's homily resonated with his perspective on losing someone so prematurely. Rather than trying to answer the impossible question of "Why did Patrick die?" he shifted our focus to, "Why did Patrick live?" When we think of all the amazing reasons why Patrick lived, our hearts and minds land in a better place.

We were so fortunate to have our friends, the Kelleys and the McNultys, make it possible for the service to be live-streamed. We thank them for this invaluable gift. It was no easy feat in an old church with technology challenges. It was greatly appreciated by our family and friends who could not be with us and was watched by thousands of people from around the world.

The music was a very meaningful part of the mass; many people told us afterwards how much it moved them.

The funeral home staff looked after Patrick and us with sincere consideration, courtesy, and respect that day and the entire week that Patrick was in their care.

Patrick's funeral booklet was designed by our Angel friends, led by Julie Hill. We were very thankful for the many hours this took, the attention to detail, and the love poured into every aspect of its creation.

The flowers in the church were beautiful; I did notice them. They were later brought to our house to join the many bouquets kindly sent to us.

Hundreds of people gathered at our house after the service. Our friends stepped in to provide their amazing food. Their restaurant, Townhall, is a favorite of ours here in Cleveland and happened to be where Patrick and I had our last lunch together just two days before he died. Patrick always ordered the beef burger, so they made special mini versions because he loved them. There was also a food truck from our kid's favorite Mexican restaurant, Barrio, which everyone enjoyed.

Without hesitation, many people contributed their time, love, and care towards the celebration of Patrick's life. It was a nightmare of a day but, at the same time, an incredibly love-filled day. We deeply thank everyone involved.

THE ACCIDENT SITE

Seven weeks after Patrick died, Annabelle and I felt called to go to the accident site. As part of our healing, we both needed to see it for ourselves, connect with Patrick there, and honor the place where he took his last breath. Our close friend, Kimberly Payne, offered to go with us.

The journey was by car, then ferry. The accident happened on an island in Lake Erie. All I could think about was how would we cope when we saw it? Would Annabelle be okay seeing it? Would it look like we had imagined it over and over again in our minds? I had never been to this place before, and neither had Patrick until that day. As the ferry came closer, the island became visible in the distance. My heart sank, and tears began to flow; we were following the exact path Patrick had traveled, just 49 days before. It felt as if we were making a sacred pilgrimage. As we drove off the car ferry, I noticed all the sights around me, again aware that these were all the things Patrick saw in the last couple of hours of his life.

We arrived at the location. It was a sickening and confronting feeling getting out of the car. I took the deepest breath I could, held Annabelle's hand, and together the three of us walked to the spot.

It was not at all what we had imagined. We now had an accurate visual. I collapsed on the ground where Patrick's body had lifelessly laid. My baby, my precious baby, oh the heartbreak. There were so many tears shed as we absorbed everything around us.

Our intention was to commemorate Patrick, so we brought many beautiful things with us for our ceremony. All the little details and rituals we chose were layered with deep meaning. We took our time with each one. We felt him there strongly. Annabelle and I were so grateful for Kim and her gentle, calming, and loving ways. We couldn't have done it without her. She knew what we needed.

As difficult and as devastating as it was, we were pleased we went. It felt right. As we drove home, the most vibrant rainbow appeared, perfectly arched across the road ahead of us.

THE MISSING

There was an emptiness, a constant missing and a relentless longing. I desperately wanted Patrick back. I was continually reaching
for him. I missed his hugs, his face, his company, his voice, his
beautiful eyes, his smell, his heavy footsteps, the way he bounded
through the door, his energy, and just knowing he was coming
home. To think that before this, I was sad about the thought of
missing him when he left home for college. I would have given anything to have that version of missing him now. The only time I
wasn't conscious of my pain from missing him was when I was
asleep.

Seeing other mothers with their sons triggered a sense of missing; it still does. I had a life with my son, and I loved that life with
all my heart, and then that life was ripped away from me in a split
second. My intention in this book is to be real, so in all honesty,
sometimes it's hard for me to see other mothers and sons together
because it's a sharp reminder of what I have lost. Tragedy tears us
from our old life while also robbing us of our future with that person. It breaks my heart that we will miss out on so much in the
physical with Patrick, and I could easily fall into deep anguish
about what has been taken away from us. Patrick would have been
an incredible husband, father, uncle, godfather, colleague, mentor,
and life-long friend. I know the way forward is to try not to spend
too long in the headspace of what could have been. These thoughts
only deepen our suffering and make our grief heavier. I give myself
grace when I do go there because it's only natural to do so, then I
find my way out by focusing on Patrick and my love for him.

In the beginning, I found it extremely challenging trying to ad-
just to caring for two children instead of three. As a mother, I have
always been aware of where my children are, how they're feeling,
what I need to do for them, making sure they're okay, etc. Even
though I was still always thinking about Patrick, my role had
changed, a role I so deeply loved. All of a sudden, a third of my
mothering responsibilities were gone. It felt so sharp. Given I had

had years of it being about mothering three, this was a very difficult adjustment for me, mentally and emotionally.

About four months after losing Patrick, the enormity of trying to live with the pain became even harder. A grief counselor told me that the three to four month mark is a common time for the shock to wear off after a huge loss and for the harshness of reality to set in. The purpose of shock is to act as a protective cocoon, a cushion for the sharp edges of loss, and once that buffer was removed, I was even more aware of the permanence of Patrick's absence in the physical. I kept picturing him coming up the back steps onto the deck and through the back door, just as he always did. Or him coming home after school and hugging me, just as he always did. This permanence hit hard.

THE FIRSTS

Patrick's death sent a shockwave through our world, and the aftershocks kept coming. Reminders of his physical absence struck me to my core every time. Setting four places at the dinner table instead of five, booking four plane tickets, not five, seeing his name everywhere, receiving Christmas cards written to Chris, Sara, Annabelle, and Matilda but not Patrick.

The firsts, as they are known, started to come thick and fast. Chris's birthday was the first of the firsts that we had to face, just 12 days after losing Patrick. It felt way too soon to have to confront such a thing, but life moved forward even if we weren't ready. I wanted to hit the pause button to spare us the pain. We did our best to be joyful for Chris, but we all felt the gaping hole. Patrick's spiritual presence was strong, however. He was with us, without a doubt.

My first trip to the supermarket and seeing all his favorite foods that I no longer needed to buy was very distressing. I cried the whole way around, with my sunglasses on, wishing I could be invisible. In the early days when I had to leave the house, I held my breath, hoping I could be in and out of a shop without having to have "the conversation" with someone I knew. Of course, I knew that anyone I bumped into was genuinely concerned for my family and me, but it was so hard to face life in those early stages. Everywhere I went, I was constantly reminded of our devastating reality. I started to get our groceries home delivered. It felt much more manageable when going to the store felt so difficult. Grief can make the tasks that weren't usually an effort feel exhausting.

The first family dinner with the four of us sitting around the table was awful. To this day, I often sit in Patrick's place at his end of the dining table because I can't bear it to be empty. The first time Chris traveled for work, I felt vulnerable without Patrick in the house. I was not expecting this reaction, but it was very obvious to me that his presence gave me a lot of security.

I remember going to have my hair done for the first time; I wasn't sure if my hairstylist was aware of our situation. The grapevine within our community was pretty strong, but maybe she hadn't heard? I knew I would be able to tell by the look on her face when she saw me. Facial expressions were my gauge when I greeted people. I walked into the salon, and her expression showed me that she didn't know. She was the loveliest person, and I usually enjoyed our conversations, but that day I was just not up to it. I sat down in the chair and took a deep breath. I looked at her but could not get the words out. I could not tell her that Patrick had died. I put my head down, leaned towards her, and kept trying to say something that resembled a sentence, which made some sort of sense without drawing too much attention to myself. I whispered and wept, and she tried her best to understand me. I told her that I really needed to be quiet, to not speak, and to just close my eyes for the whole time I was there. She held a beautiful and nurturing space for me, she was gentle, and I really appreciated her kindness. I was operating in survival mode, and honoring what I needed was the only option that day. Sometimes you just can't talk about your loss, and that's your choice.

I began to dread meeting someone new for the first time for fear of being asked the standard question, "How many kids do you have?" Would I be able to get the words out without dissolving into a pool of tears? I decided that my answer was on a need to know basis. If I was never going to see that person again, then I didn't need to invest emotionally, and I could keep my reply brief, "I have three children. A son and two daughters." I will always say three children because I still have three. If it is a more meaningful interaction, I can choose if I elaborate, "I have three children. A son and two daughters. Sadly, we lost our son, Patrick, suddenly (insert amount of time) ago." The first time I heard a stranger on a plane sitting next to Chris, ask him, "the question," my heart broke hearing his response. He did a really good job answering. It's confronting, to say the least. My first time was when a contractor at our house asked me. I did okay, as difficult as it was. I came to learn that each time you have to answer, it's a raffle as to how you will manage.

When someone greeted me with the automatic, "How are you?" my response, in the beginning, would be, "We are doing our best." While the question was asked with kind intention, it began to get harder to answer it because a lot of the time, I didn't feel good but didn't want to elaborate, so I started to avoid answering it altogether and say, "It's nice to see you." That diverted the focus from me to them and felt easier to manage.

Matilda started her first day of high school at the end of August. It was very brave of her to show up knowing that everyone knew she was Patrick Green's little sister. She embraced this with pride, but also with understandable apprehension about whether others would mention what had happened to him or avoid it.

Important days and milestones kept coming. Matilda's 14th birthday was in September. She did really well to put on a happy face, and we definitely shared some joyful moments that day. For Annabelle's 18th birthday in November, we decided to drive to Chicago, five hours west of Cleveland. We were able to enjoy some lighter moments, and Annabelle faced her day with courage and grace.

The first family photo. We were at a Christmas market in Chicago. The four of us stood in front of a festive backdrop and smiled for the camera. On the outside, I was attempting to look cheerful, but on the inside, my heart was shattering. Patrick should have been with us. I didn't want our family photos to look like this from now on; this wasn't right. Every time we pose for a family picture now, I talk to Patrick in my head, and I feel him with us because he is.

As winter started to settle in, the first snowfall brought with it a flood of memories. Patrick loved the snow.

We decided to go home to Australia for the first Christmas. It was almost six months since the accident, and I was dreading making the trip without him. He was always great company, and I liked going places with him. I loved our family holidays because I cherished the time with just the five of us. As our three kids got older, this became even more so as I knew the time would come when they wouldn't travel with us as much. Booking four seats on the plane and leaving Patrick's passport and green card at home felt wrong. Checking into our flight proved to be another challenging moment. As we walked up to the counter, the American Airlines woman's first words to us hit me like a ton of bricks, "Party of four?" That question instantly sent me into a flood of tears, and I had to walk away; she must have thought I was strange. It was the first time we had been greeted that way. I wanted to say, "We should be a party of five, that's what we have always been, I don't want to be a party of four, but now we have to be." Her words kept replaying in my head, and each time I heard them, I wanted to scream. Our first-time traveling to Australia felt different and awful. A part of us was missing. It will always be missing. But Patrick was with us. He was sitting in the seat on the plane that just happened to be empty between Annabelle and me; he was right there. His angel wings carried us all the way home.

We continued to be asked this haunting question in a variety of ways. When we arrived in Australia, the customs officer asked, "Just the four of you traveling?" Sitting down at a table in a restaurant in Sydney, the waiter inquired, "Will it be just the four of you eating today?" Over and over, it played like a broken record. Situations that used to be routine were suddenly instant triggers for my grief. In my head, my answer was, "There are five of us; there will always be five."

Christmas Day arrived, whether I wanted it to or not. I felt the grip of my grief tighten; it was a suffocating pain. Facing this day without Patrick was so difficult. I was acutely aware of trying to make it a happy day for our girls, but we were all feeling the effects of his absence. We were blessed to be surrounded by people who loved us.

Our first New Year's Eve was full of emotion for me as I reflected on everything we had been through. I didn't welcome the end to the worst year of our lives; instead, I found myself not wanting the year that Patrick was physically present in, 2019, to end. As I had done all along in my grief journey, I allowed myself to feel whatever came up. I acknowledged it all without judgment. This is generally a helpful way to process your feelings and come to a perspective where you can deal with them in a healthy way.

I felt an even deeper level of sadness with the anticipation of how we would get through the day on February 27, Patrick's 20th birthday. There was so much sorrow in my heart because it was his special day. It wasn't supposed to be this way. He was meant to be physically here, and for his birthday dinner, we were meant to eat tacos and pavlova because they were his favorites (I still made both). Many of Patrick's friends reached out to us that day, which helped a lot. Several of them traveled from different colleges around Ohio and met at Ohio State to spend the evening together to support one another and commemorate him. He would have loved that.

The month of May brought more firsts with my birthday closely followed by Mother's Day, three days later. My birthday was really hard; however, Mother's Day was extremely painful. To have to face this day without one of my children, there were and are no words. Chris, Annabelle, and Matilda were so loving in all that they did to make these two days meaningful so that my heart, although broken, also felt full.

In early June, we celebrated Annabelle's high school graduation. We had so much to be proud of, our beautiful Annabelle with her resilient nature, strong work ethic, bubbly personality, quick wit, and sensitive heart. She completed her studies with High Honors in all four years. We missed Patrick greatly on this day. His presence was palpable; he has always been so happy for his sister and all her achievements.

Father's Day is celebrated in June in the US (September in Australia). Again, our girls rose to the occasion with love and loving details. We tried our best to make the day special for Chris with Patrick surrounding him.

June 27 may have been the hardest of them all, the first anniversary of Patrick's death. I can barely write those words. I still have moments of profound disbelief, and I suspect I always will. For me, the anticipation for this day began to build about a month before it arrived. As soon as the warmer weather started, I was triggered about how it all felt a year ago. Thoughts such as "On this day a year ago, Patrick had Senior Prom," and "This time a year ago it was his graduation," filled my mind. Now the sound of emergency vehicle sirens made me feel sad; they reminded me of Patrick's accident. I used to love hearing the church bells ring; now, they reminded me of Patrick's funeral. Here we were, preparing to navigate the last of the firsts, the anniversary of the day we lost him. Once again, our communities here and in Australia rallied around us. Patrick's friends provided a lot of comfort to us. A mass was offered in Patrick's name at the church where the funeral was held. We received many messages from people telling us about the ways they were commemorating him. There was so much sadness but also so much love.

Patrick and I had always planned to get a tattoo together. We had already designed it, an outline of two hearts intertwined. It would have been the first tattoo for both of us. The day before his first anniversary, I got our tattoo. I got it for both of us, and I couldn't love it any more than I do. I know he loves it too.

Before we knew it, it was Chris's birthday again. The firsts had started to become seconds.

At the end of August 2020, Annabelle moved to college. It was another big day for our family, where we missed Patrick deeply. He should have been here to experience all the fun plans he and Annabelle had made to visit each other at their colleges. We know that

24

he is enjoying it with Annabelle as she moves through this next exciting stage of her life.

From our experience of loss, I would say that the lead up to each milestone day was usually worse than the actual day itself. Don't get me wrong, each significant day brought heavy sadness, but I think my anticipation and dread was what unraveled me. Can anyone else relate? By the time the day came, I was just so relieved that I was almost through it. I also noticed I felt depleted the day after a milestone day, both physically and emotionally. It was essential to increase my self-care on these days.

I would like to get to the point where Patrick's birthday can be a celebration again. Where we do something fun that he would love. I know this will be hard, and I'm not putting any unrealistic expectations on us here, but I think he would want us to celebrate him. I predict his anniversary will always be heart-crushing, but I know for sure we will do our best to commemorate him.

We were beyond blessed to have been given 19 years and four months with our beautiful Patrick. This length of time seems unjustly short, for him and for us. Losing him feels senseless, brutal, and unfair. He had graduated from high school just 20 days before the accident. He was due to start college in the fall. We were so enormously proud of who he was and who he was becoming. His whole life was ahead of him. More love, more fun, more memories, more experiences, and more opportunities to make a difference. In his 19 years, he touched many lives. In his death, his legacy will live on, and he will inspire us to be better people.

Over the past year, we have had many challenging days, and no day is easy. We intensely miss Patrick's physical presence. Our hearts hurt because he was taken away from us. We talk about him every single day. We smile when we recount stories and recall things that he said or did, and we acknowledge the things that he loved. This is all part of keeping his love and light shining forever and always. This is now our purpose.

KIMBERLY'S REFLECTIONS

Our dear friend, Kim Payne, was at our house when we received the news of Patrick's passing. She bravely shares what she witnessed that night, and in the days that followed:

"The terror of seeing Sara's reaction before she could say the words was telling of what was to come. She stood in silence with her eyes wide, and a few moments later, in rapid succession, the words, 'There has been an accident,' came from her, her body trying to take breaths in. I stood at her side, waiting to hear what more she was trying to say, already trying to comfort something in her that was crying out. I could see her struggling to speak. Then those terrible words burst from her about what had happened. The sheer shock, the magnitude of what she had just learned, took her breath away, drained the blood from her face, and the peace from her eyes. She fell to her knees. Her head was in my lap; she kept shaking her head, saying, 'No, no, no,' and every so often looking into my eyes, pleading, asking me if this was true. I could not believe it myself. I could not understand the tragedy that was unfolding. I could not tell her this was true. I sat quietly, unsure how this could be. Her crying out, 'Not him, not him,' circling in the air around us. The rending of a best friend, a mother, a family. It was not digestible.

The family moved in silent slow motion as if time had stopped, soaking in a new and terrorizing reality. Suddenly life felt harsh; the lights felt bright, the silence interspersed with crying taking up all the space in the house. Someone needed to call Annabelle, who had just left for a fun night of tacos with a friend. The dread started setting in as the tragic news was shared, as it would be shared many more times. How do you utter those words from the depth of your being? How do you move forward into the next moment? The baby pictures on the wall, Patrick's place setting at the table with his name on it, the photos on the mantle. All represented close family ties. Ties that were now physically shattered. The torment of watching this devastation, realizing this loving child of my dear friend, was no longer here, will stay within me forever. I wouldn't have wanted to be anywhere else in the world at that moment than with her. Time changed. Life changed forever. When I got home late that night, I heard owls crying and screaming back and forth with one another. I woke the next day to this reality that was still trying to settle in. I walked around my house, lost, those few days after. My heart with hers. Each footstep a solemn reminder of what she was enduring. How can a mother survive losing a child?

I spent the next few days at her side. Watching her, Chris, Annabelle, and Matilda gracefully handle the many decisions that had to be made. A blur in time, a hazy glaze of survival surrounding them. In my moments at home, I began seeing Patrick everywhere and in everything. It was as if he was there, in every breath, in every word. I felt as if he had expanded his loving reach beyond the physical and was asking for us to see more expansively. That was so like him, even in death, reaching his hands out to comfort and embrace those he loved. Nothing can take that away from his family and friends. In his 19 years, he reached his loving hands all around the world and is celebrated by people he has not met. He touched life in a unique way. He will be forever cherished and celebrated."

"Give the power to your love, not your grief."

"This unending love is the anchor that maintains the connection to our loved one beyond this physical life."

CHAPTER TWO

LOVE

I have great faith in love. To love deeply is to lose deeply. The greater the love, the greater the loss. When our love for someone is of the deepest vibration, and then we lose them, we feel the pain in every part of our being. It floods our body because the love is so intense. This unending love is the anchor that maintains the connection to our loved one beyond this physical life.

We are so grateful that Patrick chose us to be the ones to love him and for him to love us. His death feels like the cruelest blow for all of us. To cope with my pain, I keep returning to my immeasurable love for him; I know my healing lives in this space of love. The extent and depth of my love is what rips my heart into pieces; it also mends its shredded edges.

If you are reading this book because you have lost deeply, I encourage you to be open to a new way of feeling and experiencing your pain.

I ask you to consider this thought: your love for your loved one who has died is greater than your loss and the force of your grief. Give the power to your love, not your grief.

I know this is a difficult concept to grasp because the weight of the loss feels as if it may break you. If you can, start ever so slowly to lift yourself up from your loss. It may take a few or many attempts;

just try the best you can. It's going to feel heavy, and it's going to be hard.

Love is fierce. It has an energy, a currency, and a vibration. It doesn't require the presence of a physical body to keep it alive. Love goes beyond the physical world. Envision your love as the lifeline to the one who you have lost. This bond is unbreakable; it is eternal. Death is not the end of love. A closed mind does not see, and a closed heart does not feel. Open your mind and heart to the possibility of this lasting love connection.

Keep returning to your love for them, and you will start to feel it become stronger than your grief. Allow them to enter your heart and live within you. Commit to this new way of being together. Be open to the healing that it brings. The endless love I have for Patrick is embedded in my heart, and I take this love everywhere with me. Patrick lives in my heart, and he will live there forever. I carry his heart in mine. Where I go, he goes, and it gives me immense comfort.

The scars from our loss run deep, but our love for Patrick runs deeper. When I focus on how much he loves me and how much I love him, it helps me live with my pain, and I know our love is greater than the force of my grief. I know that our love is all that matters.

"Grief is visceral, not reasonable: The howling at the center of grief is raw and real. It is love in its most wild form."

Megan Devine,
from her book, *It's OK That You're Not OK.*

"Losing our son and brother is a type of loss that buries itself deeply in our hearts. We will continue on as the five of us because we will always represent Patrick; that is who we are."

CHAPTER THREE

THE FIVE OF US

Living away from our extended Melbourne-based family for the past 14 years, first in Sydney and then in Cleveland, we forged a strong connection as a family of five. We have always had one another.

Here is a little more about us, the five of us.

PATRICK

From the second I saw the positive result on my pregnancy test, I was in love. Totally in love with our baby. I was bursting to be a mother; I had always been maternal. I loved being pregnant and cherished each stage. My labor was a wonderful experience; I had never felt so empowered in my body. After 12 hours, a beautiful 9 lbs 6 oz healthy baby boy was born at 6:39 pm on Sunday, February 27, 2000. I will never forget holding Patrick for the first time, looking into his eyes; it was pure love. Patrick made me a mother, and I will feel forever grateful that he chose me. Seeing Chris hold our new son was also an unforgettable moment.

As a baby, I could see Patrick's wisdom in his eyes. He was an old soul who had a knowingness about him. He was engaging and social, and he didn't sleep much during the day. Chris and I would say he didn't want to miss out on being with people, a trait that stayed with him, his love of relationships. He started talking at a very young age. Other mothers would stop me at the playground when they heard him talking to me in sentences at 15 months old; they couldn't believe his grasp of language for such a young child. He was given a soft toy Labrador dog that he called Dog Dog and a woolen blanket that he called Ruggles. Dog Dog and Ruggles went everywhere with us for many years. We would say he looked like a baby bear when he wore his sleepsuit, which became known as his Bearsuit.

At 21 months, he became a big brother to Annabelle Lucy. Seeing them meet for the first time was so special. He took his new role very seriously; he was loving and protective of Annabelle.

From toddler age, Patrick was able to communicate well with adults. He looked people in the eye when he spoke to them, asked many questions, was inquisitive, and curious. When something interested him, he was fully engaged and didn't miss a detail. He was always a talker and had the cutest husky voice. He loved cars; real cars, and Matchbox cars. He would line up all his Matchbox cars in a row and talk about the different models endlessly. He "read" car magazines; family and friends were always entertained when they saw a copy of 4WD Monthly on his bedside table. His grandmother, Rita, fondly recalls one day when she was looking after him. She went to get him out of his cot after his sleep, and he was lying there listening to the cars drive by. He identified the model of each vehicle out loud to her by the sound of their engines, "That's a Mazda, that's a Four-a (what he called a 4WD)."

He loved one of the original versions of the children's movie, Jack and The Beanstalk, so much that he watched it over and over again. I kept borrowing it from the video store so often that I eventually asked to buy it from them. He was also a big fan of children's entertainers, Mister Whiskers and The Wiggles. His favorite books were Spot the Dog and lift-the-flap books.

His natural athletic ability was apparent from an early age. He could kick, catch, and throw a football with a precision and ease beyond his years. He welcomed anyone who would play with him;

he always had lots of energy.

When he was three years old, he broke his left elbow. The fracture required four surgeries for it to heal. He was a champion.

At four years old, Patrick was prime cuteness. His dark curly hair and sparkling green/hazel eyes, his freckles, and his sweet ways were all adorable. He absorbed new facts and statistics like a sponge; you could literally see the mechanics of his brain working as he stored new information then recalled it effortlessly; he had the memory of an elephant. I would lie in his bed with him each night, reading books and talking while he played with my hair and drew on my back, and I had to guess what he drew. I loved his divine husky voice, chatting away in my ear. They were such unforgettable memories. He loved Buzz Lightyear, Spiderman, and Superman. All he wanted to wear to pre-school were the costumes from his favorite superheroes. So much so that the teachers had to introduce a ban on wearing these costumes to school because Patrick started a trend and all the other kids wanted to do it too, every day!

As a young boy, we started to see Patrick's magnetism appear; people wanted to be around him; he made friends easily. He had a great awareness of others and their emotions. I used to say that his little antennas were up because he could read people like a book. He was sincere, affectionate, and complimentary.

When he was five, his second little sister joined our family, Matilda Alice Maureen. Tildy was another best friend for him to take under his loving and protective wing.

Team sports were a big part of Patrick's life from the age of five onwards. This heralded the start of many friendships and great memories made through sport that he greatly valued throughout the years. In Melbourne, his football career began when he started playing Australian Rules Football (AFL) for East Brighton Auskick.

We moved from Melbourne to Sydney when Patrick was six years old. He was nervous about starting school, and he didn't like the idea of us leaving him there. It was understandable because we had only arrived in this new city the day before and Patrick didn't know anyone. On his first day, he was upset after we left, and as the lovely principal, who was a nun, tried to console him, out of fear and uncertainty, he kicked her in the shins! I got a phone call shortly after from Sister Veronica, who thankfully had a very good sense of humor about it. When she retired a few years later, she wrote me a card and confirmed that yes indeed, Patrick would go down in history as her only student ever to do such a thing!

I'll never forget the time when Patrick was in Kindergarten, and it was his class assembly. He was traditionally very hesitant about public speaking. Patrick and his teacher, the lovely Miss Thompson, surprised me when he got up on the stage and gave a reading using the microphone in front of the whole school. My heart burst with pride; I knew he had overcome an obstacle. He was in the school musical in 4th grade. Indeed, Patrick became a confident and charismatic public speaker as the years went on and he ended up really enjoying it.

He went through a stage of loving WWE wrestling when he was between seven and ten years old. He knew every wrestler, and he and his friends had all the moves and the lingo down pat. Anything Nerf gun-related was a favorite too. He enjoyed the classic movies and musicals such as Willy Wonka and The Chocolate Factory, Back to the Future, Chitty Chitty Bang Bang, Singing In The Rain, Mary Poppins, Toy Story, and The Wizard of Oz.

In Sydney, he played AFL for the East Sydney Bulldogs as well as rugby league, cricket, and touch football. He was humble; he didn't look for accolades, although he received many of them. In AFL, he was the team captain, and he won multiple Best and Fairest Awards (voted by the coaches) and a Players Award (voted by his teammates).

In the 5th and 6th grades, all students had to play an instrument, and Patrick chose the double bass. It wasn't his favorite past-time, but it was an experience. He loved magic and magic tricks, cards, and card tricks. He taught himself from watching YouTube videos, and he loved showing us when he'd mastered a new one.

When Patrick was 12 years old, we moved from Sydney to Cleveland. Because of his age, Chris and I thought the move could be a challenging transition for him. While it was definitely hard for him to leave his great mates and the sports that he loved playing in Australia, he surprised us with how well and how quickly he adjusted. He and the girls went to the same school, and I vividly remember their first day. It was a daunting feeling dropping them off; everything looked and felt so different. There was a sea of strangers and it felt as if we were in a High School Musical movie. We were certainly the only ones with an Australian accent. At pickup time, I waited with anticipation to hear about their day. I found Annabelle and Matilda, but we couldn't see Patrick. In the distance, there was a swarm of girls, who I could hear squealing and shrieking. As they came closer, I realized that Patrick was in the center of this circle of girls. We could hear them asking him to say different words and then screaming in delight at the sound of his accent! He looked over at us with a semi-confused look on his face, yet the biggest grin. In one sense, he was wondering what all the fuss was about, and in the other, he was totally lapping it up. It was as if he was a rockstar getting mobbed by his fans. He would say that his accent definitely worked in his favor over the years.

Sports were new and exciting for him in America. He started with basketball, baseball, and skiing. In Little League baseball, he hit the most home runs in his age group, and he was an All-Star in Pony League baseball for the two years that he played. He became a great skier. He joined the Ski Club in middle school and loved the Friday nights with his friends on the slopes. On our family trips to the snow, he always skied the longest. He braved the difficult runs; the harder they were, the more he wanted to ski them. Before we moved to the US, he had never even seen snow. Each year, once it started falling and there was decent coverage, he was always the first to put on his winter layers and get outside. He and Matilda would be out there for hours; they didn't care how cold it was. Digging tunnels, building forts, sledding, and throwing snowballs, they delighted in the fun of it all.

In his freshman year of high school, he was a triple threat athlete, playing football, baseball, and basketball. As a punter, he was a three-year varsity player, Special Teams Player of the Year as a junior, Special Teams Player of the Year for the Conference, First Team All-District as a junior and a senior, Second Team All-Ohio as a junior, and Third Team All-Ohio as a senior. He loved his Friday nights playing football. While I really enjoyed watching him play, I also felt immense pleasure observing him on the sideline. He was a talented punter, but I think the sideline was where he also did some of his best work. The relationships and friendships he forged with his teammates and coaches were special. I loved seeing him in conversations with them in between executing his role on the field. I can only imagine the banter and the language! His energy was contagious, and he was always one of the first to acknowledge a teammate's successful play. He was a role model for the younger players; he took time to chat to the water boys; he made everyone feel seen and heard. As a biased mother, I must also mention how handsome he looked in his football uniform. The all maroon with black and white detail was my favorite with his dark hair. I thoroughly enjoyed watching him play every sport he participated in. I was always captivated by his agility and finesse.

He wasn't overly competitive; as much as he got excited about the big games, he equally liked the low-key times. He valued his friendships with his team-mates and coaches and enjoyed the experiences. He loved playing basketball in a local recreation league that was about camaraderie and shooting around for fun. He enjoyed meeting friends at the high school to kick the football around or going to the baseball field to smash balls as far as he could with Matilda and his mates; they called it "Hitting Dingers" and the "Home Run Derby." The basketball hoop at our house was often the gathering place for Patrick and his friends. I always smiled when I drove down our street and saw all the boys there. They were fun times, with lots of laughter and trash-talking. When it was time for a break, they would all come inside, walk over to the kitchen cupboard to get a cup, get a drink of water and chat away to me. I miss the boys being here. I miss the sound of the basketball bouncing on the concrete. "Tub Night" in our hot tub most Friday nights during winter became a regular feature with Patrick and the boys. It was a fun tradition for them.

Patrick loved people. He was the glue that brought friendship groups together. Many have joked that Patrick could juggle multiple commitments at once. In a single night, he managed to make it to several gatherings so that he could maintain his friendships across a four-year age span. From pre-school onwards, Patrick formed close connections with his teachers; I can recall many whom Patrick held in high regard over the years. He was equally able to build strong friendships with his fellow students.

In his sophomore year, he was in the Homecoming Court, and in his last two years of high school, he was a Freshman Mentor (most only do this for one year). The Freshman Mentoring Program (FMP) is a leadership development program for juniors and seniors. Their role is to serve as a peer mentor to a freshman as they transition to high school. They assist with academics and lessons covering all of the topics that a freshman needs to succeed in high school. He was also very involved in the special needs program. He excelled in both of these roles. He enjoyed broadcasting basketball games with his friend, Michael. The two of them entertained the audience with their quick wit and charm and elected themselves as the Broadcasting Club's Presidents. In his senior year, he modeled in the Prom Fashion Show.

He was obsessed with snow days (if there was a lot of snow and the road conditions were dangerous or the temperatures were extremely cold, the school might call a snow day for safety reasons, which was a day off school). He monitored the snow day app like it was his full-time job, giving us continuous updates about the percentage chance of getting one. Always the optimist!

Music was very important to Patrick. He had a good singing voice, and he knew every single word to a song after only hearing it play once. He liked a variety of music; he knew all the classics as well as the current day songs. His favorite artists were Michael Jackson, Justin Bieber, and many hip hop/rap/R & B artists. On a family trip to Las Vegas, some highlights for Patrick included seeing Cirque du Soleil's show "One" with music by Michael Jackson and the David Copperfield show where he was selected from the audience to assist Copperfield in a magic trick! We also saw Justin Bieber in concert in Vegas; that was an enjoyable night for the five of us. Patrick was exceptional at music trivia. When we played "who sings it?" in the car, he delivered the answers at lightning speed. Over the years, he went to see many of his favorite artists and bands in concert.

He loved all sorts of games. PlayStation and video games, card games such as poker and blackjack, and the gambling strategy that went with them. Other card games such as 500 and Uno have been a big part of family holidays, and he was always up for a game of Cluedo or another board game.

Patrick was a big Harry Potter fan. Chris read the books to him when he was younger, and Patrick relished in all the movies; each time a new one was released, he and Chris would watch it together at the cinema. I'm so pleased he got to go to Harry Potter World at Universal Studios on one of our more recent family holidays. Patrick loved every second of it, eyes wide open, taking in every detail, and talking non-stop about it all. As a teenager, he loved horror movies and Star Wars, which was another series that he and Chris enjoyed watching together.

Chris and I loved taking our kids to musicals, and Patrick took a great interest in the shows that we went to see, such as Wicked, Mary Poppins, A Christmas Story, Matilda, and The Rockettes Christmas Show. We were fortunate enough to see these on Broadway and at Radio City Music Hall in New York.

Patrick was proudly Australian. He didn't change who he was to fit into another culture when we moved to Cleveland, and his authenticity was attractive to others. Living in America, he didn't even get close to losing his Australian accent; he still sounded pure Aussie.

He had the most beautiful dark eyelashes I have ever seen. His eyes were my favorite physical characteristic of his. From a toddler to the day he died, he would twirl the curl in the front of his hair with his fingers. His favorite color was purple. He had a strong sense of smell. His teeth were perfect; he never needed braces. His skin tanned, and he had a lot of freckles. He had very large feet, size 14! When he walked, he turned his left foot in slightly. When standing, he swayed side to side when he talked. He was left-handed for writing and all sports.

His favorite foods were tacos, Australian foods (Vegemite on toast, meat pie with sauce, pavlova, BBQ shapes or "Matt's bickies" as he called them), apples, pears, peaches, nectarines, watermelon, biscuits and cheese, Chick-fil-A, hot Cheetos (and I'm sure plenty of other fast/junk food that he hid from his mother) and anything strawberry; actual strawberries, strawberry milkshakes, strawberry ice cream (when I was pregnant with him I craved strawberry milk and fruit). He didn't have much of a sweet tooth; he preferred savory and salty snacks.

In his teenage years, he enjoyed a variety of work experiences. His first job was at the local Brewing Company, where he was a busboy. He spent a short time working in construction, and he did some babysitting. At the end of his junior year, he started as an intern for IT Exchange Net as a data analyst. In his senior year, he continued with the internship and worked at a local Asian restaurant, clearing tables. He volunteered at St Malachi Parish Back Door Ministry in the kitchen, serving meals to the less fortunate.

As Patrick became an adult, Chris and I could clearly see where his future would take him. His greatest strength was his emotional intelligence; that was his superpower. He was going to continue to have a lasting impact on people, just as he had always done. When he entered a room, the energy lifted. The way he worked a crowd with effortless ease and a genuine interest in and desire to connect with others was a joy to witness.

When we reflect on Patrick's 19 years, we feel great comfort knowing that he knew he was immensely and unconditionally loved. He enjoyed relationships and friendships with deep meaning. Patrick knew who he was, and he was true to himself. He was a man for others. He was full of life, and he lived his life fully. He had lots of fun and enjoyed lots of laughs. He had a giant and loving heart. Some people take a lifetime to cultivate what Patrick had achieved.

We are so proud. As a family, we enjoyed many experiences together that have given us cherished memories to hold close. We were the lucky ones to enjoy this life with him. We will always be the five of us.

CHRIS AND I

Chris and I have been together since December 1995. We have shared lots of love and many adventures. In 1997-1998 we lived in the US for Chris's work, firstly in Cleveland briefly and then Dallas for a year. Chris proposed to me in New York in November 1997. We moved home to Melbourne and got married on January 8, 1999. All of our three beautiful children were born in Melbourne. We have navigated a health scare, a move from Melbourne to Sydney, living in Sydney for seven years, job changes, losing grandparents who we adored, and relocating across the world from Sydney to Cleveland. After attending university in Australia and college in the US at Ohio University, Chris has always worked in sports marketing, sponsorship, and communications. In Australia, I studied at university to become a registered nurse and worked for many years in nursing in Melbourne, and then I ran my own private chef business for four years in Sydney. When we moved to the US, I acquired my qualification as a holistic health coach, and I've been working in my own private practice for the last six years.

In our 20th year of marriage, we faced our biggest and most heart-shattering challenge, the sudden death of our only son, our first-born child, our beloved Patrick. His tragic death completely shook us to our core. As parents, your worst nightmare is to lose your child.

In my professional life, I have seen what tragedy can do to a relationship. Thankfully our strong foundation gave us the stability as a couple to hold together through this because I can imagine that those who have cracks in their commitment beforehand may find themselves with craters when the impact of trauma sets in. In the early stages, we certainly came up against our edges as we tried to find our footing in our new and devastating reality. Our grief reactions and ways of coping were different, but we kept our love and the lines of communication open and spoke our truth while making sure we heard the other and accepted their approach without judgment. I am proud of how we have survived this together.

PATRICK AND CHRIS

Patrick and Chris shared an indelible father and son bond. With all our children, Chris is a dad who is present, involved, and giving. He was completely devoted to raising Patrick to be a good man and a man for others. Patrick looked to Chris for advice on many things, especially life decisions, career, and sport. They shared a deep love, respect, and friendship. Chris's advice to Patrick before his games was always, "Be the one to bring the energy to your team." I smile when I think of the post-game discussions they had, the detailed banter bouncing back and forth. Whether it was after a game of Patrick's or a pro or college game, they enjoyed it all, and they enjoyed it together. There were also lots of discussions about Harry Potter and sports documentaries. Patrick took a great interest in Chris's job in college athletics. Here in the US, they attended many sporting events such as the Final Four, NFL and NBA games, and college basketball and football games. Chris was committed to giving Patrick opportunities to further his punting career, and they took an unforgettable trip down south to the Universities of Tennessee, Auburn, and Louisiana State. They drove from Cleveland to New Orleans via six or seven stops for punting camps, including the universities that I mentioned. They traveled with 25 guys from Prokick Australia who had flown over to showcase themselves to college coaches. A highlight for the two of them was a night in New Orleans at Preservation Hall enjoying jazz.

Here are some of Chris's reflections from the eulogy he wrote about Patrick:

"As a father, I had great pride in what Patrick had achieved and where he was headed. He and I had many wonderful times at sporting events from the MCG to Giants Stadium, from Final Fours to Notre Dame. We've had a rolling conversation for 19 years about the Tigers, the Rabbitohs, Matthew Richardson, Odell, the Giants, the Cavs, the Indians, and the Pirates. He loved nothing more than debating who was better than whom, LeBron vs Jordan – it went on and on forever. The conversation was really a continuation of one I'd had with my father and grandfather. It feels as if it's been a Green family conversation starting with Nance and Syd and continuing for more than 50 years. Annabelle pointed out that now he gets to see Nance and Syd, and we've all thought about his relatives and especially his great grandparents, who he's now joined and who will be looking after him. I especially cherish the weeks we spent in the south visiting colleges and attending punting camps with a bunch of punters from Australia in the summer of 2017. We ended the trip in New Orleans, and as you do, we spent a night going from bar to bar in the French Quarter. By about the fifth stop, I headed straight to the bathroom, and by the time I got back, Patrick was sitting at the bar and had ordered us drinks. The wise old barman just winked at me and said, 'The young gun's got you sorted.'"

My heart breaks when I think of the future father and son opportunities that Chris and Patrick will not physically experience. More trips, sporting events, laughter, stories, conversations about life, or something as simple as enjoying a drink together. While deeply devastated and trying to live with his grief, Chris is philosophical about losing his son. In his eulogy, he also shared:

"Patrick lived a full life in 19 years, and somehow that is it for him and for us."

Since our world, as we knew it, collapsed on June 27, 2019, Chris has been an incredible support for Annabelle, Matilda, and me, "My Girls," as he calls us. His unconditional love, solid devotion, steadfast presence, humor, and even-keeled nature have kept us afloat. He has stepped up and spoken publicly about our loss on behalf of the five of us when needed, which is a strength I greatly appreciate and admire. He has found comfort in the company of family and friends. His workout group, F3, has been a source of invaluable support and mateship. These men truly showed up and continue to do so for Chris and our family. Working out has been a form of therapy for him. He has also found healing through one of his most endearing qualities, his generosity. Immersing himself in doing things for others over this past year has been very therapeutic for him. One of his hobbies is smoking meat on his outdoor smoker grill. It has brought him a lot of joy to cook and share his passion for preparing and enjoying quality food. Being of service and making people happy in the process has lifted him up.

While the pain and sadness will stay with Chris forever, I can see that he draws on deep gratitude for the time he and Patrick were given. Their father and son love is eternal.

PATRICK AND I

I love Patrick with every single part of me. When you lose someone who you desperately don't want to live without, it affects you deeply. When you grow a baby inside you, you birth and nourish that precious baby, you mother that infant, toddler, young boy, teen, and man with all your heart, and then he is ripped away from you; it feels as if a part of you goes with him. To lose my only son and my first-born baby is indescribably excruciating. But I know that Patrick's soul chose me to be his mum so that I would receive the gifts from his passing and then, from there, rise up and share them to help others and continue his meaningful work.

I was the first woman who loved him; I was the first woman he loved. That, right there, is my gift. I keep coming back to our love that I know has existed through many lifetimes. I cherish every moment, even the challenging ones, because we were in it together. I treasure all that we shared. All the love, the laughter, the hugs, and the little things. We understood each other on a profound level where words were not needed. Kindred spirits. Similar hearts and sensitive souls. Throughout his life, we talked for hours about many topics; we processed our emotions in a similar way. I miss our chats so much; I miss the sound of his voice. I miss everything.

Patrick and I enjoyed many pastimes together. We played tennis, and we loved Australian movies and TV shows such as The Castle, Kath and Kim, Summer Heights High, and the Fitzy and Wippa parodies. We laughed and laughed and watched them over and over again. He would put them on just to make me laugh and then do such funny impersonations of the characters. We played the games Would You Rather and Wealthy Walrus and rolled around laughing at each other's responses. We had a lot of fun. I loved it when we went on walks, especially our beach walks on family holidays. We enjoyed great conversations; he shared things with me with such expression in his words.

I really valued the times when he asked for my opinion on things, my advice on a dilemma, or for my help with buying presents or making something special for someone. He was so cute and sincere in his efforts. It made me so happy that he wanted me to be involved.

Patrick loved rides, especially rollercoasters at amusement parks. The scarier, the better. I'm so glad he experienced both Disneyland and Disneyworld; they were very happy times. I am not a rides person; I don't like that sense of motion. On our first trip to Disneyland, he asked me to go on Space Mountain with him. I was weirdly oblivious to what was involved, so I agreed. About 10 seconds in, I grabbed Patrick's thumb with a vice-like grip as we hurtled around the 90 degree angled corners in the dark. I was petrified while he loved every minute. As we got off, he said he thought I would break his thumb; I'm surprised I didn't! Looking back, I'm so pleased I said yes. One time he asked me to go to Cedar Point amusement park with him here in Ohio. We had a great day together; I stood in all the lines with him, then he went on the rides, and I watched; it was the perfect way to do it.

I love that he wanted to be with me. In the last two weeks of his life, we enjoyed some fun times together. This moment I'm about to share feels as if it was one of the times he was the proudest of me; when I played beer pong with him at Michael Finnegan's graduation party. He kept asking me in the lead up to the party if I would be his partner, and again, I'm so glad I said yes. Our opponents were Michael and his mum, Sarah. Each time I threw a ball into the cup, Patrick got so excited. His enthusiasm was the sweetest. We ended up winning the game, and it's a memory I will cherish forever. I have a six-second video that his friend, Greta, took of the two of us playing that I often watch. The way we look at each other with such love and joy melts my heart. How lucky was I that my 19 year old son wanted to do these things with me?!

I bought myself some new golf clubs about a month before Patrick died, we intended to play as a foursome over the summer with Michael and Sarah; our beer pong buddies. Sadly, we never got our first game of golf in with them. The week before the accident, Patrick, Matilda, and I played a round to try out the new clubs. It had rained heavily the night before, and I smile now when I picture Patrick on the fairway trying to find our lost ball, standing up to his ankles in water, with no complaints. Considering my beginner golf skills, he was always so patient with me, calmly giving me instructions and never getting frustrated as my balls zig-zagged along the course. I also have some video of our game that day that I treasure.

Just two days before the accident, Patrick was working at his summer internship, and he asked me if I would like to join him for lunch at one of our favorite restaurants near the office. I simply loved spending time with him, as I do with all my children, so I jumped at his invitation. I remember thinking again how fortunate I was that he wanted to hang out with me. As I drove there, little did I know that this lunch would be so unforgettable. We sat down and chatted away, as we always did. We ordered our usual dishes, and I soaked up the moment. He looked so handsome sitting across from me in his pale blue polo shirt, so grown up and at ease. We talked about his college plans and where he thought his life might take him with his career and relationships, and where he'd like to live. I said, "I just want you to be safe. If anything ever happened to you, I don't know what I would do." He casually replied, "Mum, I'll be fine; there's no need to worry." He then went on to say, "Mum, you and Dad couldn't have done a better job with me." I felt as if my heart might burst with happiness. He spoke with such sincerity and gratitude, and I will never forget it. It was one of those moments that had such meaning at the time but would prove to be even more profound in the aftermath. A parent hopes that their child would say that they did a great job raising them. Chris and I have always put our marriage and our children first with the intention of giving them a loving, secure, happy, experience, and memory-filled upbringing. At lunch that day, Patrick gave us an incredible gift. When we lost him just two days later, we had his words as a very recent reference. They gave us immense comfort and the ability to have zero regrets. What a blessing.

It is a true honor for me to live this life as Patrick Green's mum. Even without him here physically, I will always be his mum. We have re-defined our relationship. We have found ways to still be together in the spiritual. We had the best 19 years, and our love is endless.

PATRICK AND ANNABELLE

Patrick and Annabelle were born relatively close in age. When they were little, Patrick called her many of his own variations of Annabelle: "Annie Annie," "Annie Zazzy," "Annie Zaz," "Anise," and "Neesy." As a baby and toddler, Annabelle had the biggest mop of blonde curls, and we would say she looked like a doll. "Doll" soon became her family nickname and still is today. When Annabelle started talking, she couldn't say "Patrick," and in trying to, she called him "Ga Ga" or "Ga," which became his nicknames. Annabelle and many other family members call him Ga.

When they were young, they shared a bedroom, and they would lay there at night and recount their day to each other; Chris and I called it "the debrief." It was the cutest thing. When they were older and in separate bedrooms, they would still meet at the end of the day to "debrief." It was usually Patrick lying on Annabelle's bed, they could talk for hours. They had their final "debrief" the night before Patrick's accident as they made their plans for the upcoming weekend.

Annabelle was patient with Patrick and his need to give her all the facts, he loved statistics and theories, and she listened to all of them. They knew each other so well and they balanced each other in a very complimentary way. Annabelle was Patrick's guiding light, confidante, and cheerleader. She understood him, and he trusted her. They had a beautiful friendship that was based on deep love, loyalty, humor, and fun. They were always together. She was his crutch, and he was her protector. He did an amazing job at showing her how a boy should treat a girl. He had incredible respect for women thanks to some wonderful role models in our family. We give him a lot of credit for Annabelle's healthy self-esteem. Patrick's sincere compliments and gentle nurturing of her self-confidence were invaluable gifts to her. He set the bar high for her future male relationships.

As teenagers, they loved to drive around and listen to music. They were only a year apart at school, and they shared friends and lots of fun experiences together, such as going to Prom.

With two years in between, Annabelle had ACL surgery on both of her knees from sports injuries. Patrick was with us for her second surgery. He was a protective presence for Annabelle and a calming companion for me. He brought humor to the situation as he encouraged Annabelle to say funny things during pre-op after she'd been given the relaxing drugs and then took a video that we could all laugh at later.

Annabelle looked after Patrick in a very loving way. She was his advisor; he sought and valued her opinion. She was very considerate of his sensitive nature. There was rarely a cross word said between them, and if there was, it was resolved quickly. They simply loved being in each other's company.

Annabelle shared these reflections in Chris's eulogy about Patrick:

"As one of Patrick's close friends said, anyone who talked to Patrick for as little as five minutes would add him to their list of best friends. He was special and kind to everyone he met. A few of the ways people have described Patrick since the accident on Thursday night are caring, compassionate, inclusive, outgoing, kind, loving, amazing, sweet, and unforgettable. While words can never do justice to our wonderful brother, I think we'd all be pretty honored if we were spoken about in this way when it was our time."

When Annabelle graduated from high school in June 2020, we joked that this was her second graduation, giving her some of the credit for Patrick's the year before because she definitely helped him along throughout his schooling. That's just how they were, always there for each other.

PATRICK AND MATILDA

Patrick and Matilda's relationship was equally loving. He delighted in having another little sister, and he would lie beside her when she was a baby, talking and singing to her and reciting nursery rhymes. Matilda was a great supporter of Patrick and his sports; I couldn't even begin to count the number of his games she watched over the years between football, cricket, baseball, and basketball. She was his number one fan. Whatever he was playing, Matilda learned all the rules, and she made sure she understood the game so that afterwards, they could discuss what he did well, how he could have done better and how the team performed overall.

They shared a lot of knowledge about professional sports too. As a 10 year old, Matilda was comfortable having a conversation with Patrick about draft picks, player statistics, profiles, game day predictions, anything sport-related. She loved participating in Patrick's March Madness competition; she even won it one year.

Patrick took Matilda under his wing from an early age. They played all sorts of games for hours on end, from sports to board games and video games; Matilda just wanted to be with her brother. Here in Cleveland, we live on a cul de sac, and when we moved in, close friendships quickly formed between our kids and the other kids on our street. They played countless games outside, usually wiffleball or basketball. Patrick was always so proud of Matilda as she was often the only girl playing with all the boys. There were no concessions for age or gender; she had to match it with the boys. It was all in good fun, but Patrick kept a watchful eye as he was very protective of her. If there was ever a need for him to step in and make sure she was treated fairly, he never hesitated.

When Matilda played Little League baseball for two years, she was the only girl on her team, and Patrick was her number one fan.

There were two occasions where Chris was traveling for work, and he reluctantly had to miss father/daughter events at Matilda's school. Patrick willingly and happily stepped in to fufill the dad role. The first was the father/daughter dance in middle school. My heart melted with love and pride over and over again that night. Firstly, as Patrick gave Matilda her corsage, then as all the dads (and Patrick) got up in front of everyone to learn the special dad dance, and lastly, watching Patrick and Matilda dance with all of the other fathers and daughters. He was the only teenage boy in a sea of dads, not the least bit self-conscious. He showed up fully for his sister. They smiled and laughed, and Matilda was so happy. The second was the father/daughter basketball practice. Again, Patrick willingly filled his dad's shoes, and he was the only brother to do so. They had lots of fun, and another special memory was made.

Matilda shared these reflections in Chris's eulogy about Patrick:

"Patrick was the best big brother anyone could have. He always protected his two sisters and would do anything for us. Patrick was the best person to get a second opinion from; he was honestly an angel on earth. Everyone wanted to be with him because he would lift them up instantly. Patrick was my rock; all I wanted to do was be with him. I loved my brother and will love him for the rest of my life."

Patrick got along very well with his sisters. He had a unique relationship with both of them. It devastates us that our girls have lost their brother, that this tragedy is part of their story. We wish we could spare them the pain. We are incredibly proud of how they are both doing their best to live with their grief. Getting up each day, going to school, putting on a brave face, doing the work, managing a smile, maintaining friendships, coming home and letting their guards down to decompress to then get up and do it all again the next day. Our girls are doing this with immense courage and grace.

Losing our son and brother is a type of loss that buries itself deeply in our hearts. We have had to rebuild our lives to accommodate our tragedy. We will continue on as the five of us because we will always represent Patrick; that is who we are.

"Identifying the blessings is a way to soften the piercingly sharp edges of the pain. I started to realize that from an unimaginable loss, beautiful gifts were available to us."

"For me, trying to see through this lens of gratitude felt like a good place to start. It provided a way for me to see the light when everything felt so dark."

CHAPTER FOUR

THE GIFTS

The concept of finding meaning in life while living with tragedy sparked something in me and opened me up to the possibility there could be some gifts and blessings that might arise from our trauma of losing Patrick. In the beginning, it can feel wrong to give ourselves permission to feel anything other than total despair and heartbreak over the loss of our loved one. We think we must stay in the sadness to honor our love. Rediscovering joy and acknowledging the gifts does not mean we love them any less. On the contrary, they want us to rise up somehow and experience happiness, laughter, and fun again. They want us to soak up the goodness when it shows up in our lives.

A step towards healing starts with beginning to give your grief a place in your life, a place for it to land, and be with you. It is not easy. It will feel as if it's the fight of your life, and you may feel resistant because your first instinct is to reject your awful new reality and deny it any airtime in your mind, heart, or your world. This is an understandable reaction because you are suffering. The truth can be too much to bear, and avoidance may feel much more manageable. I learned that I can feel deep sadness while at the same time immersing myself in the gifts. The two can co-exist simultaneously. It doesn't have to be one or the other. I feel as if my days are a combination of both. There is anguish about how I will endure this for the rest of my life, interwoven with gratitude that comes from the heart-opening moments when I turn my attention to the blessings.

By encouraging you to focus on the gifts that have and will come from your loss, my intention is to offer you another dimension for your grief experience. If you can broaden your view to notice the gifts that represent hope and healing, you may find that your heart feels a little lighter; there's a gentle reprieve from your pain, even for a moment.

Identifying the blessings is a way to soften the piercingly sharp edges of the pain. Some days this felt impossible for me, but slowly I began to see them. I started to realize that from an unimaginable loss, beautiful gifts were available to us. I offer my personal experience with the hope that it helps others find some peace in their struggle.

Patrick was, and will always be our gift, and his legacy is a gift to be shared.

NO REGRETS

One of the things I am the most grateful for is that I have no regrets regarding my relationship with Patrick. He knew how much I endlessly loved him, and I know how much he endlessly loved me. There was and is no doubt. We expressed our love without hesitation; he knew that I was proud of him, and our very close bond was mutual. There was nothing left unsaid. I feel boundlessly fortunate to be in this position. I understand that this is not always the case with a sudden loss.

When someone is taken from you unexpectedly, it can be so difficult to be left with regrets. If this is the case for you, professionals can help you work through this to find peace. A suggestion to lessen your burden is to write a letter to your loved one who has passed, telling them the things you didn't get the chance to say. Let your words flow uninhibited and unedited, get them all out, write them all down. Once you have finished, read it out loud to them, as if they were there with you. They may hear you and you may feel the release you need from your regret.

NATURE AND PATRICK'S GARDEN

A couple of weeks after the accident, I intuitively started to design a memorial garden for Patrick. I felt drawn to create a space where I could go to be with him and commemorate him, a place that I could nurture. He was so full of life and I knew that a garden would symbolize his life force. I would have never described myself as having a green thumb. I have always loved flowers, but I was not a gardener until now.

We have an area behind our house that's very private and enjoys lovely all-day sun; it was the perfect spot. After getting some help to clear the space and prepare the soil, I started to plant from my heart, and Patrick's garden came to life. I chose plants with meaning, such as rosemary for remembrance and others to attract butterflies and bees. Most of them have purple flowers in honor of Patrick's favorite color. I planted a magnolia and an autumn moon Japanese maple, which were both gifted to us by my girlfriends in Melbourne.

I had a piece of bluestone engraved with the words, "Patrick Michael. Our cherished son. Our much-loved brother. We will love you forever." I added a birdbath, bird feeder, wind chimes, an outdoor art piece, hearts, wooden angel wings, crystals, an angel statue, and a place to sit with a cup of tea to read, meditate, or journal. My friend Gilly, who visited us from Australia, wrapped a gold necklace that says "Love" around the trunk of the wisteria.

Early mornings in Patrick's garden are the best when the animals and birds are active. Sometimes I feel like Snow White; there is so much happening around me. Chipmunks race past, squirrels run along the fence, and birds splash in the birdbath.

Once I put some birdseed in my hand and held my arm out, hoping that the chickadee that was flying around the garden would eat from my hand, and out of nowhere, a baby robin flew over and landed there. It was so sweet. It stayed for a moment and then flew away. Another time a sparrow sat very close to me for way longer than a bird would usually stay, just calmly staring at me; its presence was so comforting. I've had three groundhogs visit me in the garden, two adults and one baby. The monarch butterflies love the butterfly bush and the milkweed.

Connecting to the plants, birds, and animals has brought me joy. They have so much to teach us. There is so much to see, hear, smell, and touch when you take the time to do so. It's a sensory and spiritual experience. They model the benefits of simplicity and innate wisdom; their soothing rhythms ground us. I began to crave nature and all of its lessons. I became fascinated with the moon and its influence on our energetic experience.

I love sitting in the garden at the start of the day with its soft light, listening to the symphony of the birds. Everything is waking up. I look for new signs of life, a flower bud that has opened or new shoots that have sprouted. In the early evening, as the sun sets and the tree frogs begin their serenade, I can feel the plants' energy slow down as they turn themselves in for the night.

As fall came to an end, many of the birds began their migration south, and Patrick's garden transitioned to dormancy for the winter. I knew I would miss it, so I created an indoor version, a place for me to tend to in the colder months and think of him.

I love that the cardinals stay over winter. They are our loved one's messengers, telling us that they are always with us. Their bright red feathers look so beautiful against the white snow.

When signs of spring began to show, with much anticipation, Patrick's outdoor garden started to come back to life. There is a divine order with which this happens, just like life. Certain plants bloom first and then others follow when it's their time. I love being the witness to this order and its lesson of patience.

Through the gift of the garden, I have seen how my love and Patrick's love can make plants flourish. Just as they respond to the energy of love, I believe that we also absorb that love and growth. In turn, we also flourish.

If you live in a place without a garden, you can still enjoy potted plants indoors next to a window or on a balcony. To soak up the positive effects of nature, you can visit your local park or botanical garden, sit by some water, find a hiking trail, or take a country drive. In some areas, there are community gardens and co-operatives you can join.

Spending time in nature this past year has been very therapeutic for me; it has felt like a healing balm. If you can, I recommend you try it. This gift has given me time to pause and reflect. I retreat to the garden for solace and time with Patrick. Nature has called me like never before. I have been drawn to its grounding and calming properties. Because the garden represents Patrick, it has provided a way for me to mother him still. I have felt him in the breeze and in the warmth of the sun.

COMMUNITY

Chris, the girls, and I have been astounded by the acts of kindness and generosity we have received since Patrick's accident. So much so that I have dedicated an entire chapter to show our gratitude in Chapter Five, titled Community. The support we have received has left an indelible mark on our hearts and has been one of our greatest gifts.

CARRYING ONE ANOTHER

When one of us is having an extra difficult day trying to live with their grief, another will carry a little more that day to lighten their load. We cannot predict when a harder day will hit, but when it does, knowing we have one another's backs is a blessing.

FREEDOM FROM ENTANGLEMENT
AND CLARITY OF BOUNDARIES

When you are in survival mode, things have a way of becoming crystal clear. I am now more intentional about to what and to whom I give my energy. This has been so freeing and affirming. Experiencing devastating loss has given me the liberating gift of saying no (without guilt) to situations that aren't healthy for me. Guilt can be a very strong emotion when you are grieving. It's exhausting in itself if you let it have power over you. Try to let go of the need to "people-please" and allow yourself to make decisions that feel right for you whether you are navigating a loss or not. Tying yourself in knots believing you have to explain your choices will deplete you.

Being entangled in a complicated or compromising situation drains our energy. When you are deeply experiencing grief, you may find you have a lower tolerance to stress. I certainly have. If you untangle yourself from the situations and people who don't make you feel good, you take care of yourself in a very loving way. I am committed to protecting my energy and allowing my intuition to guide me. Listening to your inner voice as that whisper of truth is your compass. It will always steer you in the direction that's right for you. Your deep knowing is your anchor, and as you start to trust it more, it will ground you when you feel unsure about setting a boundary.

In grief, and even if you are not mourning a loss, it is so important to guard your energy carefully because we all have our limits. This experience has taught me to listen even more closely to what feels right and what doesn't. Becoming untethered has been a transformative gift.

With what and with whom do you need to set clearer boundaries? Where are you leaking your energy?

VULNERABILITY

When given the news of Patrick's accident, I immediately fell into a deep well of emotions. It felt like quicksand as if at any minute it would swallow me up. It was terrifying, it was real, and it was raw.

Whether we like it or not, grief renders us vulnerable. We are emotionally wounded. Our fragile hearts are exposed. Vulnerability can be very daunting for some, and avoiding it is a form of self-protection. The instinct to guard our shattered hearts is strong and sometimes putting on our protective armor feels as if it's the only way to survive. That's okay. Grief takes us to our absolute edge and brings us to our knees. I am a sensitive person and I don't shy away from vulnerability or from showing emotion; Patrick was the same. I am willing to step into the pain, knowing that its intensity will change, depending on the moment. I try to let go of any resistance to my anguish, and I let it wash over me like a wave. Sometimes the waves feel as strong as a tsunami and other times, they are more predictable. Vulnerability is uncomfortable; however, therein lies growth.

To move forward on our healing path, we must be true to ourselves in our grief. Differences in personalities and ways of grieving and coping are highlighted when we are faced with tragedy. It has a way of magnifying both our strengths and our limitations. Awareness and acceptance of these differences are both critical to maintaining unified relationships. An understanding of how far others are willing to embrace vulnerability is also important. Being open to vulnerability is not a sign of weakness. If we reveal ourselves to its possibilities, it can be one of our greatest gifts.

This book truly is my heart on a plate. With courage, I chose to offer it to you because, as humans, we need connection. Sharing from a place of authenticity cultivates that connection. It feels supportive to know we are not alone when we learn about others who are also navigating loss. It's said that opening up about personal tragedy can help our mental and physical health.

How do you view vulnerability? Does it scare you? Do you avoid it? Do you welcome it?

LETTING GO OF EXPECTATION

Being the support person for someone who is grieving is a very hard job. I am in awe of those who have been mine. How do they know when to listen, when to speak, and what to say? If you have found yourself in this role but you're not sure where to start with how to help someone, my advice is that one of the most impactful things you can do is simply show up for them. Even when you are petrified that you will say or do the wrong thing, you just need to step in. Listen deeply. Resist the urge to talk too much. Be a loving witness. Tell them that you see them, you hear them, and that you acknowledge their deep struggle by saying, "I am here for you. I am listening. I am right here." Don't compare their story with your own or someone else's. They need to feel validated in their own experience, not dismissed. They don't need to hear about another person's situation at this point. Even though it's uncomfortable, try not to retreat from someone who is grieving. Don't let your inability to fix things or the daunting thought of your jumbled words make you pull away from them. Don't be afraid of their grief and their tears. They need you.

Sometimes people who are close to you are paralyzed by not knowing what to say, so they don't say anything at all. Or they assume that you want to be left alone, so they don't reach out. Or they are fearful of upsetting you further, which is unlikely. Some personalize a tragedy, where their own pain overrides their ability to be there for others. Then time passes, and they may feel as if it's too late or they're embarrassed about their absence, so they freeze in their lack of contact and remain absent and silent. This emotional paralysis response was not something Chris and I expected, so that's why I'm sharing that it's possible. While it surprised us, we have since learned that this can happen with grief; it may have even happened to you. People behave according to their personal level of awareness, consciousness, and capabilities. A tragedy can change the course of relationships and friendships. Initially, this can be confusing, disappointing, and hurtful.

Grief has a way of filtering relationships. You may find that the people you thought would be there for you are absent or, worse, have disappeared. If this has happened to you and you don't know how to make sense of it, try to have gratitude for those who stand with you and compassion for those who can't. Some people are just not equipped, even when you thought or hoped they would be. It's usually not from a place of ill-intent and it doesn't mean they don't care about you. Lovingly release all expectations of others, knowing that how they respond to your loss should not be taken personally.

In her book, *It's OK That You're Not OK*, Megan Devine explains: "Grief changes your friendships. For many, many people, it ends them. Your loss intersects with often hidden or especially painful heartbreak in the people around you. Your pain bumps up against their pain. Even when your friends want to support you, we often don't have the skills - no matter how skilled we are - to witness and withstand another's pain. The injustice of these second losses makes grief itself that much more difficult."

My friend, Andrea Vecchio, an author and storyteller, gave a compelling and engaging TED Talk about the power of human connection through uncomfortable conversations. When I asked Andrea to describe her message to me, she said:

"I believe it was a message that found me, a divine intervention of sorts. It began to write itself after an emotional exchange I had with the parents of a young boy I grew up with after he passed at a young age. I was so afraid to walk into that conversation. What could I possibly say to anyone who lost a child? I thought about turning away and avoiding the exchange altogether because I was afraid; afraid of saying the wrong thing, embarrassed that I hadn't spoken my apologies sooner, and fearful that I wouldn't emotionally handle their reaction the 'right way.' If you have a beating heart, one day you will find yourself in a space where you'll have to make a choice – a choice to walk into an uncomfortable conversation to connect with another human being who is in pain, or a choice to avoid them altogether. My message is to be brave. Choose courage to show compassion and forge human connection every chance you're given."

I was in the audience when Andrea presented her talk. She was authentic and she spoke with great compassion. It's an excellent resource; I have referenced it in the Acknowledgments at the end of the book. Her story is especially helpful for those who are struggling to be a support person for someone who is grieving. Andrea says, "Show up with a good heart. When you step into that moment, that uncomfortable moment and you forge human connection; you offer one of your greatest gifts, the gift of compassion through your humanity."

TIME WITH DR. KEITH JORDAN

I met Dr. Keith Jordan about five years ago. I had heard so much about him from my yoga community. They told me he was a gifted healer, that sessions with him were life-changing. I called the Optimal Wellness Center here in Cleveland and made my appointment. The fact there was a five-month wait to see him was a testament to just how brilliant a healer Keith was.

Over the years, Keith has been instrumental in guiding me towards living my life from a place of unconditional love, acceptance, peace, and compassion. This is the inspirational path he teaches in his book, *The Practice,* and on his interactive online learning platform, *The Practice Heals,* Keith explains, "The goal of the Practice is Living in a place of complete balance and peace. By Living the Practice, you begin to realize the Eternity you are existing in. To get to that place, you must release the parts of yourself in conflict with this Truth. When we Practice living fully and loving life unconditionally, we set the intention to do what is in the highest good. We begin to realize the totality of Life is beyond human comprehension. *The Practice* is a series of inspired spiritual teachings that show your infinite soul how to live eternally. As you practice living intuitively, the energy of ego then surrenders into oneness with all of Life. All your choices dissolve into choice-less surrender."

I am committed to my healing path and all that it has taught and given me. Every day is a Practice. I Practice living from an intuitive place, balancing my emotions, being comfortable in not always understanding Life, living my truth unapologetically, and surrendering what is not in my control (which is almost everything). Sometimes this comes effortlessly and other times, it's a real challenge; that is why it's a daily Practice. One thing I know for sure is that we are all living according to our own level of consciousness. This allows me to have compassion for myself and others. Keith has taught me that unhealthy patterns of behavior can be changed and that the perception of control is an illusion. In order to live an eternal life now, we must let go of the constraint of the context of time. I embrace these lessons of enlightenment and I try to see the Divine everywhere.

Just 10 hours after the accident, I was on the phone with Keith. He was out of the country on vacation, and Tim, our mutual close friend, had called him to tell him about Patrick. It was around 6 am when we spoke. Desperate for some guidance on how to begin to take my first healing step, I remember saying to him, "Tell me what I have to do." He immediately took me to my love for Patrick. He asked me to keep repeating the words, "I love him so much, I love him so much." Over and over, we said these words together. This mantra took me into my shattered heart, and it gave me a source of focus. It was the best direction to take. It helped me to start to put my love above my grief. He calmly explained to me that not only was Patrick gone in the physical, but our life as we knew it as the five of us, was also gone. We had all experienced a death. Patrick's bodily presence was a crucial pillar in the structure of our family unit, and with this loss, our house had crumbled down around us. We now had to start to find a way to live in our new life, and the way to do this was through our love. From thousands of miles away, Keith poured healing into me, Chris, and the girls. I have so much gratitude for this incredible gift.

A couple of weeks later, Keith and I met in person, and we have met multiple times since. We talk and he reminds me how to keep practicing living this life fully and loving this life unconditionally. Keith is my teacher, my healer, and my friend. He encourages me to share what has become available to me since losing Patrick. He tells me, "All great teachers teach from where they are now."

TIME WITH FATHER TOM FANTA

Father Tom is the reverend at a church here in Cleveland. The first time I heard him speak was at a funeral for a man who was very loved in our community, Terry Hunt, just two months before we lost Patrick. I was captivated by his presence and his words; his message to the grieving family was so meaningful and authentic; it was the most poignant homily I had ever heard. We first met each other a couple of weeks before Patrick died at a mutual friend's graduation party. We enjoyed a great conversation together and I was pleased that Patrick was able to meet him that night too. Unfortunately, Father Tom was unable to be a part of Patrick's funeral as he had a personal commitment. He kindly offered to meet with me three weeks after the accident. It was a wonderful two hours, full of great discussion, meaning, and healing intention. The insights that he shared with me from his many years of experience with people, life, and death spoke to me in the way they did that first time I heard him preach. With his permission, I am sharing his lessons with you because they were a gift to me, and I hope they will also be a blessing to you:

"Don't keep Patrick at 19 years old. Allow him to age with you."

Father Tom had many pearls of wisdom, but this one really resonated with my heart. I love the idea of taking Patrick through life with me and imagining him at age 20, 35, 52, 66, etc. It feels so wrong to have him stuck at 19. On February 27 each year, I will think of him as another year older (and definitely as another year more handsome) as he grows older with me.

"God snatched him from death; he lives on; he still has work to do.

Be open and the signs from Patrick will keep coming.

You will recognize his spirit as love when you die; you will know him by his love.

You will be okay. You might not be great for a long time or ever, but you will be okay.

Heaven is not a far-away place; it is right here all around us.

He will come to you in meditation.

Focus not on his physical body but on being grateful that you love each other and always will, and while his physical body was taken, your love can never be taken.

No regrets.

When answering the question, 'How are you?' a response can be, 'I'm living my life,' because that's what you are all trying to do in grief.

He is a shining light; he has light all around him.

Heaven is timeless; for Patrick, it will seem like a second until you meet again.

Patrick wants you to feel joy again. He knows you still have work to do, and the best thing you can do is do that for him as well as you can.

He is still very much with you, just in a different form.

This scar will make you stronger as a family. He wants you to be strong and live your life.

He will be at peace if you are at peace.

Be open to Patrick and he will guide you. Follow his way and he will bring you closer to God."

I will always be grateful for Father Tom's wisdom and the time that he gave me so generously that night. It truly was a gift that I return to often as I try to navigate our new world.

If you are struggling, is there someone you can talk to for spiritual guidance?

EMBRACING IMMORTALITY

Immortality is unending life, the power of life beyond this human existence. Our love for Patrick is eternal. While his physical body has gone, his soul is immortal. Understanding this has been a gift because I know that Patrick is still with us and always will be. Our souls are connected, and we will be reunited when we join him. When we let go of fear and doubt about immortality, and we understand we are not limited to the time constraints of this one lifetime, so much more opens up to us.

SIMPLICITY

Losing someone or something we deeply love has a way of stripping back the excess and amplifying what truly matters. Grief gifts us the opportunity to live and love from a more authentic place, and we may crave simplicity like never before. This desire to shed the unnecessary can be felt on both a physical and emotional level. Our home and work environments may be crowded with items we don't need, and our minds may be congested with thoughts that we are better off without. There is a link between clutter, the stress it causes, and the state of our health.

I have been guided to simplify by doing the following: unsubscribing from unnecessary emails, reducing my exposure to sensationalized news and what I view on social media, donating household items we don't need, protecting my energy from other people's opinions and behavior, and creating even more space in my day for self-care. I have tried to reduce everything to what I love and need.

How can you simplify your life? What areas of your life need decluttering?

THE ANGELS PUT IN MY PATH

There have been many angels put in my path since June 27, 2019. I know that Patrick has sent them to me to help me heal.

When Annabelle, Kim, and I went to the accident site, we were incredibly fortunate to meet Melissa, the lovely police officer who was first on the scene that night. She went above and beyond with the care she showed Patrick, and I am eternally grateful to her. She told me that she did so because she is a mother and she would have wanted someone to do the same for her child. She also shared with Annabelle that she too had lost a brother in an accident. Our tragedy hit close to home for her. We cried together and we hugged. It was an unforgettable moment. We were so moved to be able to thank her in person. Melissa, you are an angel, and I thank Patrick for guiding us to meet you.

Sadly, many other mothers have lost their precious children. Nancy is one of them. She came to our house one day not long after Patrick's accident and she met Chris. She left me a beautiful card with her phone number and an open invitation to connect when I was ready. I heard from a mutual friend that Nancy and I shared similar stories. We had both lost our only sons, who were similar ages when they died in sudden accidents. We lived in the same community, we also had two daughters each, our boys were well-loved and were talented athletes.

It took me nine months to feel ready to call Nancy. We talked for three hours. We cried, confided, knew exactly how each other felt, connected deeply, and became instant friends. It had been over 20 years since Nancy lost Kyle. Her pain and the way she recalled the details were as fresh as if it were yesterday. I asked her so many questions and she was honest with me about what the road ahead would look like, which I really appreciated. We talked about our beautiful boys and the immense heartbreak of having them ripped away. She was also incredibly close to her son. This type of bond forged between two mothers cultivated from a shared loss is difficult to put into words. To have someone who completely understood the intricacies of my sorrow while also being able to show me that life can still have meaning was such a gift. Nancy, you are an angel, and I thank Patrick for sending you to me. I'm so grateful for you. I know our boys are together, making sure their mums are okay.

Mark, who worked at the Apple store, was another angel who went the extra mile to help me. I had thousands of photos of Patrick from when he was younger, photos of our three kids together, and family photos stored on a very outdated Mac laptop that could barely keep a charge for me to even view them. I was desperate to retrieve and save them. This was not something they usually do at the Genius Bar. My dear friends, Odile and Gilly, were staying with us from Australia at the time and were determined to solve my problem. When we arrived at the appointment, they lovingly told me to make myself scarce while they explained my situation to Mark. Through tears, having just lost his father, Mark immediately told them he would help us. We sat for about four hours in that store while my vintage Mac slowly gained charge, and Mark worked his magic, transferring the photos onto an external hard drive. This was not easy because of the age of the laptop. A big concern was that once we unplugged it from a power source, the charge would rapidly decline. We would be back to square one if we couldn't maintain the battery life. When the battery finally reached 99%, we thanked Mark profusely for his patience, kindness, and commitment to our cause. We unplugged the power cord and bolted to the car. It was a 15-minute drive home, and instead of draining down, the charge went up to 100% as soon as we got into the car (thank you Patrick). We made it home with some life still left in the ancient Mac, plugged it in, and it then took three days to download all the photos. I am so relieved to have them. Mark, you are an angel, and I thank you for helping us that day when you didn't have to, and I thank Patrick for guiding us to you.

Chris, who worked at a local nursery where I have bought many plants for Patrick's garden, was another beautiful angel. One morning I was walking around looking for some purple flowers. I asked Chris some questions about the plants I had chosen, and we got talking. I told her my story about why I was creating the garden, and she immediately took her necklace off from around her neck and gave it to me. It was a Mother Mary medal, and she said to me, "Pray to Mary; she knows what it's like to lose a child. She will help you." I'll never forget her words and her spontaneous generosity and kindness; I was so touched. That necklace is very special to me because it symbolizes sincere compassion. Chris, you are an angel who lifted my spirits that day, and I thank Patrick for putting you in my path.

SURRENDERING CONTROL
AND THE NEED TO UNDERSTAND WHY

Control is an illusion, and the more we push and try to exert our will, thinking it will get us the outcome we want, the more challenging life becomes. We must surrender and detach from the expectation that we are fully in charge of our destiny. This is not easy because, as humans, we crave control; it makes us feel safe. There are some aspects of our lives that we can influence, such as our reactions to situations and people, but our lives are largely out of our hands. We cannot guarantee the well-being of our loved ones. I had to accept that there was nothing I could have done to prevent losing Patrick. This truth was a bitter pill to swallow because, as his mother, I had spent the last 19 years trying to keep him safe from harm. On the night of June 27, 2019, however, I could not protect him, no matter how much I wish that was not true. I would have done anything to prevent him from losing his life. In the weeks following the accident, I had to surrender the false belief that I could have influenced a different outcome.

Grief brings up many questions. For me, they have been: How could this happen to Patrick? Why do young people have to die? Why are the best humans taken? Why do some parents lose a child while others get to live their whole lives with all of their children? I have had to surrender my need to know the answers. When something feels so wrong, we cling to the intense desire to find an explanation so we can make sense of it in our minds. We are really just spinning our wheels and causing ourselves more distress. When we release ourselves from the illusion of control and the need to know why through the practice of surrender, we clear the path for a more peaceful existence.

Take some time to reflect on your relationship with control. In what areas of your life do you need to surrender more?

THE BEAUTY OF THE PAUSE

Grief makes you pause. It can sometimes feel as if your life has come to a grinding halt. I view this as a sacred pause. Appreciating this gift has allowed me to notice things I may have otherwise missed. I've heard the soothing coo of the mourning dove in the distance, the unique sound that a squirrel makes, I've heard catbirds singing their hearts out. I've closely watched bees dive head-first into clover and dahlia flowers to drink their pollen. I've sat amongst monarch butterflies in Patrick's garden and enjoyed their whimsical dance from flower to flower.

Do you take the time to pause?

WRITING THIS BOOK

Writing, like healing, has so many layers. The book writing process has allowed me to flow with, explore, and be with my grief. It has provided a place for me to both shelter and begin to heal and a purpose greater than I could have ever imagined. This opportunity has been an incredible blessing. I am humbled to have created this body of work with Patrick by my side. In many respects, it's my gift to him.

NEW TRADITIONS

A new ritual evolved organically for us that we called "Cheeseboard Friday." Each Friday at the end of the day, we sit down to enjoy a delicious cheeseboard. We plan what we will include on the board in advance, and it's become a defining and enjoyable part of our week. The thought of starting new family traditions with the four of us felt very unsettling and upsetting for me initially. The first time we did it, becoming teary, I looked out the window into the garden and saw a cardinal staring straight at me. I knew Patrick was with us that evening and that he would be there every Friday. New traditions don't mean old ones are forgotten. They rekindle joy and fun.

68

Your lost loved one would want that for you. Feel them there. Give yourself permission to welcome something new.

I encourage you to think about the possibility of the gifts that have come to you as a result of your loss. I don't begin to imply that there are always gifts available, as some tragedies feel insurmountable. However, if there is even a chance that you may find just one blessing, allow your heart and mind to be open to it and receive its goodness. In doing so, you may even experience more. For me, trying to see through this lens of gratitude felt like a good place to start. It provided a way for me to see the light when everything felt so dark.

"The word was out that our family was in crisis and crisis brings people together. Our community was showing us that they would carry us when we could barely breathe or stand."

CHAPTER FIVE

COMMUNITY

"As you can see from the outpouring of support, you don't mourn alone; the whole community lost a great young man who made such a positive impact on all those that he touched."

These words were written on a card that was sent to us. They represent the collective grief that reverberated throughout our community and beyond. Loss can feel so insular when you're in the epicenter of it, but we quickly realized that the news of Patrick's passing generated a ripple effect of deep shock and pain.

Chris, Annabelle, Matilda, and I, together with our families, would like to pay tribute to our amazing local community here in Cleveland. We have been so touched by the magnitude of love shown for Patrick and for us. Losing Patrick opened our eyes to something we, nor our family and friends who came from Australia and around the US, had ever seen or experienced before. We acknowledge that this doesn't happen to everyone and realize how uniquely blessed we have been to receive such incredible support.

From early morning the day after Patrick's accident, people began to appear at our house. Some we knew, others we didn't. The word was out that our family was in crisis and crisis brings people together. The doorbell rang and there stood four senior staff members from our city school district, two Principals, the Superintendent, and the

Executive Director. I remember being deeply moved by the vision of them standing there as a united force for us. Our community was showing us that they would carry us when we could barely breathe or stand.

THE ROCK

Near one of the entrances to the high school, a very large rock sits on an open grassed area. It gets painted by the students and sometimes the parents when there is a special event such as the first day of school, football games, sporting events, the musical opening night, and school dances. The day after losing Patrick, we received a photo of the rock. The whole thing had been painted green with #13 (Patrick's football jersey number) and a love heart in white with the words, "Once a Pirate, Always a Pirate." (A pirate is his school's symbol.) We were incredibly touched by this very thoughtful gesture by the mums of Patrick's football teammates.

The green rock instantly became a sacred and special gathering place. It gave the people in our community somewhere to go to be together in their grief, share stories, cry, and hold one another up. Flowers, plants, candles, letters, wreaths, jerseys, lights, photos, and symbols of what Patrick meant to people were left at the rock. His friends met there at all hours of the night; some slept there. A candlelight vigil burned for days. As a family, we were blown away by how essential the rock became for all of us. It had such deep meaning and Patrick would have been so humbled by how many people visited it to honor him.

On the Saturday night, two days after the accident, after the storm when the double rainbow appeared over our house, a photo was taken of the same double rainbow arched perfectly over the green rock. That photo became a symbol that was shared around the community.

Sometimes I would go to the rock late at night to sit quietly in my pain. One night I was there by myself when a car pulled up. A woman got out who I didn't recognize as she walked towards me.

72

She smiled and sat down next to me. I could tell straight away from her facial expression and body language that she didn't know who I was. She said she had never met "the boy," but she had heard he was lovely. She asked if I knew his name and I told her, "His name was Patrick." She talked about the accident and what had happened from what she had seen on the news and read online. I nodded and braced myself for what I knew was coming, "And how did you know the boy?" I took a deep breath and replied, "I'm Patrick's mother." She was mortified, of course. I reassured her, it was okay; she didn't know. I actually felt extremely honored to be lucky enough at that moment to be able to say that I was his mother. I couldn't have been prouder to tell her. I was bursting with pride while drowning in sadness simultaneously.

Six weeks after the accident, the school respectfully suggested that, with our blessing, it was time for the rock to be re-painted. It had served a great purpose, but we knew it couldn't stay green forever. It was nearing the start of the new school year and it was decided that in honor of Patrick, the football team would paint it after practice one day. Chris, the girls, and I gathered there together with the football community. It was a solemn and quiet moment as the rock turned from green to maroon, one of the school colors. It was sad to see it transform, we all felt it, but it was the right time for it to happen.

The rock had such an impact on the community that we were inspired to create a similar place at the high school for us and others to sit and be with Patrick. With the school's permission, we had a smaller rock and a marble bench made.

THE ROCK AND BENCH

The new rock has a marble inlay engraved with his name, "Patrick Michael Green," and a black and white image of him playing football. There is also a quote that reads, "And in the end, it's not the years in your life that count. It's the life in your years."

The marble bench is engraved with the words, "In Loving

73

Memory, Patrick Michael Green, Class of 2019." Patrick's class very generously donated some of the funds towards purchasing the rock and bench, which we greatly appreciated.

The process of design and selection was extremely confronting. The people who helped us were very kind, but I felt just as I did when the funeral director walked through our door, sick to my stomach for needing these people; every part of me felt resistant. You just never imagine walking around a tombstone and memorial showroom because you lost your 19 old son and brother, and truthfully, I hated that day. We reminded ourselves of why we were doing this, it was another opportunity to represent and commemorate Patrick and continue his legacy.

We held a ceremony to launch the new rock and bench on September 27, 2019, three months after Patrick's accident, and the evening of the football team's first home game of the season. Many people from our community attended. Chris gave a poignant speech about what this place of commemoration meant to us. The news cameras were there. It was another very difficult moment but also a proud occasion that we welcomed as a chance to shine Patrick's light.

We absolutely love it when people tell us that they've been to the rock and bench, when they send us photos from there, or they tell us that they needed Patrick's inspiration and advice, so they talked with him there. It warms our hearts when we find a bunch of flowers placed on the bench. We feel good about having a place for people to go to for comfort. It is a way for us to give back to our community, acknowledging all that we have received.

A minute of silence was held for Patrick at the start of the football game that evening. It was very moving and much appreciated.

On June 27, 2020, Patrick's first anniversary, a group of his friends painted the large rock at the high school green again and stenciled his initials, "PG" in white. They had a sign made that once again read, "Once a Pirate, Always a Pirate." Flowers were left at this rock and also at the smaller rock and bench. It was very emotional for us to see the community commemorating Patrick a year later.

F3: FITNESS, FELLOWSHIP, FAITH

In June 2018, Chris started working out with a local fitness group based at the high school called F3. The group had been going for seven years in our suburb. They hold six workouts a week that people can attend.

On the F3 website, it states: "F3 is a national network of free, peer-led workouts for men. Our mission is to plant, grow, and serve small workout groups for men for the invigoration of male community leadership."

Kevin Cmiel, a family friend, described the response from F3 after Patrick's accident. Kevin (F3 nickname Schottenheimer) brought F3 to Ohio from North Carolina and is the founder of the local chapter:

"One important concept of F3 is something we call a 'Shield Lock.' This is the idea of men standing shoulder to shoulder to encourage, protect, and defend those people most important in our lives. The news of Patrick's accident hit hard, and without pause, the men of F3 sprang into action. F3 fosters a sense of brotherhood amongst the group, and our brother, Thunderdome (Chris's F3 nickname), was hurting and needed support. Locally, the response of F3 Cleveland was a genuine and real outpouring of love. Men reached out directly and over the phone to offer condolences, to listen, to pray, or simply to just be there. We planted the F3 Flag in front of the Green's house and then planted F3 Flags in front of the church for the funeral mass. We wanted you to know that the men of F3 nation were there to support you and that we were praying for you. The national response was also heartwarming. Numerous regions across the nation sent their thoughts and prayers, wore green to workouts, and included your family in our Circles of Trust.

In mid-August, we held a summer convergence in which Chris hosted the Friday night BBQ. There was a huge turnout. The party went on pretty late into the evening, and many laughs were shared; it was a good night. The F3 fellowship and camaraderie over the weekend were so evident and seemed to be a very nice distraction, even for a short time, to the heartache Chris was experiencing.

We were also humbled to help in the activities surrounding the fundraising effort for Patrick's memorial scholarship fund. Contributions came from across the F3 nation and dozens attended the check presentation ceremony in September. We were there to surround and support. We were there as a shield lock for the Green family.

Our first F stands for Fitness. These are the early morning outdoor group workouts and where you would find Chris on most days. Not only was Chris showing up, but he was also physically pushing and conditioning himself to a new level. As he said, working out with maximum effort and being with the group was a distraction and provided a way to deal with the pain in his heart and soul. We can only hope that the fitness, fellowship, and faith from F3 have provided some support and solace to Chris during this time. What we have witnessed in Chris's dedication, goodness, and grace has been an inspiration to all of us. F3 is a better organization because of Chris."

Charlie Bowers, a family friend (F3 Nickname Patriot), first introduced Chris to F3. Patrick was also a member of F3; his nickname was Master Blaster. Charlie shared:

"When I first approached Chris about coming to F3, I stressed the good workouts in fear that he might be dissuaded by talk of fellowship and improving ourselves to better serve our families and community. I saw the error in my judgment as he quickly became a valued member of the group. Several of the guys already knew Patrick through their own kids and it was wonderful to see him support Chris by participating in F3 father/son days. I don't know what he really thought about the nickname Master Blaster, but he didn't complain.

I learned of Patrick's accident during our F3 workout the morning after it happened. At the close of each session, we take a few moments to make announcements about upcoming activities and share concerns. That day, when it was announced that one of our own had suffered the ultimate loss, there was a silence during which you could feel a swell of emotion rising. Not having any other outlet, grown men hugged as though it was their own loss.

In the days and weeks that followed, that emotion continued to grow and took shape through reaching out and helping Chris and his family in any way possible. Maybe the best thing the group did was signal to Chris that we were not going to leave him alone. The best thing he may have done was to return to the group. His presence gave us and him the opportunity to express our grief, but also to interact normally in a way that dissolved the tension that comes with a profound tragedy. From there, we moved on to finding ways to honor Patrick together in our workouts, and we will continue to do so as long as we carry on. If there was anything unique about the role F3 played in Chris' life at that horrible time, it occurred not because of F3, but because Chris and Patrick's shared knack for being authentic and connecting with people brought out a very genuine compassion within the group."

On the morning of Patrick's funeral, Chris attended the F3 workout. At least 50 guys showed up, with some driving from three or four hours away to be there for the 6 am start. It was a display of such incredible fellowship. Some of the exercises were done in front of the green rock. All F3 groups nationwide wore green that day to honor Patrick and our family was included in special prayers and intentions at the end of the workouts. There were many heartwarming tweets from around the country with photos of everyone in green, tributes to Patrick, and messages of support for Chris.

On February 27, 2020, the F3 Cleveland workout was dedicated to Patrick on what would have been his 20th birthday. Again, there was a large turnout, and all the guys wore green. It was a freezing cold morning and the ground was covered in snow. They finished the session standing in a circle in front of the new rock and bench.

To this day, many of the guys do their exercises in sets of 13 to honor Patrick.

On June 27, 2020, Patrick's first anniversary, Chris led the workout. The men wore green and fathers brought their sons, who were all initiated with their own nicknames. It was a very meaningful tribute to Patrick and a loving show of support to Chris.

We are extremely thankful to F3 for all they have done for Chris and our family.

SCHOLARSHIPS IN PATRICK'S NAME

We are incredibly proud and grateful to say three scholarships were established in Patrick's name.

1. The Patrick Green Memorial Scholarship, Rocky River High School

Managed by our city school Education Foundation, this scholarship was spearheaded by our local F3 community to honor Patrick's life, sustain his memory, and ensure his legacy of leadership, goodness, and commitment to service.

With many generous contributions from both our communities in the US and Australia, the initial revenue goal of $20,000 was exceeded in just two days. The fund ended up at triple the goal, and, to this day, donations are still being made in Patrick's memory.

On September 27, 2019, the same night that we unveiled the new rock and bench, together with the F3 community, we presented the scholarship check to the Education Foundation in a ceremony during half time of the high school football game. This was a proud moment; the four of us felt very supported by F3 and our community.

Chris, the girls, and I set the criteria for the scholarship recipient:

"This scholarship will be awarded to a graduating senior who best exhibits the characteristics Patrick stood for, including generosity of spirit, inclusiveness, and friendship to all. Most of all, the student will have demonstrated a willingness to embrace all staff and students at the high school with a caring and loving attitude."

Our intention was to make a significant difference to the academic life of the student; therefore, we set the amount to be awarded at $10,000.

In May 2020, we chose the first scholarship recipient, Mahdi Salti. Mahdi is a wonderful young man from a beautiful family, and he is incredibly deserving of this recognition. He's kind, gentle, humble, polite, respectful, a leader, involved with special needs programs, an athlete, and is held in high regard by his peers. He shares such similar qualities to Patrick. It was an emotional process from the selection to the presentation. We spent a very special afternoon with Mahdi, his parents, grandmother, and siblings, and we will never forget their hospitality and gratitude. We are so happy for Mahdi and we know that Patrick is too. It felt really good to have something positive come from our tragedy.

Mahdi shared this with us:

"Yet again, Patrick Green has found a way to make me smile with joy. Being selected as the first-ever recipient of the esteemed Patrick Green Memorial Scholarship has cemented itself as a great life achievement. From the moments of happiness and shock from when I received this award to the later years of my life, I will always hold this award close to my heart. It brings feelings hard to describe. The overwhelming emotions of happiness and joy keep me speechless to this day.

Knowing Patrick Green was an honor like no other. I had the opportunity to play football with him and learn from him as a mentor in our high school's Freshman Mentoring Program. His leadership style stood out to me. Patrick was kind and accepting of all. No matter what grade you were in or who you were, Patrick treated everyone equally and fairly. As one of the captains of the school wrestling team, I conveyed Patrick's leadership style to my own team, using it to affect all in a positive and encouraging way.

Not only was Patrick a great leader and role model, but he was also a great friend with his outgoing personality along with his loving and caring attitude, which I have learned from and admire greatly.

For the rest of my life, I will always look to Patrick in times of hardship and times of prosperity. The Patrick Green Memorial Scholarship means the world to my family and me. We are ever so grateful for the generosity of the Green Family."

Around the time of Patrick's first anniversary, more generous donations were made to his scholarship fund, which we greatly appreciated.

2. The Patrick Green Scholarship, Bay Village High School

From our friend, Amy Bircher Bruyn:

"The reason that I started this scholarship for Patrick at Bay Village High School is a simple one. I, like many families around the world, was completely shocked in June 2019, when Patrick lost his life in a sudden, tragic event. While I knew Patrick only for a brief time, it was clear to me that he was a special kid and that his legacy must live on in our community where Patrick was also well known. For me, it was a chance to spread the love to Bay Village and honor Patrick for the wonderful person that he was with the hope that it impacts the scholarship recipient for the rest of their lives."

3. The Patrick M. Green Scholarship, Ohio University

Chris attended Ohio University's graduate school as an international student in 1996-1997 to gain his Master's degree in Sports Administration. It was there where he met Kevin Abrams, who became a life-long friend. When Chris and I moved to Dallas in 1997, we were introduced to Mark Harrison, a fellow Australian, and his wife, Suzanne. They had both been through the Sports Administration program a few years before at OU and also became our very close friends.

Here Mark and Suzanne and Kevin and Sarah-Jane share why they decided to create the scholarship:

"We started an annual scholarship to honor the beautiful life of Patrick Green. The donation to fund the scholarship was placed in an endowment fund, which will ensure the Patrick M. Green Scholarship will be given to an international student, in perpetuity, who has been admitted to the Masters in Sports Administration program at Ohio University. We hope this donation will help change the lives of many, just as Patrick changed the lives of all those he touched."

DONATIONS IN PATRICK'S NAME

We chose St Malachi's Back Door Ministry and Autism Speaks for those who wanted to donate in Patrick's name. St Malachi's was where Patrick volunteered. We chose Autism Speaks in honor of Thibault Plante and Paul Witzigreuter, who are both dear friends of Patrick's and our family.

FOOD

Food is a symbol of love. In the days after losing Patrick, we were blessed with many donations and gifts of food. Our friends, who own one of our favorite local restaurants, Cleveland Vegan, kindly made food to help feed the hundreds of people who visited us. The lovely owner of the Chinese restaurant where Patrick worked called me in tears after hearing the news and donated food. The owners of the local brewing company where Patrick also worked were very generous in their gift to us. We received gift cards to grocery stores and restaurants. People left coolers full of drinks on our back deck. Community groups gathered funds to deliver us meals. Our close friend Kim made us many beautiful home-cooked dinners (and still does). Another dear friend, Katie, has made us dinner every single Tuesday since the accident (and still does). She has shown such devotion and her delicious meals are made with love. We are so grateful for her nourishment and unwavering care for our family.

We are very thankful for all of the immense generosity. It really helped us, especially in the beginning, when we couldn't even think about preparing a meal.

TRIBUTES TO PATRICK AND ACTS OF KINDNESS

Our community showered us with tributes to Patrick and incredible acts of kindness that will never be forgotten. These gestures came in many forms. Some were things people did or words they wrote;

others were things they made with their own hands or had made so that we had lasting symbols of Patrick that represented what he meant to so many.

In the days following the accident, all the houses in our cul de sac showed their support for us by displaying Australian flags. This meant a lot to us because it represented our homeland, which, at the time, felt so far away.

Bouquets of flowers, arrangements of fruit, and potted plants began to arrive, and our house was quickly transformed into a florist. Although in a daze, I appreciated and noticed all the beauty.

Our lovely friend, Celeste, offered her house for our Australian family to stay in for the 10 days that they were here. This was such a kind gesture to open up her home so willingly and lovingly. Celeste's nurturing nature ensured our family felt comfortable and cared for, and we were so grateful for her generosity.

People took the time to tie green ribbons around the trees in our suburb, which was incredibly touching.

The night before Patrick's funeral, we came home from dinner to see our entire street lined with candles in white paper bags. It was a magical sight to see. The gentle glow lit up the dark night and our hearts. We found out it was our friends from the school Patrick first attended when we moved here who organized it. It was such a heartwarming message of love and support on the eve of what felt like an impossible day ahead. The next morning when it was barely light and raining, I looked out the window and saw my friend, Colleen, out there by herself picking up all the wet and soggy paper bags. That vision of her is etched in my mind; it was such a beautiful example of friendship and community.

The school choir came together on their summer break to rehearse and perform at the funeral, and they were amazing. The school choir director cut her vacation short to come back to rehearse and lead the choir. It was such a generous gesture for which we were very grateful. The church choir director, who had only started in this position just two days before the funeral, gathered people together to play the instrumental pieces. He was very accommodating of our song requests. We thank everyone who worked so hard to make it all happen.

There were multiple sticker designs created in Patrick's memory: PG13 stickers in green and white for the players to wear on their football helmets. Chris, the girls, and I gave each player their stickers at the start of the 2019 season. Similar stickers were also made for the school hockey and baseball teams' helmets. There was a green and white 13 with a heart and a maroon and white football jersey with Green 13 that many people put on the back of their phones or on their cars.

The high school golf team wore Australian badges on their team caps.

The Freshman Mentoring Program's logo for 2020 was a tribute to Patrick.

Jack Corrigan, Patrick's close friend, hand-painted a beer die table in Patrick's memory. Beer die is a game played on a rectangular table. There are four players, two at each end, and each player has their own dice and cup. The objective of the game is to toss the dice above the opponent's head at the other end of the table and try to land it in either of the opponent's cups for three points. Jack painted one side of the table depicting an Australian flag with an outline of Patrick's face in the center, and on the other side, he painted a Cleveland Browns design with Odell Beckham Jnr taking his famous catch. Jack worked on it for the entire summer after the accident. My observation was that this creative outlet was very therapeutic for him and provided a beautiful way to process his grief. The finished product was amazing, and I know for sure that Patrick absolutely loved it.

One of Patrick's classmates designed PG13 purple and white wristbands. Many kids and adults still wear them.

Annabelle and Matilda designed white and purple wristbands with Patrick's initials, PMG, for our family for Christmas that year.

Patrick's aunt, Sarah, along with Annabelle and Matilda, designed a Green family t-shirt that featured significant family symbols on a crest on the front and Patrick's initials, PMG, on the back.

In October 2019, our friends named their baby after Patrick.

Our neighbor chose the name Patrick as his Confirmation name.

There were news articles written in print and online in Cleveland and Australia about Patrick. The stories of the accident and our unveiling of the rock and bench were shown on the local TV news.

A friend whose sons were football teammates of Patrick's had a set of coffee mugs made for us with photos on them from memorable football moments.

We received hundreds of letters, cards, emails, and text messages from our local community, around the US, and in Australia.

A former student of the high school and a friend of Patrick's organized a Go Fund Me in his name. We weren't aware of this until it had started. It was a very thoughtful gesture and much appreciated.

The initial thought by Patrick's football coaches was to retire his #13 jersey. We appreciated this mark of respect. Chris then had the idea to ask Patrick's teammate and friend Owen Bebie, who was a year below Patrick, to wear his #13 for the 2019 football season. Owen did so with pride, and we know Patrick loved it. It was Owen's senior year, so now his younger brother, Tommy, will wear the #13 jersey for the 2020 and 2021 seasons. Then it will continue through the family with brothers Johnny and Michael to follow.

It has been heartwarming to see family and friends who are athletes choose #13 in honor of Patrick for their team jersey in other sports too, such as touch football, basketball, and volleyball.

Patrick's cousin, Tom, chose to wear #12 as a tribute to Patrick as he embarked on his first year as a professional Australian Rules footballer for the GWS Giants in 2020. (Patrick wore #12 when he played football for his school in Sydney.)

Patrick's accident happened just three weeks into our summer break. The football team practiced most of the summer and the players and coaches had to find a way to continue on and cope with the devastating impact of losing one of their much-loved teammates. The football mums stepped in to carry the load.

Head Coach, Josh Wells, had this to say:

"The football moms had to take on a different challenge this past season. Over the summer, the team experienced the tragic loss of a player who had just graduated. This was an extremely hard time for players, parents, and coaches. In the days leading up to the funeral and after, this group of moms helped support the team in countless ways. No player should have to experience this type of tragedy, but with the support of the football moms, the program was able to navigate its way through the loss of a former teammate."

The football mums were later awarded the Northeastern Ohio Chapter of the National Football Foundation, "I'm a Football Mom" Award for their dedication to the team during this very difficult time.

I have friends who continue to text me to acknowledge the 27th each month. Some even text me on Thursdays, which was the day of the accident.

Two days after Patrick died, friends in Sydney organized a memorial at the church where our kids went to school, Holy Cross. We are very thankful to those who attended that night to remember Patrick.

In August 2019, we were blessed to have our close friends, Odile and Gilly, visit from Sydney and Melbourne. I will never forget the moment when I looked up and saw them walk towards me when I picked them up from the airport. We dissolved into tears. No words were needed. This was going to be a very special 10 days. It was their first time in Cleveland. They were able to experience our life here, meet our friends, and see all the places that were meaningful to Patrick. We did a lot in the time we had, and I soaked up every minute, knowing that this was such a treat and solace to have both of them here. Thank you, Simon and Paris, for holding down the forts at home. Thank you, my darling girls, for traveling across the ocean to be with me when I needed you the most.

The University of Cincinnati, where Patrick was due to start college, wrote to us to say that they would include him in their memorial slideshow at the start of the 2019-2020 school year that commemorated students and staff who had recently passed away. It was so touching that they still embraced him as part of the Bearcat family.

Catherine and Sarah Green, Patrick's aunts, together with Father Michael Sierakowski, Patrick's great-uncle, organized a memorial service for Patrick in October 2019 at St Peter's Church in Melbourne. This was an incredible act of love for Patrick, for us, and for all who attended who were unable to be with us on July 3, for Patrick's funeral in Cleveland. It provided an opportunity to commemorate Patrick in his birthplace, where most of our family live. Patrick's aunts and uncles, cousins, grandparents, and friends gave readings and prepared the altar with meaningful objects that represented Patrick. Patrick's uncle, Matthew, sang a breathtaking version of Hallelujah, which was also sung at the funeral here. Father Michael led the congregation through tears and laughter. We were fortunate to have a priest in the family. Mikey, as we all call him, has married and baptized many of us. He has also had the very challenging job of leading funerals for much-loved members of our family. Patrick's mass was filmed so that we were able to watch it. It was heartbreakingly beautiful. The memorial booklet was full of lovely photos. All the details were chosen so thoughtfully. There was a gathering afterwards so that people could stay and be together, remembering Patrick. Chris, Annabelle, Matilda, and I would like to deeply thank everyone who made this day happen.

I would like to thank my health coaching clients for their loving support over the past year. Many of them have been seeing me for several years and we know a lot about one another's lives. They were so saddened to hear about Patrick. I was also very fortunate to be cocooned in friendship by my communities at Inner Bliss Yoga Studio and Centered Soul Retreats. Centered Soul is a wellness retreat offering started by my dear friend, Megan. I helped her facilitate the experiences and over the years, we have met many lovely guests who have become friends. Equally, Chris has received an outpouring of kindness from his work colleagues here in Cleveland, the athletic directors and collegiate sports community across the US, and the Australian sports industry.

In the six months after losing Patrick, we were lucky to have many other visitors too. We really enjoyed our time with Andrew, Adam and Karoliina, John and Elissa, Lincoln and Jasper, and Mark and Suzanne.

There have been many creative ways that Patrick has been remembered through poems, paintings, many tattoos, and a song.

Patrick's friend Connor wore a t-shirt with the letters "PG" printed on it under his uniform for every one of his high school football games. He pointed up to Patrick after he scored the winning touchdown one night. Connor also put a purple shooting string on his lacrosse stick for the season.

Our neighbors and friends, Cindy and Tim, handmade dozens of necklaces, one with a green heart (for the girls) and the other with a silver disc stamped with PG13 (for the guys). They then generously gave these to many of Patrick's friends.

A bracelet was left for Annabelle at the high school office eight months after the accident that had "Never Forgotten #13" engraved on it with an anonymous note. This very thoughtful person was not looking for any credit, they just wanted to make Annabelle happy and acknowledge that Patrick was still very much with her.

Amy, our friend and owner of Witzi's Raw Granola, included an Australian flag in the design of the label of her banana berry flavor to honor Patrick. Patrick was very close to the Witzigreuter family and he often taste-tested Amy's granola. He would be smiling at this kind-hearted tribute.

We have a tree in the center of our cul de sac that our neighbor, Annie, decorates for all the holidays. On Valentine's Day, she placed a red heart with Patrick's name written on it at the top of the tree facing our house. At other times during the year, she puts a star on the tree with Patrick's name on it and an Australian flag next to it. These sweet gestures are appreciated by us all.

On Patrick's first anniversary our neighbors, Debbie and Cindy, thoughtfully arranged for our families to release butterflies to honor Patrick. It was a very special moment; we gathered in a circle and did this together.

I would like to say a special thank you to Patrick's friends. I always felt lucky that Patrick wanted me to be close to you. He had you over at our house often, and as a result, I know you well. Since we all lost him, you have been so caring towards me. I appreciate all of your texts and I love it when you come over and visit. I really enjoy talking to you about Patrick and the funny stories that you share with me because you know I want to hear them forever. You make me feel better when I'm around you. You have also taken Annabelle and Matilda under your wings and I know that Patrick is so grateful for all that you do to look out for us.

Chris, Annabelle, Matilda, and I would like to extend our deepest thanks to our communities both in the US and Australia. For everyone who paused their own lives to look after us and who traveled to be with us. For every card, letter, text, phone call, email, tweet, and message we received. For every prayer that was said for Patrick and us. For every meal, bunch of flowers, gift card, and gift that was left at our front door. For close friends who, upon hearing the news of Patrick's accident, left their vacations to be with us. For the flowers, symbols that represent Patrick and the handwritten notes left at both of the rocks. For every mass and circle of prayer that was said in Patrick's memory. For every tree that was planted in a national forest to commemorate him. For the three scholarship funds that have been so generously set up in his name. For every donation that was made to the scholarship funds, St Malachi's and Autism Speaks. For the Go Fund Me donations. For the accommodation that was given to our Australian family. For the contributions to Patrick's garden. For all the creative ways that Patrick has been remembered.

We were honestly blown away by all the love we received and the amazing tributes that were paid to Patrick. From our hearts to yours, we sincerely thank you.

Lastly, for the countless hours that we likely don't even know the half of that were put in behind the scenes, especially in the first week after losing Patrick. Lovingly led by one of the best humans, Brenda Kirk, our incredible support crew included many dear friends who know who they are. How do we say thank you?

Chris said this to you at Patrick's funeral and I want to say it again, "We know what you've done and the ultimate compliment we can pay you is that Australians love the actions that have defined the word 'mateship' in our country for over 100 years. One of the core tenets of mateship is when things are bad, you don't talk about what you are going to do, you just do. You drop everything and do. And I can pay no higher mark of respect and love to you than to say that is what you have done for us."

We are so very grateful for you. We love you.

Patrick's uncle, Matthew, shared his admiration for our community and the generosity that he witnessed in the 10 days he was here with us visiting from Australia before and after the funeral:

"They were able to pick us up as a family for that time and do all the 'domestic and nuts'n'bolts' work to run a busy house so that we as a family could purely focus on being together and sharing this time with no distractions. This may happen with other communities for a day or maybe the day of the funeral, but they did it for weeks. From food and drinks, cleaning the house, fixing household items to organizing the logistics. It was like they were an organized community 'grief operation' that came in and took care of everything' – it was AMAZING.

They were so willing to ensure Patrick left a lasting legacy and footprint in the community from the scholarship, rock, bench, etc. They didn't need to do any of that, but the generosity and willingness to help really stood out.

As a mark of the effect that Patrick (as a 19 year old) had on the local community, I had the sense when I was there that whether it be a kid from school, a teacher, coach, or an adult friend that yes, they were there to support Chris, Sara, and the girls but also they were there to help with their own personal loss of Patrick and to deal with the specific relationship they had with him. For a kid of 19 to have that influence on people, it was incredible."

"Learning to love and be compassionate to one's self is our life's work. "

CHAPTER SIX

SELF-CARE

Learning how to live with devastating sadness and pain after having one of the most precious people in my life taken away from me has been a huge challenge. If you had told me that losing one of my children was going to be on this life's path, I would have told you that I couldn't do it. Yet, here I was, somehow doing it. Without a doubt, it was, and still is, the worst thing I've ever had to endure. In the first few weeks, I began to feel depleted from having to get up every day and live the same nightmare. No days were good; they all felt hard. I know for sure that the key to me being able to function for myself, my family, and Patrick was committing to consistent self-care practices from the very start of my grief journey. Due to my profession as a health coach, I already had the tools; I just needed to make sure I used them while feeling all-consumed with a grief that was so raw and painful, I could hardly stand it.

From day one, my inner knowing led me to prioritize looking after myself the best I could. I kept things very simple and focused on the following areas: sleep, nutrition, yoga and movement, meditation, journaling, healing sessions with my holistic practitioners, setting strong boundaries to protect my energy, accepting help, taking supplements and drinking herbal teas that supported my nervous system, immunity and digestion, saying no when I needed to, and allowing myself to only take on what I was able to manage.

Self-care is a term that's used a lot in the wellness world. As a health coach, it's one of the core foundations of well-being that I teach my clients. I believe it is fundamental to living a balanced and happy life. Self-care looks different for everyone, and there is no right or wrong way when it comes to choosing your approach. It is about understanding which rituals or activities nourish you the most, bring you joy, peace, and inspiration, give you energy, and make you feel whole. Self-care is not selfish; it's essential. Without it, we can become resentful, even when that is not our intention.

Grief is a heavy weight to bear. It is always with you. As I continue to navigate all of its variables, I keep self-care at the forefront of my mind. I identify my priorities and focus on them the best I can because I know that helps me manage my grief, day in and day out. I am very aware of my limits and I don't overextend myself. Finding that equilibrium is necessary, whether you are recovering from a loss or not. Imbalance in our priorities definitely has a negative domino effect on core areas of our health, such as our eating habits, sleep, relationships, motivation to exercise, mental state, energy, happiness, job satisfaction, home environment, and more.

Learning to love and be compassionate to one's self is our life's work. You are worthy of this love and compassion. Keep returning to kindness rather than self-criticism. If you feel fragile, be gentle, and loosen your expectations for how you think you are supposed to be handling your loss. You don't have to hold it together all the time. Don't let others influence you with their opinions on how you "should" be coping. You do not need to "move on." Those who imply you should be "over it" after time has passed have clearly not stood or walked in your shoes. I certainly do not feel that my family and I will ever "get over" losing Patrick; it's just not what it's about. Starting to heal through self-love gives you the courage to keep moving forward, but there is no specific place you need to be apart from where you are in the moment. Your grief journey is yours, no-one else's. Only you know what is truly right for you. Allow all of your feelings to come to the surface, without judgment. Let self-love and self-compassion be your guides. If you lose your way, I recommend returning to these guides as your anchors.

ROADBLOCKS TO SELF-CARE

I have observed three common roadblocks to self-care:

1. Guilt. This is closely connected to our self-worth. Sometimes we don't believe we deserve to focus on ourselves. If you feel guilty, try to shift your perspective to a place of self-love. Allow yourself to tend to your needs. The amount of energy we have to give to others is dictated by how well we care for ourselves.

2. Time. The misconception with self-care is that we don't have enough time in our day. We couldn't possibly fit another thing into our busy lives. Here's the truth, even 10 minutes a day will make a difference to how you feel, and most of us can find 10 minutes in a day.

   Think about how much time you spend watching TV or Netflix beyond a reasonable amount, mindlessly surfing the internet, sleeping in late, falling down the rabbit hole of social media, saying yes to things that you later regret, and booking your schedule back to back with non-nourishing commitments. Hidden amongst your time wasters is your self-care opportunity; it's easy to find it when you start looking.

3. Money. Money does not need to be a barrier to nurturing yourself. Many self-care rituals don't cost a thing. For example, going for a walk or a run, meditation, deep breathing, talking to a friend, asking someone close to you for a massage, taking a free online exercise class, spending time in nature or writing.

STEPS FOR SELF-CARE

1. Identify what you enjoy. Ask yourself, "What truly nourishes me?" Write down your self-care list.

2. Make a promise to yourself to practice self-care without guilt.

3. Determine how it will realistically fit into your schedule so that you have the best chance for consistency. There is no point in choosing a time when you are likely to get interrupted, as this can easily derail your good intentions. Are you better at doing it in the morning, during the day, or in the evening? What time of the day do you have the most energy?

4. Add it to your calendar as if it's an appointment or a meeting with its own time slot so that you take it as seriously as you would another commitment. Protect this time carefully; don't trade it unless it's absolutely necessary.

MY SELF-CARE RITUALS AND PRACTICES

I acknowledge that this is my experience and you must choose yours according to what's most healing and nourishing for you. My intention for sharing what has helped me soften my pain is to give you some suggestions to try as you gain confidence and clarity about your own situation if you need it.

SLEEP AND REST

Grief can make you feel bone tired, even if you haven't done much at all. You can literally feel your bones aching. I really value sleep and its healing properties. I believe it is one of the cornerstones of health. When you rest, your nervous system re-sets. If you have suffered a loss, you need to rest. In the early days after Patrick's accident, I found myself needing daily afternoon naps. I was mentally exhausted. My brain was tired from the relentless nature of the grief. I experienced brain fog and had difficulty recalling information and words. My mind felt congested. This lasted a few months and then it began to lift. Now, if my mind and body tell me to take it slowly, I listen and create space in my day to rest and reduce overwhelm.

ACCEPTING HELP

Responsibilities don't disappear when grief lands in your lap. At this time, you may need help to lighten your load. Asking for, and accepting assistance, when you are overwhelmed is a critical component of self-care. It's not easy for many of us. We don't want to be a burden and we feel as if we should be able to do it all ourselves. Embracing help requires us to be vulnerable. It can make us feel uncomfortable, which may lead to self-imposed feelings of guilt and inadequacy. If this sounds like you, consider how you would do anything for your family and friends if they needed it. They want to do the same for you. Allowing them to help you gives them the opportunity to show their love for you.

After Patrick's accident, we quickly surrendered to accepting help, it was definitely what we needed, and we were very appreciative.

YOGA

It's hard for me to put into words the immense gratitude I have for my teachers and my yoga practice. This sacred self-care ritual is a huge part of my life and has been instrumental in my healing after losing Patrick.

Before I elaborate on my love of yoga, I want to share that while living in Sydney for seven years, my passion was swimming laps every morning in the Bronte Baths ocean pool. In the colder months, I wore a wetsuit, which meant I could swim year-round, and I just loved it. The ocean has always called me, and I felt so lucky that I lived in a place that allowed me the opportunity for this to be my exercise. While it was daily movement, it was also more than that to me. It was my meditation, the place where I cleared my head and felt a lot of joy. I adored and craved that exhilarating feeling every single time my body first entered the cold water. The painted black line on the sandy bottom of the pool was my friend, and up and down, I swam. I never counted the laps; I just swam.

Moving to Cleveland meant leaving the ocean behind and finding my new happy place. This was when I discovered yoga. From the minute I walked into Inner Bliss Yoga Studio, I knew I had struck gold. I kept showing up, slowly building my confidence, and meeting many lovely like-minded people. When I practice yoga, I get lost in the flow. When I move my body with my breath, my mind feels quiet and free, and my body feels strong. It reminds me of how I feel when I swim, and it strikes me how kindred ocean swimming and yoga are to me.

Yoga is an ancient practice and vinyasa yoga is a style that connects breath to movement. There are many mind-body-soul benefits of yoga. We know for sure that it's good for our health. It calms the mind and any racing thoughts, reduces tension and stress, makes us strong, improves our flexibility and circulation, and it keeps our spine and connective tissue supple. It encourages us to breathe deeply, teaches us to tune into our body, and listen to what it has to tell us. It allows us to turn inward and be quiet.

A week after Patrick's accident, I returned to the studio for a class. I was nervous, which felt strange as I'd never felt hesitant to walk through that door. I was worried about seeing people and how I would cope with speaking about my monumental loss and horrific pain, but I realized that it didn't matter if I sobbed uncontrollably, or if I didn't say much at all.

Unbeknown to me, Chris had thoughtfully texted my support crew to tell them I was coming. I got there extra early and lay down on my mat in my favorite spot in the room - the back corner, in front of the heater. I closed my eyes and soon I started to sense other people arriving around me. Without even needing to open my eyes, I recognized the beautiful energy of my dear friend, Kim, as she lay her mat down next to me. I knew it was her. As I sat up to hug her, I saw other friends placing their mats down to surround me; they had all shown up to carry me through this first class back since June 27. It was such a beautiful sight to see and my heart filled with gratitude. No words were needed. Tammy Lyons, our teacher and close friend, led us through a soulful class, and I felt my practice go to another level of meaning and healing.

Yoga is my medicine. I always feel better afterwards. Since losing Patrick, there have been moments in a class when I've felt very emotional and questioned whether I should stay, but the open invitation to move into a child's pose is always there. I have used it and the space it has allowed me until I could pick myself up again. Since Patrick's passing, I've had times when I have felt highly anxious with my stomach doing backflips. In these moments, I chose to get on my mat and breathe as deeply as I could manage, and by the end of the practice, my nervous system and stomach were calm again. That is the power of the breath. The long inhales and the even longer exhales are so restorative for the parasympathetic nervous system, they relax the "fight or flight" state.

Yoga is a tonic for the soul, a doorway to deepen your spiritual connection with yourself and the Universe. A more vigorous class will take you to your edge and a gentler flow will feel like a soothing bath for your nervous system. Yoga builds resilience. It is not about being the best; it is a judgment and competitive free place where you are encouraged to be yourself and to look after yourself. If you haven't tried it before, I encourage you to be open to receiving the gifts of a breath and movement practice and feel the transformation happen.

Occasionally Patrick used to come to yoga with me and I loved it when he did. He said he liked it. I think he did, but knowing him, he also said that to make me feel good, and it worked. I smile now when I remember the way he scrunched up his nose and squinted his eyes when trying to move through some of the poses.

If you are going through any kind of loss, consider giving yoga the chance to ease your pain. Your yoga mat and its four edges may start to feel like your sacred space. You may begin to crave its comfort and security. Inner Bliss Yoga Studio has been my sanctuary over the last seven years. I have much to be grateful for. It has given me so many happy times, close friendships, countless "yoga highs" (the blissed-out feeling after a class); it has cocooned me when I've felt homesick for Australia and sheltered me in my darkest moments of grief.

BODY LISTENING

The persistent nature of grief can deplete even the healthiest person. I know that has been true for me. Every day is an opportunity to have an honest conversation with yourself about where you are at regarding your mind, body, and spirit. Ask yourself two simple questions: "How do I feel today?" and "What do I need today?" Notice I said "today" because every day is different, every hour can be different. Tuning-in to your body and asking what it needs is called body listening. It's a skill that can be learned and fine-tuned. Based on the information your body gives you, you are guided to make decisions based upon your needs for that day. Everyone's body is different; listen to your own and try not to compare it to someone else's. It's your own personal narrative with your internal home.

My clients often ask me, "How do I know what I need?" Learning how to follow your intuition is a practice. It's an invitation to go deeper and connect to your inner knowing. We have the answers within us; sometimes the outside noise is just too loud for us to hear them clearly. Developing your awareness starts with being still and quiet, then taking notice of how you feel. Focus on your energy, mental state, digestion, and cravings. Write down how your food and lifestyle choices affect how you feel. For example, if you eat "x," you feel "y," if you don't get enough sleep, you feel "x," if you talk to yourself in a certain way, mentally you feel "x," or if you're feeling emotional, you crave "x."

Listen to your hunger cues and cravings and challenge them. Sometimes we mistake hunger for thirst, where we are actually dehydrated, not hungry. We may crave sugar and carbs when we are tired or upset. If you're not truly hungry, then ask yourself, "What am I really hungry for?" Listen to the honest answer. Are you trying to fill a void in your life with unhealthy habits or food? Are you, in fact, bored, lonely, anxious, fatigued, sad, in pain, or agitated? Grief can be a gateway to emotional eating; we literally eat our emotions in an attempt to escape and numb ourselves for a while. This is a common self-soothing reaction to loss and if this has been your response, there is nothing to be ashamed of.

Our body is amazing; it will do all it can to keep us balanced and healthy. As we move throughout our day, so many functions are going on inside us without us even thinking about them. Our body will make allowances for temporary poor choices; however, continuous unhealthy behaviors will catch up with us before too long. Honor your body and give thanks for all that it does for you. As you live with your grief, forgive yourself for choices that have not served you. Pivot to a mindset of nourishing your mind, body, and spirit the best you can. To do this, ask yourself, "What is the healthiest choice I can make to nourish myself right now?" These can be food and non-food related choices. We are not aiming for perfection here. There is definitely room for fun and indulgences.

When I practice body listening, I tune in and have a truthful conversation about what I need. I listen to what my body is telling me; then I make conscious choices from a place of self-love. When I do this, a beautiful synergy happens; it's my body saying, "Yes!" and it feels wonderful.

CRYING

I have never cried so many tears than I have since losing Patrick. Crying is a normal response to loss. There is no shame in it, nor is there any benefit in suppressing your emotions. Sometimes the feelings are deeply submerged and it's difficult to find any release even though you feel sad. If you can relate, there is nothing wrong with you. Try permitting yourself to feel it all, to allow the feelings of grief to emerge and be free. A good cry may sound like sobbing wails; make noise if you need to; this is a way for you to feel relief from your pain and to self-soothe. Crying can be an expression of emotion when we can't find the words. You are not weak if you cry. I'm not sure why crying sometimes has negative connotations. I see crying as an opportunity to cleanse and comfort myself in my sadness. Losing my child will always be devastating; therefore, crying is a part of living with my grief. I have found a cold compress relieves my puffy and tired eyes. I also recommend extra hydration, as I definitely notice I am drier and need to drink more water after crying. Do you allow yourself to cry?

STILLNESS

Stillness is where we can be quiet enough to listen to our intuition, our inner knowing, and our truth. I have learned to love stillness. Here, I can connect to my heart and to Patrick. It feels very restorative to allow myself to enjoy deliberate time in a peaceful place that is the opposite of busy.

SPACE IN MY SCHEDULE

In my healing this past year, I know I am able to cope better when there is space in my schedule. Anxiety builds for me when my day includes too much back-to-back activity and meetings without the chance to re-set. I make sure I honor my needs and plan each day so it is balanced. Be honest with yourself and others about this. What do you need your day to look like?

TALK OR DON'T TALK

Talking helps me process my thoughts and feelings. Patrick was the same. Some people are more verbal than others. It's important to remember that just because someone doesn't talk about their feelings, it doesn't mean they don't feel them. Talking or not talking are both coping mechanisms, and both are normal reactions to grief. If you need to be verbal, find your person or people who you trust, who you feel comfortable sharing your personal thoughts with, knowing that they will guard them carefully. Sometimes I don't feel like talking, and I know that it's okay for my grief to be private. Don't feel as if you have to divulge all the details of your experience to everyone you encounter; it can be very draining to go over and over it repeatedly; you are allowed to protect your heart and your energy.

MUSIC

Music has been a lifeline for me since Patrick's accident. I created a playlist for us and when I listen to it, I feel connected to him. Many others who were close to Patrick have also created playlists to commemorate him.

MANTRAS

Mantras are positive intentions or affirmations that take you in the direction you want to go. For example, "I am calm," "I am strong," "I am free," "I am letting go," "I am enough," "I am brave," or "I am healing." For your self-care, perhaps you could create a mantra for yourself. Think of a word that describes how you want to feel. Breathe in, and in your mind say, "I am," then breathe out and in your mind, say your word. Mantras are a simple tool I have used to help me change my state and lighten my grief. You could also have a word of the day to give your mind an anchor. Some of my words have been: perseverance, warrior, rest, breathe, nourish, and stillness. What could your mantra or word be?

MORNING DRINK

My morning drink is a daily ritual that I look forward to from the night before. There's something so soothing about it. The process of making it, taking that first sip, feeling the warmth of the mug in my

THE GIFTS FROM LOSING YOU

hands, sitting outside if possible. Chris and I enjoy this time together. I love to make my own nut milks, usually cashew or almond. I then froth the milk and make a superfood latte, either cacao, maca, or turmeric. Do you have a morning drink that you enjoy?

HEALTHY EATING

Nourishing our body with healthy, clean, whole, and real food is essential for us all. If you're not sure where to start with this, focus on trying to eat the colors of the rainbow. This is a great way to make sure you absorb a variety of valuable nutrients. To fuel our body properly for long-lasting energy, we must eat mindfully rather than mindlessly. Healthy habits are more maintainable and sustainable when we take a balanced approach. Allow treats in moderation. Food is meant to be enjoyed. Eat plants, good quality protein, and healthy fats. Stay well hydrated. Know where your food comes from and support local farmers and growers if you can. Eat seasonally, when possible. Avoid processed foods containing ingredients you don't recognize or can't pronounce. Minimize sugar. Value your body enough to nourish it optimally and then notice how you feel when you do.

I practice intuitive eating. I ask my body what it needs, and I listen closely to the answer. I have come to know what makes me feel good and what doesn't. This is something I teach my clients and it's a joy to witness them make the connections and reap the benefits.

Incorporate superfoods into your diet as they are nutrient-dense and very beneficial to our health. For example; blueberries, salmon, spirulina, maca, goji and acai berries, coconut, turmeric, green tea, kale, flaxseeds, cacao, raw honey, cinnamon, camu camu, chia seeds, hemp seeds, medicinal mushrooms, and ginger. I love adding Philosophie superfood plant-based protein powder to my smoothie each morning because I know I am giving my body pure and whole nutrient-rich ingredients that will energize me and optimize my health. When we start our day well, we are more likely to stay on a mindful track with our food choices throughout the rest of the day.

When coping with grief, if you don't feel like eating in the beginning (I didn't), then try to have liquids such as smoothies, juices, soups, broths, kombucha, kefir, superfood lattes, lots of water, and herbal teas. They felt the most manageable and nourishing for me.

COOKING

I believe food is an expression of love and there is nothing better than sitting down to a home-cooked meal. It can be a really simple recipe with a few healthy ingredients, cooking doesn't need to be complicated. There is a lot of unnecessary expectation centered around it. Cook from your heart and you can't go wrong. I can hear my non-cooking friends laughing and saying that there's a lot that can go wrong, but I promise, fresh and simple is best. Those you feed will feel the love that you have infused into the meal when they eat it.

I am a self-taught cook and it was Chris who got me interested in cooking when we first met. He learned a lot from spending time in the kitchen with his mum, Rita, when he was growing up. He has always had a great intuitive knowledge about food, and we enjoy creating meals together. In my private chef business in Sydney, I cooked and delivered delicious and nutritious meals to my clients. Being in the kitchen preparing nourishment for my family and friends is a form of meditation and self-care for me. It brings me joy to make others happy through food.

In the beginning, after Patrick's accident, I didn't have the mental capacity or energy to cook or decide what was for dinner, so all the meals we were kindly given helped a lot. Once I was able to get back to it, cooking provided a way for me to find some happiness again.

MOVEMENT

During this past year, I have found that when I am in my head too much, I feel better if I move my body instead. Exercise benefits us physically and mentally. With my clients, I have noticed that there is a lot of pressure and expectation around exercise, just like cooking. People get caught up in the "shoulds," such as, "I should be a runner, or I should go to the gym." We need to drop the "shoulds" because they create guilt and shame, and they can be paralyzing to the point where we do nothing.

There are some important factors when it comes to establishing a regular exercise routine. Take the time to understand some things about yourself. Be honest about your relationship with exercise and what you need; it is a personal preference. Try not to be influenced by what others are doing. What works for one body may not work for another.

- What sort of exercise do you like to do?

- Are you a solo or a group exerciser?

- Are you self-motivated, or do you require a class with a start time to make sure you show up? Do you need to commit to doing it with someone else to stay accountable?

- Do you prefer to exercise in the morning, during the day, or in the evening? When is your energy the best? When are you more likely to do it?

- Do you have any injuries or limitations where you need to modify? Do you need help with finding options that will work for you? Be compassionate with yourself and focus on what you can do, rather than what you can't.

- Do you like variety or do you prefer to do the same thing?

If you don't like what you're doing, it doesn't make you feel good, and it does not fit in with your life, then you are less likely to make it a habit. You will find all the excuses to avoid it. Whereas if you love it, it energizes you, it integrates well into your schedule, and you look forward to it, it's going to be more sustainable and enjoyable.

I like to let how I feel on the day dictate what I do. I tune in and ask my body and mind what is needed. Some days it's a more vigorous workout; other days it's to move at a slower pace. I have different movement options that I love, and I make the choice that suits me best at the time. This is intuitive movement and it works very well for me. What type of movement works best for you?

CONNECTION TO OTHERS

When grieving, just as in everyday life, some people need to be social while others need more time alone. It's a personal choice. I find that a combination of both works well for me.

A few months after Patrick's accident, I joined the Rockstar Coaching Collective led by Robyn Youkilis; a wellness coach, author, and gut health expert. I wanted to connect with a like-minded wellness-based community. My intuition told me to sign up and I'm so glad I did. The program was online, with a live video call each week. Robyn was amazing, I learned so much from her, both personally and professionally, and I found the inspiration to further develop my health coaching business that I had been looking for. Rockstar gave me a place to be myself. Joining something new and putting yourself out there can seem daunting when you are deep in grief, but I encourage you to do so, if you feel you can. It gave me something to look forward to, something else to focus on, it felt meaningful to connect with others who each had their own challenges, I felt inspired, and I met a lovely group of women.

A couple of months after Rockstar finished, I signed up for Gabby Bernstein's Bestseller Masterclass Digital Course. This was another inspirational experience where I learned so much about the book writing, publishing, and marketing process. I loved Gabby's work and her writing style, so to have her as my teacher was wonderful. The resources were of such high quality. The course affirmed my direction for this book and gave me another online community for connection.

If you are navigating a loss, I recommend you connect with others as much as you are able. These days there are so many options;

choose one that works best for you, you never know who you will meet, and as my Grandma Florence used to say, "You don't know what it's like until you get there."

As a way to feel less alone in your grief, find comfort from others who have walked this path before you. They know your pain. Seeking out those who have experienced the same type of loss as you can be very therapeutic. While the details may vary, you will most likely share a common understanding, which creates connection. You may feel validated, seen, and heard. When someone else gets it, you don't have to put on a brave face; you can just be you.

Humans are social creatures by nature. Connection nourishes us, but at the same time, we all have our limits, and we need to honor them. Isolation is considered a risk factor for poor health. If you are concerned about someone who is grieving and has completely withdrawn themselves, I would gently suggest to them that you would be happy to help or encourage them to seek guidance from a professional.

JOURNALING

Having a place to write down all my thoughts and emotions has been an incredibly therapeutic experience. I started journaling regularly 12 days after Patrick died. It became a daily ritual that I craved, and it really helped me get through the first few months. It enabled me to move out of my head and into my heart. Journaling allowed me to sit with a feeling and then explore it through writing.

REDIRECTING EMOTIONS AND THOUGHTS

As important as it is to be with your emotions and thoughts so you can process them, I have found it's also necessary to not stay in them for too long. The mind can take us down some deep rabbit holes where it can be difficult to separate from them. If I'm getting too bogged down, I know I need to actively choose a more self-loving path and infuse some lighter moments to relieve my congested mind. Movement will do this for me, as will meditation, sunshine, cooking, music, gardening, or talking to a friend. Before I know it, my unproductive emotions and thoughts have loosened their grip, and I feel more balanced. What's the best way for you to get out of your head?

DEEP BREATHING

The simple practice of deep breathing can change your state. It can be done anywhere, anytime; all you need is you. In my breathing practice, I take a slow and deep breath in for a count of four seconds, pause then hold my breath for four seconds, then breathe out for four seconds, pause for four seconds in that empty breath, then start again. This self-care ritual shifts me to a more peaceful place. If I feel anxious, restless, irritated, or overwhelmed, I return to my breath. Notice how you feel after a few minutes of deep breathing. Feel the tension begin to wash away.

COPIOUS CUPS OF TEA

I am a tea-lover. When that first sip is at that perfect tea drinking temperature, it's simply the best. I love tea and the healing properties of the herbal ingredients feel nurturing, calming and soothing to me.

MEDITATION

Many years ago, in Sydney, I completed a meditation course that gave me a solid foundation for my practice. Since then, most mornings, I start my day with meditation. It's a soothing ritual I look forward to. Many clients tell me they cannot meditate, that shutting off their thoughts and racing minds is impossible. My advice is always the same; let go of expectation; meditation doesn't have to feel a certain way. It's okay if thoughts come and go; it's actually a nice opportunity to sort out any thoughts that have needed a place to land. A meditation practice can be really simple. Find a comfortable place to sit or lie still, close your eyes, and focus on your breath, inhaling in, and exhaling out. Invite in peace and love. Notice your body start to relax and feel heavy. Allow yourself to totally let go and sink into the earth beneath you. I like to visualize a white light of protection around me. Stay there for as long as you can, then when you are ready, slowly come back out and soak in the feeling of calm. Even a few minutes is beneficial to your health. Eliminate all barriers to meditation, such as a busy mind or lack of time. The positive effects of meditation are life-changing.

I think it's important to note that meditation can be any activity that takes you to a place of inner peace and washes away stress, such as exercise, gardening, listening to music, writing, crafting, being in nature, cooking, singing, playing an instrument, dancing, etc. If you find it hard to be still and meditate, choose another way that works for you.

HOT WATER BOTTLE

This self-care ritual is one that I especially love. The warmth of a "hottie" as we call it in Australia, is so soothing; it releases stress and pain. Its calming quality is also a favorite with my health coaching clients. When they come to see me, I offer them a hottie and a cup of tea to enhance their experience with me; they tell me they love that.

PET THERAPY

The healing presence of a pet is well-known and over the past year, our family has been uplifted by the gentle, joyful, and loving energy of our two dogs (Willow and Milo) and our two cats (Bronte and Billy). Their affectionate and faithful ways have been a vital part of our recovery.

ACUPUNCTURE

To support me in my grief, I started acupuncture treatments with Malerie Giaimo, OM, L.Ac. I felt the healing benefits immediately. Malerie is a talented and knowledgable physician of classical Chinese medicine and time with her feels very nurturing and restorative.

NEURO EMOTIONAL TECHNIQUE (NET)

Dr Sam Bahan is a friend, chiropractor, and holistic physician. Her expertise in NET helped me release emotions associated with my grief. NET is a language used to express subconscious emotional patterns in organs. Sometimes we unintentionally store these emotions as a protection mechanism following emotional trauma. These can manifest as physical symptoms in the body if they are not addressed. Sam is always able to identify where my body needs support and sessions with her are very therapeutic.

MASSAGE

My family and I are fortunate to know Cara Perez, the owner of Jade Massotherapy. Cara has been working with all of us for the last few years. Since Patrick's passing, she has supported us with her healing hands and kind heart. The mind and body benefits of massage are so therapeutic. You can massage yourself on the accessible parts of your body, or you can ask someone you feel comfortable with to massage you.

Grief does not have a timeline. There isn't a checklist to be completed in the healing process. If you are recovering from a loss, let go of any expectation with your healing. Some days you may feel as if you've got your feet under you and others, not so much. Know that these ups and downs are completely normal.

Sometimes, in the early days after losing Patrick, I would wake up, and to be honest, I was so tired of it. I just wanted the whole thing to go away and for Patrick to be back with us in the physical. It's hard work to keep facing a reality each day that you don't want to be living in. I carried out all my self-care practices, and while I knew that they helped me, sometimes I just wanted a break from the continuous effort it took to try to be okay. A leave pass from the pain, even for a day. I just wanted my son back. Can any of you relate to this feeling? I am certain this is a common reaction to loss. The feelings of agitation and frustration were usually only temporary, and as much as I would give anything to change our reality, I understood we had to move along with it and accept all that it forced us to face.

I have learned that just because someone says that they are coping, they may not be; grief can have many faces. Someone can be smiling on the outside while falling apart on the inside. Sadness can manifest in visible tears, or it can hide behind a courageous façade.

The effects of loss can present in different ways: exhaustion, anger, appetite changes, body aches, headaches, brain fog, memory disturbance, social withdrawal, and insomnia, to name a few.

Self-care becomes even more critical on the harder days. When you have lost someone or something, you will feel a void. Try to choose self-loving rather than self-sabotaging ways to fill this void. Nourish yourself deeply, even when you feel as if you don't have the will or the energy to do so. Ask yourself, "What would be supportive for me right now?" When the sadness is consuming me, I tell myself to do one thing that I know will make me feel better.

If you're looking for a way out of your pain, try walking towards it. Our tendency can be to want to escape, to be numb, or to push it away. Step into it with courage and grace. This may seem like an impossible approach; I hear you. Your goal is not to move on from your loss but rather to move with it. It's a daily battle. You have to keep fighting; you have to stay fierce for yourself and for others who need you as well as for your lost loved one. You may feel as if you go to bed at night, grateful that you made it through the day only to wake up the next morning having to face it all over again. This relentless nature of grief is why you must be intentional about how you nurture yourself during your recovery. In the extra challenging moments, be loving to yourself. Be gentle; you are carrying a heavy load. Self-care is not indulgent; it is necessary. Like a lotus flower, you will begin to rise up out of the mud. Keep rising. Self-care starts with self-love and self-compassion. I know you can do it.

"Our purpose gives us direction and eases us into healing. It opens us up to the possibility that even though our world has been turned upside down, there is still something more for us."

CHAPTER SEVEN

PURPOSE

I t's recommended that a grieving person should try to return to a version of their normal routine as soon as possible to help them cope with their loss. The time frame for this is a personal choice. In my experience, I can definitely say having purpose in my day has been one of the most important aspects of my healing. How we define purpose is different for everyone.

In the beginning, after losing Patrick, my purpose was to survive the pain, connect with Patrick, and look after Chris, the girls, and myself as best I could. My energy was limited, and my daily routine was focused on the basics to get the four of us through each day as we tried to find our footing in our unwanted new reality.

Caring for our family has given me purpose; it always has, but after Patrick's accident, it was even more important. I created a home environment that was a haven for healing that included nourishing food and cozy spots to rest and restore. It exuded an energy based on unconditional love with an understanding of, and respect for, one another and our different ways of coping with our loss.

The day after the accident, I emailed all my health coaching clients to tell them what had happened and to let them know that I would be taking some time off indefinitely to focus on our family's healing. They were all very supportive and most attended the funeral; many had met Patrick because I work from home.

In late August the summer break had come to an end for Annabelle and Matilda, and it was time for the academic year to start. It was hard for them to face returning to school because our experience was so well known in the community. They did so with immense courage and grace. Chris and I were very proud of them, and Patrick was too. Having the routine of school was important for their recovery; it was a part of their daily purpose. Chris had returned to work, and 10 weeks after the accident, I decided that it was the right time for me to resume my health coaching; intuitively, I knew that I needed this purpose. I am a women's health coach. I guide and empower my clients with sustainable and holistic recommendations to prioritize their health and wellbeing. I teach them how to nourish and love themselves unconditionally. I listen deeply and I love what I do.

My clients had respectfully given me the space I needed, and I missed them and our work together. I started my schedule slowly and made sure I paced myself so that I didn't become depleted. I knew straight away that it was a healthy choice for me to be back doing what I was passionate about; it felt good. When I was with them, I was all in, and I found that focusing on someone else gave me a mental break from my grief. It didn't drain me at all because it had meaning, it was fulfilling, and it was a privilege. When I'm coaching, I give a lot of myself energy-wise, and I also receive so much goodness back, it becomes a mutual exchange of energy. I also find on the days when I'm missing Patrick even more than usual that a session with a client really helps me positively change my mental state. It shifts my mindset because I choose to show up for someone else, be present, and work at my best.

Writing this memoir has given me immense purpose. It has allowed me an opportunity to honor Patrick and to continue his legacy. It has provided an avenue for healing and many moments of reflection as well as a place to release my pain. It hasn't been easy and it has taken more courage than I anticipated. What we have been through is a very personal experience, and while I have guarded our privacy and kept the more intimate details just for us, there is an immense vulnerability in sharing our story. However, when I considered all that has happened, all the heartbreak, the generosity, the emotions, the kindness, the conversations, the way people have shown up for us, and the gifts we have received, I just knew that they must be shared.

Early on after Patrick's accident, writing to share wasn't even remotely on my radar. Many people had said to me that I should write a book, but it didn't spark any interest in me. My emotions were still too raw; my writing was for my private journal only. It was too soon to write publicly. While I had made a conscious effort to start my healing from day one, I wasn't ready to even consider a book until I had made it past the initial trauma and shock. I remember the exact moment when my perspective switched from a narrow focus to a bird's-eye view. I was able to look at our experience through a wider lens, like an eagle who flies highest in the sky and is the witness. It was then that I got the nudge that I needed to write a book and I was able to move into the headspace to do so. From this broader perspective, this book came to life.

I believe this new view came after I had accepted that this had happened to Patrick and to us. This acceptance was accompanied by a sense of relief. I can clearly recall that feeling; it was definitely a turning point for me. I think it was simply the release I felt from freeing myself from the noose of my resistance to what was. I was fighting an unconscious battle against our reality because I so badly wanted it to be different. I so desperately wanted it not to be true. Acceptance of where we were at helped me begin to move forward. Acceptance gave me some room to breathe and a glimpse of peace.

At the start of my writing experience, there were times when I questioned whether what I had to say was original or had any value. The good old, "Who am I to write a book? Is what I have to say even relevant?" reared its ugly head. This is very common amongst writers. When that doubt crept in, I reminded myself to keep writing from my heart. If I spoke from there, then I couldn't go wrong. I reminded myself that Patrick was with me on this journey, helping me find the words. I truly felt that. If I ever thought about the many other books that have been written about grief, I told myself that there may be similarities in our stories, but no two journeys were the same. Once I gained this belief and confidence in what I had to say, the book's energy shifted dramatically for the better. I began to see that somewhere amongst the unspeakable heartbreak; there were nuggets of valuable insight that I could share to help others.

In my work as a health coach, I see people who struggle to find meaning and enjoyment in their daily purpose. I have witnessed how this negatively impacts their health and happiness. There is a direct link between how we view our contribution each day and how we feel in our mind and body. Dissatisfaction can have a ripple effect on our eating habits, sleep, joy, motivation to exercise, mood, energy, self-talk, relationships, and more.

A great way to tap into our purpose is to identify our core values, which are at the crux of our inner belief system. They give us guidance and a moral compass. They are our truth. When we live according to our core values, we feel aligned and authentic. Internal conflict arises when we ignore our own morals and live according to others' values or who we think we "should" be. Some examples of core values are: adventure, balance, belonging, choice, commitment, connection, equality, faith, family, freedom, fun, honesty, independence, intuition, kindness, love, privacy, respect, routine, security, sharing, teamwork, and wisdom. It's a worthwhile exercise to look up the full list of core values and determine your own. They are a helpful place to start if you are having trouble defining your purpose.

I encourage you to take a moment to think about who and what gives you purpose. Then commit to placing some of your time and energy there. Not sure what your purpose is? Here are some questions to ask yourself:

- Who and what feeds my soul and brings me joy?

- What are the essential things I need to get done in my day?

- Who needs me to show up?

- What activities align with my core values and how can I bring more of them into my life?

- What's my superpower?

- What is that quiet whisper inside of me telling me to do?

- How can I be of service to others?

Once you've identified your purpose, write down a few actionable steps that will help you integrate it into your days. Keep these steps simple so that they feel manageable. This is not meant to feel heavy.

Living your purpose in grief takes perseverance and courage. It's easier to remain numb and to avoid. Some days you will feel as if you are making some headway, and other times, it may feel as if you are sliding backwards. It's okay. Ask for help if you need it. If you are dealing with loss, I encourage you to look for ways to find hope. I know it's hard, but it is possible. In our grief, we could easily withdraw from life and be sad every minute of every day. The despair can be all-consuming if we allow it to permeate every part of our lives. Our purpose gives us direction and eases us into healing. It opens us up to possibility, the possibility that even though our world has been turned upside down, there is still something more for us. Life does not have to be over, even though it may feel as if it is in our darkest moments.

Be open to the possibility that your purpose could be something completely different to what you have done before. I did not plan to write this book; it evolved organically. Losing a child and brother is unspeakably traumatic. From our family's tragedy, we can help others who are in pain from loss because we understand how it feels. This book has allowed us to be of service and to make a difference. Our calling as a family has been to model healing for those we love and for those we haven't met.

What is your purpose? From your trauma experience, how can you serve?

"I am who I am because of Patrick, and now I'm learning who I am without him physically by my side."

Annabelle

"I love Patrick with all of my heart, and I will always be grateful for the amazing moments we shared."

Matilda

CHAPTER EIGHT

PATRICK'S LITTLE SISTERS

For Ga, love Doll:

"Patrick's little sister," the label I was honored to be gifted from the moment I entered this world and the three words that have shaped me into the person I am today. I have always been called Patrick's little sister from attending the same preschool and primary school in Australia, then moving halfway across the world and attending the same middle school and high school, being only one grade apart. We are twenty-one months apart in age. Twenty-one months that have always felt extremely insignificant because age was never a factor in our relationship as brother and sister and as best friends. Ga and I grew up practically as twins, experiencing each other's accomplishments and hardships as our own along the way. Growing up, Patrick protected me from all things bad in the world: mean girls, insecurity, and the plethora of issues that arise when you're a young girl. He didn't protect me in a way where he shielded me; instead, he sat on my bed with me and listened to me vent, he offered amazing advice, he cried with me, and he taught me how to get back up after being knocked down by all the bad the world had to offer.

In a way, it now feels as if he was preparing me for the time when he would no longer be there in the physical to be my protector. He was preparing me for the cruel reality that we all face now. The one where Patrick isn't in the bedroom next to mine, or sitting in the driver's seat in the car we share as we drive to school, or dancing with me in our bathroom as we get ready to go out together, or sitting at his place at the dinner table as we share a family meal. Four will never feel complete.

Since June 27, 2019, the hole in my heart and in my life has only grown larger. Just as Patrick protected me, I spent my entire life trying to make sure he was okay too. After Patrick's accident, the truth set in, I could not protect him from everything bad he encountered. I have struggled with this realization since that night. How could his life be taken so quickly? How could I not protect him? While I will never understand why or how this happened, I am now starting to understand my new role in his life and his new role in mine.

A large part of my mourning process has involved redefining the relationship Patrick and I now have. The dynamic has shifted from being inseparable to now finding other ways to feel close to him. Ga is now the little voice in my head, the one I have constant conversations with, the one who helps me make tough decisions, goes on drives with me through the Metroparks listening to all of our favorite music, and reassures me that I am not alone, even when I feel most isolated from those around me. I have made a habit of consciously spending some of my day with Patrick. This time with my brother has quickly become the best part of my day, and it's a time where I don't feel so crushed by my grief. Whether it is a trip to Target, a coffee run, or simply a drive around town, this is the time

I spend hanging out with my brother. I tell him what is going on in my life, even though he already knows, I play him new music I think he would like, and I try to imagine the advice he would give me if he was around. While nothing can ever compare to having Patrick in the physical with me, this is our new relationship, and I am learning to navigate this new life the best I can.

Another part of my grieving process has been redefining the relationship I have with myself. Until Patrick was gone, I never realized how much of myself I derived from having him around me. Growing up as the luckiest little sister in the world, Ga consistently made me the center of his universe. He laughed at my jokes, liked the music I showed him, never excluded me from any game we played, told me I looked pretty as we'd get ready for school, and allowed me to join his friend group without any questions asked. These acts of love say a lot more about his good nature than the person I am because I know he didn't think I was THAT funny, and I have shown him some pretty bad songs. I believe he was teaching me how to love myself and attempting to help me build healthy self-esteem, two things he knew were scarce in girls my age. Reflecting on the amount of time he spent validating me and my feelings, again, I feel as if he was preparing me for life without him.

The standards for the men I surround myself with have always been extremely high, thanks to the men I grew up with. From my great grandfathers to my grandfathers, uncles, my dad, cousins, and of course, my brother, I learned from an early age what to expect from a man. Many of these lessons were instilled early by my family and reiterated by Ga at every stage of our lives. Patrick treated everyone with kindness, but those he loved, he loved fiercely. He loved me fiercely for 17 years, and now I have to learn how to function without this love each day. I am who I am because of Patrick, and now I'm learning who I am without him physically by my side.

While trying to be more like Patrick each day, I have been searching for any ounce of positivity that could come out of this darkness. In the last three years of his life, Patrick and I were lucky enough to share a group of friends who we spent almost every day with, which allowed us to hang out together each day too. I cherish these years so much now, feeling so lucky to have made some of my best memories of high school with my brother by my side. Patrick somehow carried on hundreds of friendships without making anyone feel as if they were less important than another. His plethora of close friendships became apparent when, hours after the accident, I received hundreds of texts from people expressing their sorrow and sharing my grief. Fortunately, Patrick made sure to take care of me even after he died. He surrounded me with the most magnificent support system of friends I could have ever asked for. Patrick's passing strengthened the friendships I already had, rekindled the ones I missed most, and created beautiful new friendships with people I now consider to be some of my best friends. They are all my people. United by their relationships with Patrick, friends from Tildy's age, 13, through to graduates from college, all remind me that the love we share and feel for Ga is greater than any other emotion. While it can be easy to dwell on the loss and grief we feel, whenever we all meet up at Brian's pool, we just cannot feel sad. We know we are at Patrick's favorite place and that he would be so mad if we wasted the great weather, our time with one another, and any time that could be spent playing Die. When surrounded by my people, the love outweighs the pain. We can talk about Patrick casually, whether telling our favorite Pat stories or simply stating that he would have loved to be there. We can also talk about him sadly, without judgment.

Putting on a brave face is not something I have to do around my close friends, and for that, I am so grateful. We are all bonded by the tragic loss we have experienced and sharing this pain makes the grief feel less consuming and lonely. My friends no longer leave a hangout without everyone receiving a hug and saying a collective, "I love you," on the way out, now knowing our time together is precious and limited. The immense love we share has become a glimmer of hope for me in this heartbreaking time. I don't say it enough, thank you to all of my friends. You do more than you know for me, and I love how much you love my brother and me.

I feel upset when I hear songs that I know Patrick would have loved; he loved music so much. I promise to play them loud enough in our car so you can hear, Ga. I'll even sing them super loud like you used to get annoyed with me about. I am scared about getting married because the thought of living the "happiest day of my life" without Patrick is terrifying. I am scared to have children for the gut-wrenching truth that they won't know their uncle, but mostly I feel sad because I know the amazing person they are missing out on. I am very grateful that my mum wrote this book so that my future husband and children can sense the incredible amount of love we all have for Patrick, hopefully translating into their own love and relationship with him. Thinking about having to go through all of these life stages without my brother is something I don't think I will ever get over, but I know he will be with me through them all. I know he will be proud of me. I don't have a greater supporter or a better friend than my big brother.

Even though I am now burdened with this grief for the rest of my life, I still consider myself the luckiest girl in the world to have had a brother like Patrick. While only 19 years will never feel fair, thank you Ga. Thank you for making me love roller coasters. Thank you for teaching me how to drive. Thank you for making me watch so many horror movies that even the scariest ones don't phase me now. Thank you for being so competitive when we were growing up so that now I can hold my own in any competition. Thank you for teaching me unconditional love, for others and for myself. Thank you for showing me how beautiful it is to be unapologetically yourself. Thank you for the signs you give me to show me that you are okay. Thank you for giving me a friendship that some are never lucky enough to experience in their lifetime. While some may now attach sadness and grief to me being Patrick's little sister, I wear this label with more pride and strength than ever before. How could such a beautiful relationship be viewed tragically, ever? In trying to figure out who I am without Ga, I am confident that I will find my way because I have the best big brother guiding me from up above.

I love you so much, Ga, and I miss you. Until we meet again.

For Ga, love Tildy:

Writing about Patrick has been hard because I didn't really know where to start. Reminiscing back on all of our times together and wishing for more has been difficult. My struggle with grief has been tough in general. Being a 13 year old girl at the time and getting ready to start high school, then having a life-changing event like this happen has been hard. My stages with grief have been very personal and independent. The way I have been dealing with this has been by myself, which is what I have wanted. I prefer to process my loss on my own, it's how I've always been. I don't love to talk about my feelings, so when June 27 happened, I had to open myself up to what the world was throwing at us. This past year has forced me to grow up and mature very quickly, and it has changed my views on life completely. I have really struggled with being far away from all of our family in Australia. Not being able to be together through the year of firsts and going through this unimaginable pain without all of the people who raised and grew up with Patrick has been very difficult. Something that has been very important to me during these hard milestones has been to surround myself with people who really knew Patrick, like his close friends, to be able to hear new stories, and just be with people who really understand. There have been times when we have been all together, and we have felt his presence so strongly that everyone in the room could sense it and see all of his signs so vividly.

One of the things I enjoyed doing with Patrick was sharing our love for music. We both enjoyed similar kinds of music, which bonded us together when we would go on long car rides and listen to my favorite songs. I always loved it when Patrick showed me a new song because he knew I would love it, but there was never a new song that I could show him; he knew them all.

Sport was another thing Patrick and I both enjoyed. He would always come and cheer me on at all of my sports games, and we liked to talk about what was going on in sports at the time. When I played Little League baseball, he told me that if I ever scored a home run, he would go and strip on the field after I scored. He was always so genuinely happy about my successes in sport or just in general life. We never really got into serious fights because if I was ever mad at him and I stormed off, he would come to find me and instantly know what to say to make me forgive him.

Patrick was always so good to me. I know that it would get a bit annoying sometimes when I always wanted to tag along with him or just spend a lot of time with him, but he never complained about it. One of my favorite traits about Patrick was his love and protectiveness over Annabelle and me. Patrick did anything he could to look after us and when I wasn't being treated equally or was getting made fun of in some situations, he was always there to protect me. He truly wanted the best for everyone in life. He just wanted everyone to succeed and be happy, which is something I really admired about him. I still do. Another thing I really admired about him was his confidence in himself. He was never ashamed of who he was and was not scared to show his emotions and be real with others.

Patrick and I had things we did together, such as playing video games and getting mango smoothies every Sunday morning. One of my favorite memories with Patrick was when Mum, Dad, Patrick, and I went to Texas to go on college football tours for him. We traveled around and visited all of these amazing schools, and at the end of each day, we went back to our own hotel room, watched movies together, and talked all night. It was rare that it was just Patrick and I hanging out, and I was so excited because I got to spend so much time with him, just the two of us.

Over the past year, I have enjoyed seeing signs from Patrick and have found comfort in knowing he is always there for me. Even though what we have been through has been something unimaginable, hearing, and learning new things about Patrick every day still brings me joy in dark times.

I love Patrick with all of my heart, and I will always be grateful for the amazing moments we shared.

"I believe that there is no better way to judge success than leaving this earth but not really leaving it in spirit because your legacy lives on."

Patrick

CHAPTER NINE

PATRICK'S WORDS

I would like to share some words from Patrick himself. One of my intentions with this book has been to ensure Patrick's legacy lives on. He gave me a beautiful place to start because he wrote an English paper in his junior year of high school titled, *Legacy*.

Below are some passages from this essay written by Patrick, dated October 27, 2017.

"I define success as leaving a mark on the world, also known as leaving a legacy. Imagine being successful enough that people remember you, or maybe they don't know you, but they have heard your name. I believe that there is no better way to judge success than leaving this earth but not really leaving it in spirit because your legacy lives on."

Throughout his essay, Patrick referred to two people he greatly admired; his grandfather, Michael Green, and NFL player, Odell Beckham Jnr.

"I consider myself lucky to have someone like my grandfather to look up to and receive advice from. The way he is able to take care of his whole family and his generosity are the reasons he is the man I aspire to be one day.

Odell is my biggest athletic role model on the planet. As a Giants fan, Odell means everything to me.

My grandfather is a true inspiration and a blueprint of the kind of man I can only dream of becoming. Words cannot do him justice; he's truly just an amazing man.

Overall, I consider myself lucky to have these great influences and true legends in my life to give me something to shoot for and a good idea of how to really leave my mark on the world, a true legacy."

Our darling boy, you have more than left your mark. Eternally, you live in our hearts. Your legacy will inspire others for many years to come. We will do everything we can to keep your light shining brightly. You are already doing it. You are showing people how to live a more meaningful life through your genuine kindness, inclusivity, generosity of spirit, care and interest in others, ability to lift others up, listen deeply and truly see people, your authenticity, and unwavering certainty of who you are.

As you can see from Patrick's reflections above, he had a very special relationship with his grandfather, Michael. Below is another piece titled, *My Hero* that Patrick wrote about Michael, this time in his freshman year of high school, dated January 13, 2016.

"When my grandfather was recently here for Christmas from Australia, he said something to me that really hit home, and I know I'll remember it for the rest of my life. He said, 'In Australia, not much more matters than just being a good bloke, and mate, you're growing up to be a great bloke.' This meant a lot to me because I've always looked up to him and it was great to hear that he's proud of me like that. I believe my grandpa is a hero because he's an extremely devoted husband, father, and grandfather, and also because of all the wisdom and knowledge he passes down to me and everyone he talks to.

Everything he does, he puts love and 100% effort into it. It's one of the many reasons I look up to him. He had his own law firm and has worked very hard his whole life to look after his family. He is also very caring towards his five children and nine grandchildren. I aspire to be the man he is someday when I grow up. His influence has had an extremely positive impact on me because it is what I want to do in the future.

Another reason my grandfather is my hero is all the wisdom he has and will continue to pass down to me. He played professional football for the AFL (Australian Football League) and was very good. His team won the Premiership (Superbowl) four times. As the siren sounded at the end of the '69 Grand Final, everyone knew that Michael Green had been best on the ground. He won an award after the game similar to winning the MVP in the NBA finals, and I think that's amazing. He has shared so many stories with me about his career but also just about life in general too, which I will use to make the right decisions and think about every day. It has helped me so much to learn from him, not to mention he's always been my role model, so I've tried to listen to everything he's told me. I hope I can make him proud in the future.

In conclusion, my grandfather is my hero because he is a very devoted man as well as a very wise one. I try to emulate him every day, and I always think about all the great things he's told me. He's the best possible influence I could ever have, and I hope I can be like him when I'm older because if I am, it means I'll be a great man."

Patrick attended a Jesuit school in Sydney, where the motto was "Men for Others." He demonstrated this quality many times in his 19 years. These next two pieces of writing are both examples of his kindness to others:

When Patrick was in the 5th Grade in Sydney, a friend of his, Eloise Littlefield, was battling brain cancer. He came to me with the idea of organizing a fundraiser to help pay for her medical bills. He decided to organize a crazy hat competition and a dodgeball tournament at his school. It was a fantastic event and he coordinated the whole thing. His classmates were very supportive and $1200 was raised to give to the family. We were so proud of his compassion, genuine desire to help, and his initiative.

This is the letter he wrote to the families in his class:

"Dear Parents and Students,

My name is Patrick Green. I am a student in 5:2.

One of my classmates from my primary school was diagnosed with an aggressive form of brain cancer. Over the past year, she has endured two brain surgeries followed by radiation and chemotherapy. She is now in a hospice full time with her mum and dad.

Both of her parents have given up their jobs to care for her full time and the family is under significant financial pressure. A friend of the family has set up a fund to assist in paying for the medical costs as well as day to day expenses.

I would like to do something to help her and her family. I am going to hold a fundraising day on Thursday 22nd September.

I ask that each boy wears a 'Crazy Hat,' and we will also be playing some dodge ball.

The activities will run from 11:15 – 12:15.

If each student could make a gold coin donation on the day, it would be much appreciated.

Thank you very much for your support.

Best Wishes,
Patrick Green"

In his junior year at high school, he wrote this essay about his time volunteering at St Malachi's Backdoor Ministry in Cleveland:

"I have always had a goal that I would do more community service and help those less fortunate than myself. I was lucky to find an amazing place for me to achieve this goal at St Malachi's kitchen, feeding the homeless just outside of downtown Cleveland. At Malachi's, I was faced with many different challenges that shaped me in multiple ways. While serving food, you never knew what you would encounter, potentially running into more than you think you could handle. An example was when I brought my younger sister, Annabelle, along. We were confronted by a man who used inappropriate language towards my 16 year old sister. I handled the situation, kept my cool, and made my sister feel comfortable about being there. There were certain situations, however, that were not handled in such a manner. For example, a man who was clearly under the influence was causing trouble at the food window. We could not get him under control and we eventually had to close down the window. These are just a couple of examples of the obstacles I had to overcome, and although they were not always pleasant, they have shaped me as a better student and a better man. Being the source of someone's happiness who has so little makes me appreciate how lucky I am and puts life into perspective. St Malachi's has humbled me, and I am glad I persevered through the challenges to receive countless benefits from this amazing place."

Patrick and our girls faced our family's move from Australia to the US with courage and trust in Chris and my decision to relocate the five of us across the world indefinitely. We will always be proud of how they embraced the opportunity. Patrick wrote this essay in his senior year of high school about his transition:

"In November of 2012, at the age of 12, I said a very tearful goodbye to my best friend Alex, my other friends in Sydney, and my family in Melbourne, Australia, and moved with my sisters and parents to Cleveland, Ohio. I left behind the only home I had ever known and landed in a place as foreign and unfamiliar to me as landing on Mars. But as scary as it was at times, that move impacted my teen years in more positive ways than I could have ever imagined.

I had my first shopping trip to Walmart shortly after our arrival, and I convinced my mum to buy Twinkies, that strange American 'delicacy.' And I was pleasantly surprised to find Vegemite and Tim Tams in our local grocery store. Before I knew it, Cleveland was starting to feel more like home, except for the weather. Cleveland was entering its winter months while my friends back in Sydney were enjoying their summer. The first time I saw snow falling, all I could think was how magical this new home was becoming.

I always missed my friends in Sydney and thought of them often, but I made new friends quickly and adjusted to my new school in the American school system fairly easily. I started playing American sports that I'd never played in Australia; to this day, I still love

131

playing baseball, basketball, and football. And every chance I got, I played in the snow.

When we boarded that plane all those years ago in Sydney, I never imagined how great a place I was headed for or what amazing new opportunities awaited me on the other side of the world. I never imagined what great friends I'd make or how lucky I'd be to go to a great high school and play on their sports teams. And I certainly didn't think I'd find myself at age 18 caught up in the excitement of my senior year alongside my classmates. But here I am, looking forward to attending college here in the States, and to all the new experiences ahead."

I am so happy that I was able to include Patrick's words in this book. They are a true reflection of him and how much he cared about people.

"I think my favorite part about Pat was the way he would look at you when he had something to say that he was pumped about, which was pretty much everything. Whether he was in the passenger seat of your car or sitting next to you on a couch, he would turn towards you and look you right in the eye as he joyfully told you what was on his mind, and it was almost like everything he had to say was the best thing that had happened to him in weeks; he just loved life and wanted everyone to see the best in it the way he did."

Jack Corrigan

CHAPTER TEN

IMPRINTS ON HEARTS

After losing Patrick, many people shared personal stories with us about how he touched their lives for the better. These stories represent his legacy; the impressions he left on people's hearts, the intense love, the great times, the funny moments, the deep connections, and importantly, how he will be remembered. They mean more to us than we can ever express, give us comfort in our immense despair, and make us so proud of Patrick and the person he was and still is.

My intention for sharing these in this book is to radiate Patrick's goodness, keep his light shining, and ensure that future generations of our family may also know him and learn about his essence.

For those who knew and loved Patrick, I hope you can turn to this chapter time and again when you feel like reading a good story about him or when you miss him.

Thomas Green (Tom)
Patrick's cousin, 19 years old, Canberra

"Losing Patrick was the toughest moment of my life, and it shook our family to its core, as it still does today. The day I found out was one of the greatest rollercoaster rides. From the extreme high I had been feeling of performing as well as I could have hoped to make my professional football dream come true, to finding out in the changerooms after the game about the tragedy that had unfolded on the other side of the world. Luckily, I was able to spend time with our family in Melbourne as we all came to terms with what had happened. That night we all cried our eyes out together.

Since that day, I haven't cried about it again. Early on, and occasionally now, I feel guilty about not crying. I can see the devastating effect it has had on everyone, and here I am, unable to cry again. But I know the reason. Every memory I have of Patrick is of us laughing and adventuring. No matter what it was, we were always having fun. I look back on those memories so fondly that I cannot help but be happy. Despite his life being cut cruelly short, I am grateful for the time we did get to spend together and the memories we did get to make. He brought so much happiness and joy to my life, as well as so many others that I'm sure will be detailed in this wonderful memoir, that I feel that it would be a waste of time for me to wallow in grief over what has happened. Patrick was always about living his life to the fullest and, as I said at his memorial service in Melbourne, the best way I can honor his legacy is to continue to live my life to the fullest.

So that is how I try to live, and I would encourage all to do the same. I understand it is difficult to deal with such a terrible thing in a positive way, but I feel it has really helped me and served me best for the life I have ahead of me. In his passing, Patrick still serves to help lead others on the right path of enjoyment and fulfillment. It is a legacy he should be truly proud of, and Chris and Sara as parents should be proud to have raised such a fine young man."

Joshua Green (Waaz)
Patrick's cousin, 17 years old, Canberra

"I have a long list of favorite memories because every time we all saw one another, more were created. Christmas in Melbourne with the whole family was the highlight of each year when we were younger and only got sweeter as we grew and moved further away from one another. I distinctly remember the old house in Brighton and how each morning on December 25, all of us kids would get each other up to see if we could guess the presents to be opened later. Some of my best memories that I will never forget were made in that house. The amount of cricket and footy I played with Patrick in those years was ridiculous, and I wouldn't change a thing.

By far, the best memory I have was before you all moved to Cleveland, the day Tom and I played football for Riverview alongside Patrick - the only time we ever got the privilege. As it turned out, between the three Green cousins, seven goals were kicked out of eight or nine of the team's total, but that's not what made it special. It was having the opportunity to all play together that was so much fun, and I will always remember it.

Other memories from our youth include going to Don Camillo's and the Vic Market on a Saturday morning - something we got to do once more in April 2019 - and the jam doughnuts that came with it. Also, every game of footy that we went to watch was always great, despite our team, the Richmond Tigers, not being so good for a lot of our childhood. I distinctly remember Patrick wearing his #12 footy jersey every time we went to any Tigers game - he loved Richo, who wore #12 for the Tigers.

Holidays on Magnetic Island (Maggie) were the best holidays. I remember the house that we all rented out one year in Arthur Bay, with the big rock in the middle and the sign out the front that read 'Private Property.' We explored the mangroves for hours on end, finding nothing in particular but chatting and just pretending we were Bear Grylls or Indiana Jones. Water skiing with Alby was another good memory; Patrick, of course, was the first to get up.

Maybe the highlight of our time though, was every morning when Mikey would pick us up in his Moke and drive a little dangerously around the island. It was then that we learned that perhaps priests weren't exactly perfect men of God, with his questionable language and example setting for five kids under the age of about 10. The journey would eventually take us to a bakery on the southern side of the island, where we would each get a doughnut of our choice, except Annabelle, who would have a meringue. I loved those holidays on Maggie so much, and it was the time that we all got as cousins together that I now treasure.

As the years went by, each time we saw Patrick, it got a little better and a little sadder to see you go. Even though the periods of time between visits were long, each time we got to see everyone again, it was like you had never left. It was so easy to talk to Patrick - about anything - which is one of the things I loved about him. Cricket always seemed to be a topic of discussion as well as sport in general, but I always knew that if I needed Patrick, he was all ears if I wanted to talk about life, school, or whatever.

The last two times we all saw one another were no doubt some of the best weeks of my life so far, and always will be. I cannot express enough how much I enjoyed the Green family holiday in California for Christmas 2018. From Disneyland to exploring the cliffs and kicking the footy in Carlsbad, to the cricket we played in Venice Beach. I will always cherish that holiday, especially because of the memories I created with Patrick.

Perhaps the time that I will remember the most, though, was the night that Patrick, Tom, Sarah, Grant, and I went out in Melbourne when they were all here for Matt and Sam's wedding. That whole night, the band we saw and then the Casino was just so much fun, and a big reason that I was even there was because of Patrick. This was maybe the thing I loved most. He was so much fun to be around and always loved spending time with all of his cousins, a feeling that was clearly mutual.

Above all, I'm just so grateful that I was privileged enough to have been so close to someone like Patrick, and the bond we have as cousins is so special to me. I can't say enough how much I loved all of these memories and how much I love to remember them. I wish I could do it all again with Patrick, but I'm thankful that I was able to do them at all."

William Green (Will Pill)
Patrick's cousin, 16 years old, Canberra

"The reason why I love Patrick so much is because of the one-on-one time I got to spend with him, the times when it was him and I talking and sharing stories, and because he always included me.

As his younger cousin, Patrick could have very easily palmed me off and gone and hung out with Tom and Waaz, but he never did. He always let me tag along on our adventures, and he cared about my opinion. One of my favorite moments was one night on a family holiday in Carlsbad, California, when we were climbing on the cliffs. We were making our way down to the beach, and Patrick and I had reached the bottom first, so we decided to start walking along the sand while Tom and Josh finished their descent. I loved this moment so much. We didn't talk about anything in particular, but it was so amazing for me to be talking to my eldest cousin, someone I looked up to, and for him to be clearly enjoying spending time with me.

Another example of Patrick always including me was during the times when Patrick, Tom, and Waaz played cricket. Patrick always asked me if I wanted to play, and although I didn't often accept the offer, he was always happy for me to stand nearby and watch and join in the conversations. He would also come over and talk to me whenever Tom or Josh were fishing the ball out from under a car, and if the ball ever got stuck up a tree or in a high place, Patrick would always come to me first to ask me to retrieve it. I was always excited to do this, especially if the ball was in a very high up spot, and this was why he asked me because he knew I loved to climb.

One of the major things that Patrick and I bonded over was Harry Potter. We both loved Harry Potter, and I was always trying to convince him to read the books instead of just watching the movies. I remember the night in San Diego when we went out for dinner; Patrick took time away from his endless sports discussions with Tom and Waaz to talk to me about Harry Potter. We would share our opinions on different parts of the story, and Patrick always enjoyed me telling him about anything that happened in the books that wasn't in the movies. I also remember when we were in Carlsbad, and a Harry Potter movie marathon was on, we spent hours sitting in the home theater watching together. When Patrick asked me things about Harry Potter, it was so amazing for me to have my older cousin listening so intently to what I had to say.

The reason why I love Patrick so much is because he always made time for me, and he saw his relationship with me as just as important as his relationships with Tom and Waaz. I deeply miss all the time I had with Patrick, but I am also extremely thankful for the time we had together. I am now trying to learn from him and live my life the way he lived his, always being inclusive and caring about everyone, not just the people my age."

Francesca Noble (Frankie)
Patrick's cousin, 12 years old, Melbourne

"Patrick was always really fun and like the leader of all us cousins. Even though he was older, he wanted to play with us and sled, throw snowballs, or play cards. He never made me feel young or left out."

Lachlan Green (Lochfin)
Patrick's cousin, 10 years old, Canberra

"I liked it when Patrick and I would wrestle in his bedroom every night in Carlsbad. He was and still is, a very kind and lovely person to have as a cousin and was always there for me when I needed him. I love him and miss him."

Elizabeth Noble (Sid)
Patrick's cousin, 8 years old, Melbourne

"I always remember being on Patrick's shoulders or sitting on his lap. Even though I'm the youngest cousin and he's the oldest, he always played with me and included me; he even introduced me to his friends when we were in Cleveland."

Rita Green
Patrick's grandmother, Melbourne

"My relationship with Patrick gelled in the early years when I babysat him on a Monday before Annabelle was born. He was a gentle, happy boy, inquisitive, and great company. Actually, I didn't have much choice but to spend his waking hours with him, as he always wanted to do things together. He wasn't a child who would play on his own for long; he much preferred company.

For me, the next stage in his life was seeing and looking after him with his sisters and 'the swarm'; all of the cousins, who he loved. My role was just to 'feed and water' them.

I cannot remember Patrick fighting, arguing, or acting superior to 'the swarm'. If he wanted something, he did it through the art of persuasion. I strongly felt the definite bond of love amongst all of the cousins. They all just loved being together. Sometimes different ones were doing different activities, but they were equally happy to spend time with everyone, no matter the age difference. No one was left out or ostracized, including the adults. Examples of this were our wonderful times on family holidays on Magnetic Island, Byron Bay, Sydney, and of course, the last big one in Disneyland, Carlsbad, and Venice Beach. In Disneyland, I expected to be looking after the young ones, taking them on simple rides appropriate to them, while the big kids went on the scarier rides. But as it turned out, I never saw them; they all went off together and looked after one another. There was such excitement, it was palpable. How blessed we were.

The memorial service we had for Patrick in Melbourne in October 2019 was a wonderful example of the outpouring of love for him. Even though it was so difficult to do, the whole family insisted we did it to honor our darling Patrick."

Michael Green
Patrick's grandfather, Melbourne

"I don't reflect on Patrick and my interactions and connections with him during his life. Instead, every day I think about and feel close to him by trying to learn from him.

To me, the overwhelming story of Patrick is his reaching out to the person on the edge, on the margin. This has come out repeatedly since his death, and so I try to honor Patrick and connect with him by reaching out to people who might need some connection with another person.

It doesn't come naturally to me as I tend to feel I shouldn't intrude upon people's privacy, but Patrick has taught me that is not the best way. The best way, 'the Patrick way,' is to reach out. So, I'm trying to reach out more to the person on the edge or on the margin in conscious imitation of Patrick.

This is my Patrick story and it is not about the past. It is about his continuing presence in my life and me learning from my grandson and trying to live like him. He's my teacher."

Richard Green
Patrick's uncle and godfather, Canberra
Rich read the following at Patrick's Melbourne memorial service:

"On behalf of Chris and Sara, I'd like to thank their many friends who have provided support over the past few months. Due to the fact Chris and Sara haven't lived in Melbourne for so long, many of you will not know Patrick very well, but instead, you are here today out of love and respect for Chris and Sara. They have been inundated with cards, meals, flowers, and visitors. I'd like to thank you for your love and support, I know it has been somewhat overwhelming for the family, in a good way.

One of the memories about Patrick that I would like to relate was his love of family. Although the Cleveland Greens lived on the far side of the world, he maintained regular contact with his family through social media, and he had a private chat group with his uncle and cousins so they could talk about teenage boy stuff like who was better, Michael Jordan or LeBron James (Jordan, obviously). He loved coming back to Australia to spend time with family, play sport with his cousins, and to find out more about the places and the stories from where his father and his grandfather were raised.

In the aftermath of his death, however, having listened to the stories of his friends and witnessing the spontaneous outpouring of emotion from both their local community in the US and back here in Australia, I realized that while he had a special love for his family, it was actually people he loved (something that must have come from his mother). He was genuinely interested in your individual story and didn't care whether you were young or old, male or female, one of the cool kids, or not. One of the reasons there has been such a strong response to Patrick's death has been because of the many and varied relationships he cultivated in his life. In light of this, I think it's fitting that the memorial at the high school, the rock and marble bench, is a place where people can spend time together.

To quote Matthew 18:20: *'Where two or three are gathered in my name, there I am with them.'*

As a father, I think I know how I'd handle a situation like this, and I can see how Chris is working his way through it, as best one can. But when it comes to understanding Sara's perspective, I think about how my wife Mel would deal with such a tragedy. After having nurtured another human inside her for nine months, I think an event like this would be like cutting out a piece of her heart. For the rest of your life, there will be something missing, and there is absolutely nothing you can do about it.

Sometimes, life can be capricious, and events can often be a harsh reminder of how little control you actually have. While Chris

141

and Sara have been handed a life sentence, the next twelve months will be particularly difficult. The first of everything. First Christmas, first Easter, first Father's Day and Mother's Day, birthdays, graduations.... the list goes on.

Unfortunately, this is not the first time this has happened to someone close to me. As such, my advice to Chris is to accept his fecklessness in this situation and, like swimming in the surf, when the waves of emotion unexpectedly swamp you, don't fight it. Take a deep breath and let them drag you under and tumble you around, all the while knowing that there is nothing wrong, that this is just another part of life you have no control over, and you have enough breath to make it through.

My request to everyone here is to keep in touch with Chris and Sara in the coming months. Not every day or every week, but maybe every month or so, give them a call or send a text. Not to talk about Patrick, but maybe to shoot the breeze, to talk about cricket or footy. While you may think it's a small gesture that will have no impact, you never know. You might just get them on the day when they feel as if they are drowning under the waves."

Melanie Green
Patrick's aunt and godmother, Canberra

"Patrick, I'll never forget the first day I met you. You were a couple of months old, and I'd come down to Melbourne from Townsville. When I got to your house, you were asleep. Sara took me into your room, and you woke up immediately. You stared at me, wondering, 'Who is this?' Your dark hair. Your dark and intelligent eyes. You were taking everything in. You were engaged, inquisitive, and 'there.'

Then came the talking at such a young age, so chatty, a communicator. Then the activity, your energy, running up the street, slightly pigeon-toed but FAST, especially when you didn't want to go home after playing with your cousins or for us to leave. You were best friends. Your love of Richo, who played for the Tigers, something I wholeheartedly agreed with (the Richmond Tigers not so much!). Running through the house at 3 Normanby St, leading the way for your cousins who could not sit still. The walks we had at Maggie. I'd feed you chocolates before dinner. Your husky voice. You were older beyond your years.

We love you so much, a role model and friend to the boys, sharing a kinship and bond that will never break."

Catherine Green
Patrick's aunt, Melbourne

"To get the superficial out of the way first; Patrick was always so beautiful. He was a beautiful looking baby, a beautiful toddler, kid, teenager, and man. Sara would say people stopped her in the street to comment on what a beautiful boy he was, and I definitely had that experience when he was younger when I was with him. But it wasn't just that he was classically handsome, which he was; he also had a twinkle in his eye and a cheeky smile that was just so attractive and magnetic.

When I think of Patrick over his 19 years, I always think of how openly affectionate he was. We had a very close bond when he was a toddler, so 'Minna' (my nickname) always got big cuddles, and as he grew up, this never faded. No matter what age he was or who was around, he would give you the biggest hug and genuine physical affection. And he was exactly the same with my husband, Lochie. I love that as a 19 year old man, he'd come over and give Loch, 25 years his senior, a big hug when he saw him.

Patrick loved people. He loved hearing their stories, asking about their lives, having a laugh with them, and having larger discussions about bigger issues. I've looked at so many photos over the past months, and one of the many things that stands out is how often, at large family gatherings, Ga and I were sitting next to each other, chatting away; on the couch in our ski lodge in New York, our final night dinner at a restaurant in Cleveland, around the table at Mum and Dad's place, on the couch at my house. I am so incredibly grateful for each and every one of those conversations. And I know for a fact that Ga sat and had the same one-on-one time with every member of our family. I have just as many photos of him either talking directly to or listening intently to his aunts, uncles, cousins, and grandparents."

Lachlan Noble (Lochie)
Patrick's uncle, Melbourne

Lochie is the assistant principal at a high school in Melbourne. He gave a speech to the senior class at the opening session of their school camp at the beginning of the school year. He used Patrick as his example with a slideshow of photos of him. This is what he shared with me about his speech:

"I asked the students to think about what they fear. We looked at how to process this and put the school year in perspective. We are all going to die. It's what we do with the time that is given to us that counts. That is what Patrick taught me.

To explain this, I shared the story of Patrick's life and the pain we are enduring. My points were: Live well. Love and treasure your relationships. Be empathetic and inclusive. That is what Patrick did."

Matthew and Samantha Green
Patrick's uncle and aunt, Melbourne

Matt:
"What I loved about PMG was his ability for friendship and connection with people of all ages. He really showed a level of care and interest in everything people did - he liked to know and understand people. He was a gentle and caring person fundamentally, so it's no surprise he attracted so many people to his life.

Memories:

- Babysitting him as a kid - calling him 'stinky' and him laughing.

- Patrick sitting in the car with Syd and loving cars as a young boy.

- Teaching him things as he looked up to me as an uncle - sports, BBQ Shapes - 'Matt's bickies', as Patrick called them.

- Playing cricket and footy at the park in Bronte, Sydney.

- When he was in his WWE wrestling phase, he convinced Doll and I into watching it, telling us about the different wrestlers - who was a goody and who was a baddy.

- He loved playing cards - so we played lots of 21, Poker, and 500 on family holidays.

- Over the past few years, Patrick, Tom, Waaz, and I had an Instagram DM group where we'd share stuff and basically argue about basketball players - how much he was into LeBron (completely one-eyed) reminded me of myself with Jordan at the same age."

Sam:
"Whilst I only knew Patrick for a brief time, it's somewhat incomprehensible the friendship that was created, not just with myself but also my family.

After physically meeting Patrick for the first time (in the US for Christmas 2018), it was only two days later that he already started cuddling me and telling me how excited he was that I was his future auntie. From then on, it was non-stop hugs every day. It was as though we'd known each other forever but just hadn't seen each other in a while.

On the day of our wedding, he was the very first of all our nieces and nephews to come up to me outside the church and give me a big hug and say, 'Finally, I can call you my auntie!!' - my little heart melted.

Similarly, all night long at the reception, he kept coming over to give me a hug and say, 'I'm so glad you're my auntie, I love you so much.' He would've said those words to me over 10 times that night, bless him."

Sarah Green
Patrick's aunt, Melbourne

"Patrick was the first baby I held. I remember I didn't hold him until he was a few months old because I was scared to drop him, but he was such a good baby; he made it so easy for me. I had the joy of spending a lot of time with Patrick. We both lived in Sydney at the same time, and I traveled to see him and the family in Cleveland a few times. Every moment we spent together was filled with laughter and fun. We would watch music videos and learn the dances, go driving so we could blast music, and talk for hours.

Patrick was so interested in life. He was interested in everyone's story, the values they had, the fun times they had, the sad times they went through, and the plans they had. He wanted to know about you. He wanted to understand who you were because he genuinely cared about people, and I think he used these conversations to help form his own opinions and learn about the world.

I cherished the conversations I had with him. He made me feel so special and important. He made me feel as if my opinion mattered and that my life was interesting. He was funny, charming, and a great conversationalist. As soon as he could talk, he was great at having a deep, honest, and meaningful conversation.

Some nights I go driving alone just so I can blast music and talk to him."

Grant Douglas
Patrick's uncle, Melbourne

"I met Patrick and the Cleveland Greens a little over a year ago. Being the new boyfriend and meeting new family members is always daunting, but the moment I met you, Patrick, there was an instant connection that put me at ease. I've since been told you had this impact on just about everyone you met. Although I only got to meet you and spend time with you ever so briefly, I cherish those memories and return to them daily. To see the effect that you've had on people is truly awe-inspiring. I was really looking forward to a lifetime of chats and laughs, but memories will have to do for now. I promise to keep your Aunty Sarah smiling and laughing for as long as I can until we meet again; you will always be missed."

Beverley Chambers
Patrick's grandmother, Melbourne

"Patrick, my first grandchild, it was 'love at first sight.' A gorgeous little boy who would give me great joy in the early years of looking after him. We had lots of excursions, such as me wheeling him in the pram around to Gigi's place or going to Carnegie Station to watch the trains come and go.

As he grew, the outings were a little more adventurous. The Collingwood Children's Farm, where his eyes lit up at finding another egg to put in his basket - later on during another visit Patrick was able to show Annabelle 'the ropes.' They also had great fun at the Children's Museum, enjoyed visits to Hay's Paddock, as well as my local playground, where the old round-about could barely go whizzing around fast enough for Patrick - such heart-in-mouth times for Nanna!

I'll never forget our visit to Scienceworks. With a broken arm in plaster and a sling, he ran like the wind against the Cathy Freeman interactive - there was no stopping him! Nights at Nanna's playing board games, card games, and Guess Who?

Even from a very young age, it was obvious that Patrick's determination to compete and succeed would take him far. So many treasured memories of a special boy who grew into a lovely, thoughtful young man."

Kevin Chambers
Patrick's grandfather, Melbourne

"My favorite memories of Patrick go back to my Melbourne babysitting days and playing games in the backyard, especially those involving a fishing rod. A 15-20 meter cast to 'right on the spot' was easy for him. Even then, at five years old, his excellent hand and eye coordination was evident, and this obviously led to the sporting prowess he achieved in his short time with us.

I also really enjoyed my birthday time in Cleveland with the family and all the fun emails that I subsequently shared with Patrick and Annabelle. I was really looking forward to his time at college and perhaps assisting with his budding interest in music and his business studies."

Olivia Foulds
Patrick's second cousin, Melbourne

"Patrick Green, the little brown-haired, doe-eyed boy who was the first, proudest great-grandchild for his Gigi Foulds. I have one fond and clear memory of him sitting in his pram, all of 18 months old, and my dad (his great uncle) staring down at his little face saying to him, 'Hello cheeky bugger!' Patrick's big hazel eyes glanced up; he tilted his head to the side while smirking and replied, 'Chee-kee bug-a' right back at him.

Patrick was charismatic, the apple of his sisters' eyes. On my Sydney visits, and later across the globe on my visit to Cleveland, I witnessed the way his parents idolized him.

He had a graceful ease in the way he moved around both the world and those close to him.

His quiet confidence was magnetic. A knowing boy. The glimpses I got into his later youth were nothing short of him being a fine young man with his head screwed on well, measured in all aspects of his life. Considerate and engaged, everybody's friend, an ace sportsman, and very family-focused. An all-time kind of human."

Andrew Brushfield
Patrick's second cousin, Melbourne

"As many Australians do, we had escaped the Melbourne winter and had just started our family holiday in Italy. I had decided to head out for a quick run in Rome before the tourist buses arrived. When I returned, my wife Robbie looked worried. My mum had called multiple times and left a message asking that I call immediately. It was unusual. What's going on? Was it an elderly relative? Had something come up with my estranged brother?

I called Mum and the news was shocking. This can't be real. Not Patrick. No way. After sharing the news with Robbie and the kids and hours of tears later, the realization began to sink in. I kept thinking, this sort of stuff doesn't happen to our family; we had only seen him a few months earlier in Melbourne for Matt and Sam's wedding. He was fit and healthy and looking forward to his summer and a move to college. This can't be happening.

How I wish I was wrong. Such a superb young man. So friendly and genuine. Despite the distance, Patrick was always so interested and connected with his cousins and wider family back in Australia and was so comfortable being the person he was. I thought of Chris, Sara, Annabelle, and Tildy. How would they be feeling? I couldn't imagine. Michael and Rita. This was too hard to comprehend.

Chris is my first cousin and someone I love. We were raised in a tight-knit family, spent Christmases together, holidays and birthdays. He was the year above me at the same school, and when he met Sara, she quickly became part of the family too. When I look back on my life and significant events, Chris has been there for most of them. Although we live on opposite sides of the world now and we don't speak all the time, things really haven't changed between us. I knew I had to call Chris straight away, and I vividly remember the spot in the Airbnb apartment where I was standing, feeling completely numb. When he answered, the reality of the loss of Patrick struck hard. The shock and pain in Chris's voice, and the pain they all would now carry was devastating.

I was fortunate enough to spend three days in Cleveland in September 2019. I was nervous and a little anxious about seeing them all for the first time since Patrick's passing. I shouldn't have been as it was such a memorable weekend. There were heaps of tears, of course, as we all shared stories of Patrick, but as is typical of Chris, Sara, and the girls, they welcomed me into their daily life and all its ups and downs with gusto, and I loved that. I will always treasure sitting up talking with Sara and Annabelle until the early morning hours, covering every detail of Patrick, sitting on the deck for hours with Chris while meat smoked on the grill, talking footy, our grandparents, and our basketball heydays. Annabelle taking me on a tour of where they live and where she and Patrick spent time are moments I treasure. Sometimes we cried, sometimes we laughed, but I really appreciated that at no stage was any topic off-limits. This is truly a testament to Chris and Sara, and the honesty and openness with which they live their life is how I know they will survive this.

There are so many great memories of Patrick that demonstrate what a unique kid he was; babysitting him as a three year old, he liked to listen to 3AW in bed. As a young boy, he could reel off the competing prices of sausages at their local Sydney butchers. Most recently, though, only shortly before he died, Chris and Sara and the kids had returned to Melbourne for a family wedding, and we wound up walking with Patrick to the wedding venue. It had been a while since we'd seen him, and it was a 10 minute talk I replay in my mind often. Robbie was so impressed by Patrick. He truly had a natural charm about him. So interested in others. So content in being who he was. I thought this kid is going places. What a champion."

Jane Brushfield
Patrick's second cousin, Melbourne

"When you were in Melbourne for Matt and Sam's wedding, Patrick made such an impression on me that Sunday afternoon at the Half Moon in Brighton. I can't tell you how glad I am that we were able to see you all. I loved it at the time, but I cherish those memories now, so much more than I ever realized I would.

Looking across the room and seeing him engaged in conversation with Lucy, Alice, and Ted (who, let's face it, would probably struggle to keep it interesting unless it's about gymnastics, soccer, or lollies) was an absolute joy. He really had an incredible way about him - he made the people he was with feel important. What an amazing quality. I'm sad that Charlie wasn't with us. Dave and I hope our boys will become young men just like Patrick. Smart, kind, thoughtful, and emotionally aware.

The loss of Patrick is horrendously unfair - the world has lost someone important and special, but no one will feel this loss more than you, Chris, and the girls. I know you must be in a world of pain, and I want you to know that there are so many people all around the globe who are thinking of you constantly, sending you all our love and best wishes. I have been taking solace in the idea that Patrick is safe in the care of Nance and Syd now. If anyone can love him as much as you and Chris did for 19 years, it's them."

Alex Hooper
Patrick's friend, Sydney

"Patrick was my best friend, but he was a best friend to everyone and friend for those who needed one. His kind nature and comforting attitude made for a humble but talented person. Although we only got to see each other once a year, our connection as brothers never wavered and never will."

Michael Konrad
Patrick's friend, Cleveland

"When I think of Patrick, there are endless memories that run through my head. He is my best friend in the whole world, and I love him so much. We loved each other so much.

My favorite memories are: calling each other Daniel; beating him in ping pong, then listening to him tell me that he's the goat because Lebron always lost in the finals; having so many inside jokes that we would accidentally run across the forgotten ones in a normal conversation and use them way too much from that point; playing countless hours of NBA 2k13, MLB 2k11, Madden 11, Tiger Woods PGA tour 2005, GTA, and NHL14; waking up to him coming in my room at 2 am half of the summer nights and watching him lay down on his couch in my room; watching him flirt with every mom on my street and get away with it; getting a text at any time that wasn't the right time to hang out and having him still barge into my room; watching him leave a party or a hangout multiple times just so he could be with different friend groups that night.

Playing countless hours of basketball on his court - games to 100 by 1s and 2s; going out in the snow and being the only two kids childish enough at our age to make snowballs and forts; playing ice basketball with him where a two-pointer counted as negative seven points and a three-pointer counted as two; waking up at 7 am to Patrick opening my garage and walking up to my room because he couldn't sleep and he needed someone to hang out with; hot tub nights; driving through the Metroparks or all around the city listening to random songs that only we knew about; making lunch for him every single day for an entire year and starting his mustard addiction; him asking me to do an impression or retell a joke because he loved it so much; sitting on the plane that was never going to take off to Miami and running through every Mario baseball character and rating them while he died laughing; walking around the streets of Miami trying to convince ourselves for hours that we were old enough to get into a bar!

Meeting him for the first time at a high school football game I was so fascinated by him because he knew how to play cricket; how well he knew everything about me because he asked me everything there was to know about me; him flirting with my grandma and making everyone in my family think he was the best thing ever; walking around and having every girl scream 'Oh my God, are you Patty Green?!' and being completely ignored as they stared at him; Geneva with Pat and Finn and how much he loved being with us in the little house on the lake; the Green's back patio and all the schemes we thought of back there; football Sundays where I would tell him the most absurd things and he would egg me on to keep saying stupid things; going to John's Diner (that we called Don's Jiner) before or after every Rec basketball game and making fun of the old ladies at the counter as we ordered the same meal every time; having every bet we made result in somebody buying a dinner box for us to split; 'Mikey' coming out of his mouth in so many tones in so many different phrases.

Patrick loving every single one of my family members, friends, and girlfriends to the extent I did; double dates with Pat, Callie, Liv, and me or Pat, Eve, Sarah and me; Patrick helping Sarah and me get through the long-distance by being a best friend to both of us and always making us laugh; every text he sent me that was followed by my sarcastic response and him laughing; how I've never had a best friend turn into family before Patrick, and how it takes a special person to leave behind so many friends that were so involved with his family; walking through the Green's back door and screaming upstairs for Pat to come down.

Finding every second we could to hang out after school, during school, on the weekends, in the summer, or whenever; all the Skyvenka nights and how much he loved being down there asking my dad endless stories saying, 'We have to get Chris down here with us,' every time; talking about our futures and him asking me what I thought he should do for his profession; every jersey we talked about getting each other; watching him get so upset when I rubbed it in his face that I won the 'Bownet Hat' in football more weeks than him just because it was my last year kicking and Coach Massad knew that Pat was exponentially better than me; how we never left each other's sides whenever possible; Patrick getting fake upset thinking that I was Sara's favorite son over him; the way he talked about his family and how he was so excited for me to meet everyone in Australia; me asking if I could come over to your house all the time because Patrick and all of you made me feel like a Green; all the plans we had - what our weddings would be like and countless visits to Cincinnati and OSU; our big trip back to Miami when we were 21; going to Australia with Patrick; who we would marry; things we had to do before we died; being each other's best men, and always being best friends.

When I think of Patrick, I think about all the amazing qualities he has: he is a best friend to everyone; he is so curious about everything;

he is so beautiful; he is hilarious beyond anyone's imagination; he never finds a bad trait in a person; he could eat a house if he was hungry; he is the most athletic kid I've ever seen; his brain works so well in so many ways that nobody else's can; his love extends to everyone; his smile is perfect; the way he talks could fool anyone; his time management is incomparable; he is loving; he is the best at comforting everyone; he is the most fun person you'll ever meet; he is always thinking about everyone; he always keeps you in touch; he loves everyone; he is my rock.

There will never be a moment where you don't miss your big little angel. He loved you guys more than he loved anything in the whole world. That kid was everywhere he wanted to be when he wanted to be there. I've never been the comforting one or the one to cheer everyone up like Patrick was, but he's been guiding me through this whole grief thing. Patrick has been telling me exactly what to say to every single person, and I have been thanking him every second for that.

For Chris, Sara, Belle, and Tildy, Patrick has just three words that he wants me to say, 'I love you.'"

Michael Finnegan
Patrick's friend, Cleveland

"It was Summer of 2016, Pat and I had just finished our freshman year of high school. We decided to play a round of golf down in the Metroparks at Little Met. Since Pat was older for our grade, he had already turned 16, and he'd been driving for months. As a result, we figured that we would easily get a golf cart until the worker, an older guy probably about 70 years old, informed us that you had to be 18. After asking to see our IDs, Pat brought out his new driver's license. The worker checked his date of birth and saw that he was only 16. He gave Pat a blank look and said that we wouldn't be able to take a cart. Without hesitation, PG began inspecting the ID as if he was surprised by his own age. Chatting up the guy with a bit more Australian in his voice, Pat went on to explain that since he wasn't from the US, the date of birth didn't transfer correctly and that he was actually 18. The worker responded, 'So you're telling me when you moved to the States you magically gained two years?' 'Exactly, mate.' Pat said. The guy was still not budging; however, neither was PG. They went back and forth for a good five minutes until Pat 'Aussie'd' the poor guy to death. He eventually got so sick of hearing Pat's 'BS' that he just said screw it and let us take the cart. I've never seen someone work so hard for a golf cart, but I must say that the round was much more enjoyable because of it.

In our sophomore year, Pat and I both had Health class 7th period. Mrs. A, God bless her, made a terrible mistake and let Pat and I sit next to each other. For weeks straight, the two of us talked nonstop through her teaching until the sex education unit started, and the talking between the two of us turned into laughter. Pat had a field day asking Mrs. A all sorts of questions about the unit, knowing that she had to answer him since technically it was appropriate. He eventually crossed the line with a question I can't put into writing that sent me out of my chair, laughing. Mrs. A finally understood what we were up to and sent us to the assistant principal's office, who had a reputation of not being lenient in terms of punishment. I opted to go into her office first and find out my fate, to be done with it. I was in there for maybe 30 seconds and just accepted my three days detention. I walked out of her office and told Pat what the punishment was. I figured I would just wait for him so we could get all of our laughs out on the walk back to Health class. A full 20 minutes later, Pat walked out with a grin on his face - I knew something was up. We took the long way back to class, and he explained what went on in there. He said, 'Yeah, so at first, we were talking about why we were sent to the office, but then I totally steered the conversation onto something else. We were just talking about her dating life and other stuff about her, 20 minutes went by, and she completely forgot to give me the detention. Sorry mate.'

It's always been my belief that Pat would want to be remembered in the manner in which he lived - with positivity. Though the past year has been one that none of us expected, reflecting on moments like these has been my savior. I often think to myself, man, he would've absolutely hated 2020. A pandemic has consumed the better half of the year, and we're all cooped up inside. I think he would've gone crazy not being able to burn his social calories. Since his passing, PG has had no trouble being the uniting force that he always has been. He single-handedly meshed multiple friend groups of differing ages into one, and we now all have a texting group chat named after him called 'The Kid's Legacy.' In fact, as I'm writing this, a text just came through from Brian Lowry inviting all the lads over for the first swim of the year in his pool - something that would never have happened unless Pat brought us together. There was no chance he was going to miss this swim, there was a brief storm with heavy rain, and afterwards, a double rainbow appeared. There he was.

We've laughed, cried, and grown as a group since June 27, 2019. Out of all the blessings that PG provided in our brief yet unforgettable friendship, I'll always be most grateful for 'The Kid's Legacy.' After all, it's in the name - the kid left a legacy."

The story of Patrick's passing was broadcast on the local TV news here in Cleveland, and many articles were written about him and the accident online and in print in Cleveland and Melbourne. Cleveland.com featured Michael Finnegan talking about how much Odell meant to Patrick:

"'Rec basketball, football, baseball - he was #13 always,' said Finnegan, one of Green's closest friends and the Pirates' former starting quarterback. Finnegan said Green first became a Beckham fan in 2014 when his father Chris' good friend, Kevin Abrams, assistant GM of the Giants, told Chris the Giants were thinking of drafting Beckham out of LSU.

Green started watching his LSU highlights and was instantly hooked.

'Pat was a fan right away, way before The Catch,' said Finnegan. 'Everyone knew Odell after that, but Pat beat everyone to that punch.'

Finnegan recalled the time the Pirates called a fake punt, and

Green emulated his hero:

'He had to roll out to his left, and then he had to tuck it and run, but he always remembered the way Odell carried the ball if he was about to score a touchdown,' Finnegan said. 'Odell wouldn't put it under his elbow as most players do. He would hold it just in his palm, and Pat did that, and he got the first down for us, and then we went and scored. He came up to me and said, 'Finny, did you see how I carried the ball just like Odell?''

Anyone who knew Green knew that he was all OBJ, all the time.

'Everything was Odell-centric,' Finnegan said. 'If Odell posted a video on Instagram of him dancing to some new rap song, Pat was going to blare that song for the next two weeks in his car. He tried to dance just like him, doing all the funny moves that Odell does.'"

Odell Beckham Jnr
NFL player and one of Patrick's sporting heroes
Odell tweeted the following two days after the accident:

"R.I.P Pat Green. Heard you've been a fan from Day 1, and I appreciate U. My sincere condolences to the Green family on their loss. You are in my thoughts and prayers. LUV."

Patrick would have been ecstatic! Annabelle tweeted the following reply to OBJ:

"Thank you for the happiness my family is currently feeling, something that has been missing the past 48 hours. It is a lot easier knowing that Patrick is smiling up above us."

Brian Lowry
Patrick's friend, Cleveland

"I have been trying to rake my mind for my absolute favorite memory of Patrick. I decided to tell you the full story about when he learned about the deaths of my mom and someone who I considered

157

my brother. I don't know if you know about Alex Chamberlin, but a little back story is that he was my neighbor for my whole life, and my brother and I grew up with him, hanging out with him every single day. He was basically how Pat was with all of the kids on your street; we looked up to him and loved him. He was diagnosed with leukemia in, I believe 2010, and he ended up beating it, but one day, two months after his blood transfusion results came back clean, he did not wake up. One of my fondest memories with Alex was that every year we would sit in my front yard and watch the fireworks from Fairview days. The day after he passed was the day of the annual fireworks and I sat there alone, bawling my eyes out. This sets the scene for my favorite memory with Pat and when I knew that we were going to have a special bond.

As the case was on most summer days, Pat and I were at my house hanging out and swimming. Then the fireworks started going off, and I got emotional about all of the memories, and all of the feelings about those tragic days washed over me. Before this, I had never really opened up to Pat about my mom or Alex, who had both died. Patrick had come into my life after both of these things had happened, and he never pressed me about them. Pat sat next to me and watched me cry throughout the whole fireworks show. After that, we talked about my mom and Alex. Pat, being the person he was, didn't even take a moment to look away. He embraced every story, and when it was all said and done, he thanked me for telling him about them. He told me that he would have loved to have met both of them, and I assured him that they both would have loved him (I mean, how could you not?). I knew after that day that I could talk to Pat about anything, and he would drop everything he was doing to listen.

Here are the text messages that we exchanged once he got home that night, just to reinforce something you already know - how much of a great and caring son you raised:

Patrick: Thanks for a great chat, brother. Always here if you ever want to talk or just need anything, love you Bro.

Brian: Love you brother, I'm glad you got to hear the whole story.

Patrick: It was an honor, your mum sounds like she was an amazing woman and Alex sounded like an unreal dude. I wish I could have met them.

Brian: I really wish you could have, they were such great people.

Patrick: I can only imagine how great they both were, thanks for sharing, it truly means a lot. They are with you every day mate, you know that. And they are super proud of you, you are super strong. I've always got your back for life.

I have gained a little peace knowing that when Patrick got up there, he was embraced with open arms by Alex and my mom, and knowing my mom, she thanked him for being such a great friend."

Jack Corrigan
Patrick's friend, Cleveland

"When I met Pat, I was a senior in high school, and he was just a freshman. We both had girlfriends who were sophomores at the time and best friends. I had no idea who Pat was, but Callie had told me how excited he was to meet me, and I thought that was pretty cool, but I had no clue who was about to walk into my life and the impact he would have on me. As I finished my senior year and went off to college, Pat started to talk to my friends and me more and more. When we both went through breakups with our girlfriends towards the end of my freshman year of college, we really became close. Several of our friends, including Patty and myself, started a group chat in the spring of 2017 called 'Da Boyz' which ended up being the beginning of an incredible friendship for us all. For the next couple of years, we all spent endless hours hanging out, swimming, playing beer-die, having parties, bonfires, getting food together, playing video games, visiting one another at our different schools, and anything else we could think of. When we all weren't together, we were talking daily in 'Da Boyz.'

Besides Pat, all of us boys had known one another since we were six years old, all being in the same grade and playing the same sports. So, for Pat to come in out of nowhere and be so accepted and liked by all of us; it wasn't a coincidence; we knew he was special. Through the next couple of years, I began to realize Pat was becoming one of my closest friends, and there were many reasons for that. Every time he walked in the room, or got in the car, or came through Lowry's twin garage doors into the back yard, he brought a level of energy and joy that you couldn't help but smile at. He always put others before him, constantly asking you about your day, or hyping you up for something that you were excited about; he always wanted to see his friends happy, and that's why he had so many of them.

Looking back, I think my favorite part about Pat was the way he would look at you when he had something to say that he was pumped about, which was pretty much everything. Whether he was in the passenger seat of your car or sitting next to you on a couch, he would turn towards you and look you right in the eye as he joyfully told you what was on his mind, and it was almost like everything he had to say was the best thing that had happened to him in weeks; he just loved life and wanted everyone to see the best in it the way he did.

During the first half of 2019, he began to introduce his other group of friends to me and the rest of our older group. In a way, it was as if he knew that it was almost his time, and he wanted all of his best mates to be together. Over the past year, those kids that Pat introduced me to have become some of my closest friends, and it's something that only Pat could've done. He spread more love in his short time than most people do living to a ripe old age.

Every decision I make, I think about him, and I try to share that same positive energy that he had in everything I do. For me, the hardest thing to do is think about everything we would have done together in life and all the experiences we would have shared; I knew Pat and I would always be close friends, and we loved talking about the future and all the awesome things we would do. I can always feel him, subconsciously pushing me to never settle for anything and to always go for what makes me happy. And even though he won't be standing next to us during the good and bad times, he will be with us, watching over everyone he ever loved. While it's easy to think about how unfair this all is, I know he would want everyone to think about the time we did have with him and how to spend the time we have going forward with the best possible mindset, carrying his legacy with us each day. It was the greatest honor of my life to have known someone so special, and I will always cherish that fact."

Callie Cmiel
Patrick's former girlfriend and family friend, Cleveland

"One of my favorite memories with Pat was serving meals at Saint Malachi's Church. Pat, Belle, and I would drive downtown together. I joined the mix after they had been going there for some time. I'll never forget the first time I went. When Pat walked in, everyone was so excited to see him. He had made friends with the workers and also the men and women who we served meals to. We usually got right to work, and I was given the opportunity to meet the people with whom Pat would spend his Sundays. Looking back, I am so grateful to have seen him in this element, which was helping the less fortunate. The way they looked at him, you could tell that he was truly making an impact on their day, and it was amazing to witness. Pat's outgoing and selfless personality shone. He had this light in him that made every single person feel better about themselves. By spending time with Pat at Saint Malachi's, I truly understood his gift of helping and caring for other people.

Other fond memories include attending my brother, Connor's, sporting events with Pat. No matter the sport or the game, he always wanted to go. My parents usually asked me to film parts of the games on our iPad, which was my least favorite thing to do. Luckily for me, Pat offered to do it. When Connor would go into the game, Pat would jump into action and make sure he was recording. The part that made it so amusing to me was that Pat made sure to give commentary on every single play, of every single game. He would shout and yell at Connor things like, 'Okay bro I see you,' 'Ooh look at that fit!,' 'Nooo don't do it to them CC,' and 'GOAT!' Pat was often the loudest fan. Because of this, I found myself wanting to go to more games if Pat was with me. We laughed the entire time because of his hilarious comments. At home, Connor and I would re-watch those videos and laugh. Pat made going to Connor's sporting events the highlight of each week. I am so grateful that he took the time to film because now we have a dozen videos featuring Pat's enthusiastic audio and Australian accent!

One of the many times Pat helped me was when I tore my ACL. It was definitely a difficult time knowing I would miss the rest of my volleyball season and have another nine months of physical therapy. Pat showed up almost daily with encouragement, kindness. and tons of ice cream. Even though it was a minor incident in my life, there was no way I could have gotten through it all without Pat's support. For the entire time, he pushed me to get better, he was there for me on good and bad days, and he helped me to stay positive. After I recovered, he attended almost every single one of my volleyball games and made sure I knew he was there through his cheering and clapping. I am forever grateful to Pat for his strength during a difficult time.

Although I have countless memories of Pat that I will forever hold in my heart, my absolute favorite times were when we were doing absolutely nothing. Pat's presence and personality made any kind of experience the best. Whether it was challenging each other to talk with the other person's accent, driving for hours listening to Justin Bieber, or walks in the Metroparks, Pat was my go-to and made every outing much more fun.

Patrick was generous, caring, selfless, passionate, funny, adventurous, grateful, loving, gentle, considerate, energetic, compassionate, and kind-hearted.

Even though someone may have just met Pat, he made them feel as if they had been best friends for months. Pat was not concerned with what people thought; he was focused on what made other people happy. This is something I try to practice every single day. Pat was patient; for some crazy reason, he would not get upset when I would talk for three-plus hours. He was a very loving person, and if you got lucky enough to be in his close circle, he did anything for you. I admired the way he treated Belle and Tildy. By being close with his sisters, Pat showed me how to be a better older sibling to my brother. He had the most contagious energy and smile and would absolutely light up the room when he entered. The thing that set Pat apart was his unforgettable and one-in-a-million personality - you were just drawn to him. You felt happier when you were with Pat; he had that effect on everyone.

I believe the most important aspect of Pat was how he made me feel. Many of the qualities that he possessed are the qualities I strive to incorporate in my life. These attributes are also what I look for in my best friends and people I continue to meet. What makes a person someone you want to have in your life forever is someone who loves you and sincerely wants the best for you, no matter what. Pat would take the time to personally know every single person I cared about. I knew he would always be in my life based solely on the way he made me and others feel.

I have amazing memories of Pat and will always keep them dear to my heart. I certainly know that if it was not for him being such a big part of my life, I would be a different person than who I am today. I am a better person because I knew Pat."

The Cmiels
Family friends, Cleveland

Kevin:
"When I think of Patrick, here are some of the attributes that come to mind:
- Incredible spirit and positive energy.
- Kindness, goodness and deeply caring person.
- Curiosity and interest in so many things.

- Confidence - the way he carries himself with a sense of self-assurance without even a hint of arrogance.

- An emotional intelligence level and people skills beyond his age.

Reflection...

You feel better when Patrick is around; he puts a smile on your face because of his infectious and positive personality.

I love how he walks into our house with a big smile, an energy, and a warmth that is truly unique. We know the questions will be coming and that there are going to be discussions about anything and everything. Having Patrick join us in the kitchen for a meal and conversation is something I always look forward to. And then when it is time to go home, he is always so appreciative; he has a way to make you feel special.

It was fun to see how he made Callie light up every time he was around. I love the fact that they were always on the go; they did so many fun activities and outings together. There was never a dull moment; his energy wouldn't allow it.

A special bond developed between Patrick and Connor. He went out of his way to include Connor and took the time to foster that relationship. In addition to a friendship, there was an element that was more like Patrick playing the role of an older brother, which made Connor proud and happy. That bond continues today.

We feel so blessed to have Patrick in our lives; his impact is felt by all of us. As a family, we have discussed that a great tribute to Patrick and to the Greens would be to act and live our lives a little more like Patrick. Let's live by and incorporate some of his characteristics; how can we be strong leaders, be inclusive and kind to everyone and look for and find what's good in people? Patrick is in our hearts forever, and his influence will carry on."

Eileen:

"Did you know we had a handshake? Rather than hugging Patrick every time he came over, I thought it would be more comfortable for him to have a fancy handshake like professional athletes. What 16 year old wants his girlfriend's mother hugging him all the time like some crazy aunt, I reasoned. I wish I could have those visits again; he wouldn't have gotten away with just a handshake.

I have one daughter and she had one first love. I am so grateful that Patrick was Callie's first love. He is a tough act to follow but also a great example of what standard she will expect in a mate.

To this day, I am still surprised at the depth of my shock and anger that Patrick was taken from this world. There is a greater purpose I have yet to understand, but I still search for that answer.

We cherished our time with Patrick and are so grateful that our families have remained close. This is also part of his legacy."

Connor, who wrote the following essay about Patrick for English class:

"'What's up GOAT?' spoken in an Australian accent is the typical greeting I received from Patrick. Patrick is one of those kids who lights up every room he enters. He is outgoing, funny, and kind. He has the unique ability to make every single person feel that they are valued and loved. Patrick's zest for life is contagious, and his ability to live in the moment, every moment, is something to be imitated. I consider myself lucky to call Patrick a friend.

To say that Patrick's death affected me is an understatement. It was the first significant loss that I had experienced. Patrick was so young, and his passing was so shocking. It took me several days to even accept that he was gone. I have always had strong faith in God, but my friend's death made me seriously examine my faith. Questions like, 'How does God let something like this happen?' and 'How does someone like Patrick get taken away from us?' haunted me. The real question I struggled with was, 'How do I exist in a world in which Patrick isn't?' I saw no need to go to mass. It was hard to pray. It was hard to go a day without thinking about what I had lost.

Many signs helped me to regain my equilibrium and rethink my approach to faith. The Saturday after Patrick died, a huge thunderstorm rolled through. In its place was an enormous rainbow that arched over Patrick's house. My sister and I pulled into a nearby beach and our headlights illuminated table 13. We said a prayer in a church while on vacation that summer and coincidentally sat in row 13. I used these signs to help me understand that Patrick was still with me. I also decided that my faith was the one thing that would get me through this dark period.

I put #13 above my bed to remind me of him and how he lived his life. My faith will always be with me, and so will Patrick."

Eve Witzigreuter
Patrick's former girlfriend and family friend, Cleveland

"Patrick made me feel like I was the most important thing in his life, like I was his priority. He made me feel so beautiful and he gave me a lot of confidence in myself. I don't even recognize the person I was before he entered my life. We brought out the best versions of each other. Whenever he was around, I was happy. I love his compassion for other people and his ability to read other's emotions; he read me like a book. He was funny; our relationship was filled with laughter. He wanted everyone to be happy and be the cause of all laughter and smiles. He accomplished that with every person I saw him interact with. In fact, we could barely be in public places without having to stop and talk with someone he knew. I loved that about him. He made it a point to speak to everyone in a room, even if he had never met them before. He was the person who went up to someone who was sitting alone and asked them how they were; he made everyone feel important.

People felt as if they could confide in him; he was loyal. He interacted with Paul in a way I've never seen before, and I'm not sure I'll see again. Patrick and Paul had a special bond and I feel blessed to have been able to witness that. There was never a dull moment with Patrick. We could be doing absolutely nothing and have a good time together. In fact, some of my most favorite times with him were just sitting in the basement doing nothing. I miss those times. With my entire heart, I loved him. I feel so lucky that I got to experience his love and that he chose to love me. I don't think I'm capable of loving another person the same way that I loved him. He was truly one in a million and I thought he was my soulmate.

Things I loved:
- The way his Australian slang rubbed off on me and all the terms he taught me, and he used.
- How much he loved music and movies, he made me watch all the 'classics' - Harry Potter, Seven, The Shining, Silence of the Lambs.
- The way he swayed back and forth when he talked.
- The way he twirled the front piece of his hair.
- The way Paul would lay with him on the couch.
- How passionate he was about things he believed in.
- How he was totally and completely himself and never ashamed of it.
- The way he interacted with his family and how close-knit of a group they were.
- He loved showing me Australia and his old house and the old family photos/videos.
- His YouTube channel and nerf gun review he had when he was younger.
- I could never show him a new song. Every song I thought was new, he had heard. He used to pretend he didn't know it, and right when I got excited about finally showing him a new song, he'd belt out every word.
- 'Meatball banter' with my mom.

- Watching him play football, I loved going to his games and watching him punt.

- Brian Lowry's house, so many memories there.

- How he ran down the stairs or flung the door open to my house and kind of stood there waiting for applause, just the overall way he carried himself."

The Witzigreuters
Family friends, Cleveland

"We have so many fond memories of our time with Patrick. One winter afternoon, Patrick helped Dan, Eve, and I rearrange the furniture in Paul's bedroom. Music was playing. Paul was bouncing around and we tried several arrangements until we settled on the current set up. This led to investigating all the medical supplies in Paul's closet. Patrick asked countless questions about Paul's experience. Soon we were taking everyone's blood pressure, listening to one another's heartbeats, and just laughing and having fun. Pat's blood pressure readings were terrific.

Silly Stunting: We loved seeing Patrick 'cheer' with Eve. He would willingly mimic her jumps and clap along with the cheers, often lifting her into various stunts. We still can't believe she never hit the ceiling.

Family: Patrick was very popular with my siblings and In-laws. Everyone enjoyed his joyous nature and ability to fit right into the family-fun at Thanksgivings and other gatherings. He was considered another grandson, nephew, cousin, and son. Many of our family members attended the funeral and came to town to offer support. They all loved Patrick.

On the Job: Dan feels so fortunate to have had so much time with Patrick when they worked together in Massachusetts. He especially enjoyed the time after work, just hanging with Patrick and Luke. He was very proud of how hard they worked that week.

Cincinnati Children's Liver Transplant Picnic June 2018: We were so glad to have Pat join us at the transplant picnic in Cincinnati.

Coney Island was more fun having Pat along to play putt-putt-golf, ride paddle boats, swim, dine out, and just travel with. He brought so much energy; it truly lifted all of us.

Gift of Life Walk and Run August 2017: Pat and Belle joined us at Blossom for the annual Gift of Life Walk and Run. It was special to share this event with them and warmed our hearts.

Witzi's Raw Granola: Pat was the ultimate granola fan. Numerous recipe testings, photoshoots, and even bag filling. He was so sure it would dominate the health food scene and was always asking about the business and the latest updates.

4th of July: We had fun going to the local 4th of July parade each year. Pat was such a sport wearing red, white, and blue, and embracing the USA for the day.

Pirate Hockey: Patrick was the ultimate hockey fan. We loved it when he came to the games with us. He cheered loudly and with great enthusiasm. His Australian accent bellowing and his fists pounding the glass when a check was well-executed, 'DIRTY!'

Other memories:

Eve, Patrick, and I made home-made spaghetti and meatballs. Patrick willingly rolled the meatballs and engaged in what he called 'meatball banter.' We laughed really hard at this new term.

One night, Eve, Pat, and Paul went to Target. They came home with a few things, but the funniest was a fart gun. Oh yes, there were many giggles as we all demonstrated our ability to act out the various fart noises. Paul still pulls it out and blasts us.

We loved to hear the way Patrick pronounced various words. Our favorites were aluminum, garage, and NOar.

We loved Patrick's awesome listening skills. He listened intently and looked you right in the eye. It didn't matter what else or who else was around. If you were talking with him, he gave you his full attention.

We loved seeing Pat and Eve playing on the trampoline, shooting hoops, skating on the rink, bike-riding, and wrestling. He was always up for fun. We loved how happy he made Eve.

One night, in the dark, Pat and Eve helped me cut some lilacs from behind Vosh. It was like we were on a secret mission - acting quickly and keeping a look-out for anyone who might see us. So silly, but we laughed as we drove away with a big bundle.

It is hard to describe how special Pat was with Paul. It was magical. He seemed genuinely curious about how Paul perceived the world. It was as if he didn't care about the things that were different about Paul, but more about the things that made him special. Paul doesn't care what others think; he wants everyone to be happy in-the-moment; he doesn't judge anyone; he doesn't hold grudges and truly lives in the moment. Sounds just like Pat! Pat was the first person (other than trained tutors and specialists) we truly felt at ease with, in regard to Paul and his disability. He saw some of our toughest moments with Paul, yet it felt comfortable having him with us. He didn't shy away; he observed and aimed to understand and support Eve, Paul, and all of us.

It was special to see the brotherly-like bond Pat had with Luke too. Sometimes they had to work through things, but there was a mutual respect and genuine fondness. As Luke's mom, it warmed my heart to see Luke connect with Pat in a way he'd never be able to connect with Paul.

We were especially happy that Eve found Pat. He brought her so much joy and taught her how to love someone. She was happiest when with Patrick, and that meant the world to us.

Dan and I were excited about Pat's future. We looked forward to watching him grow and 'rock-it' as an adult. We anticipated great things for him as he moved through the University of Cincinnati and into his career and life. We truly felt Pat was a part of our family. We will keep him in our hearts forever."

Chris Baxley
Patrick's friend, Cleveland

"Patrick made every interaction he had with people enjoyable, memorable, and impactful.

The first time I ever saw Pat was at the Little League fields. I thought that he was pretty much the coolest kid in our class. He was one of the few people in my life with whom I have felt a genuine connection. Being around him honestly boosted my confidence and fueled my charisma, something I've never seen anyone else do; it was just easy to be around him.

One of Pat's best qualities was his ability to connect with people. He made friends with anyone and everyone and truly had a way with his words. He was also the best at any sport or game we ever played and always offered to play with me. One of the best parts about Pat was that he always reached out to you and made you feel special. No matter the circumstances, he would bring positivity and enthusiasm.

All our lives are going to change so much when we go to college, and the worst part about it is that Pat won't physically be here to grow and experience so many new things with us. We would always talk about the future and things we or our friend group would do. There are so many things that I never got to tell him and there are too many things that we will never get to do. One thing all of us share is a love for music, and Pat's was one of the strongest. Everything about him was just fun. He was an emotional person, and he really wasn't afraid to do or say anything; Pat was truly judgment-free."

Jake Reali
Patrick's friend, Cleveland

"Pat had just arrived from Australia and my friends and I asked him if he wanted to hang out on a Friday night. Alex had an ice rink in his backyard. We were playing hockey and Pat was the goalie. Alex ripped a shot at Pat and the puck nailed him right in the mouth. We all felt so bad - what a welcome to America. This was my first memory of Pat.

He had the most contagious laugh. I remember joking around at school or just hanging out on weekends, rolling on the ground laughing.

We both loved video games. A normal NBA 2k game takes about 30 minutes to play. We loved playing so much that we changed

. the quarter length to 12 minutes. It then took around two hours to play and it was a blast playing together.

My family has an annual party the day before Thanksgiving. Pat was there three years in a row; it was so fun every time. I still think he only came for the chicken we got from K&K Portage Meats. He absolutely loved it and my dad would know to get extra when Pat was coming."

Evie McNulty
Patrick's friend and Senior Prom partner, Cleveland

"Pat mastered the concept of being a good friend, whether he was actually your best friend, or you simply just knew him from school, everyone I have talked to has said one thing, 'Patrick was an amazing friend.' I had the privilege of being Pat's friend, and whether it was him waiting for me at Belle's locker just to tell me all the coffee I drink will make me crazy, or sitting outside on the Green's back patio for hours and hours on end talking about anything and everything, he never failed to make me smile.

A trait very specific to Pat and one that I don't believe a lot of people possess was his unwavering kindness. The type of kindness that comes naturally. One of my favorite memories of Pat was when we were driving home from work, Belle handed me a coffee, and of course, I spilled it everywhere. I knew how much he hated the smell of coffee and even worse, they had just had their car detailed. Instead of acting annoyed, even though I totally would have been if I were him, Pat erupted in laughter and said, 'Gosh Evelyn, you really are special,' and tried to help me clean up before Belle noticed.

On the way to our Senior Prom, Pat gave me his Ray Bans to wear, and he wore the Five Below sunglasses he kept on him at all times. We took our time just driving around before actually going to Westwood because Pat believed there were too many hype songs we had to listen to before actually making our big entrance. Being best friends with Patrick taught me how to be kind, compassionate, and confident. His light will never dim and his impact on my friends and I will carry us through for the rest of our lives, strongly and positively."

Sarah Robertson
Patrick's Homecoming Court and Prom Fashion Show partner and friend, Cleveland

"Pat, I remember the first time I met you. It was at the rehearsal on the football field for Homecoming Court during our sophomore year. You were, of course, my king. I remember being so nervous to talk to you. You were such a stud. An amazing athlete, so handsome, charming, kind, and funny, and I knew that everyone adored you. I vividly remember our conversation because the second we started talking and cracking jokes, my nerves instantly went away. It was like I had known you for a lifetime.

Flash forward to the summer entering our senior year when I met Michael. Here I was again, needing to impress you because there was nobody else's opinion that Michael valued more than yours.

In senior year we took Fashion and Design class together. The instant I walked into that classroom and sat across from you; I knew there would never be a dull moment. We loved each other's company so much that we decided to take Child Development class together just so we could have that hour of the day with each other too. I would look forward to that class because of you. You'd greet me with the biggest hug and smile every time and instantly made me beam from ear to ear with some crazy joke. You were the ray of sunshine in my days. You made my cheeks hurt from smiling and my stomach hurt from laughing. I miss our Prom Fashion Show dance rehearsals, where we sang our little hearts out every time Dancing Queen played. I miss our walks down the hall and our car jam sessions on the way to Ohio State listening to Spotify's '2010 Hits' because you knew that's exactly what I wanted to hear. We sang every word so loudly. I miss you making fun of me for everything I did and talking about visits to Denison to watch my tennis matches dressed in 'Denison Dad Gear.' I miss the way you lit up every room you walked into and the way you filled my life with so much joy. You touched the lives of so many people and I am beyond blessed to have been one of them. Life will never be the same without you, but I know you will be right here with us through it all. I knew you were an angel sent from heaven the moment I met you. I love you always and I can't wait to see you again."

Angela Diab
Patrick's friend, Cleveland

"Pat's kindness, charm, and charisma were something rare. He had a way of making you feel comfortable within just a few moments of talking to him as if you had already been friends for ages. I loved it when he told stories or recounted funny memories because he spoke with such animation and humor that you would be crying from laughter by the end of it. Pat gave the greatest advice when you were stressed; I admired his 'go with the flow' attitude and the way he wouldn't dwell on problems. It's like he was always confident that things would work out in the end, and now I apply this mindset of his to my life every day. I will forever cherish our memories from school, work, and countless weekends. I was always excited for Mondays and Wednesdays because we worked together at the Pearl of the Orient Restaurant. No matter how busy or slow the nights were, we had a blast. Pat, our co-worker Cassie, and I called ourselves the 'Dream Team,' and we had a habit of rewarding and celebrating ourselves for doing even the simplest tasks, truly believing that we were the best trio to ever work at Pearl. He made those shifts go by so quickly because of how much fun we had.

I am eternally grateful to have been a friend of Pat's. Although the pain of losing him will never go away, I find comfort in knowing we will meet again someday. In the meantime, I am blessed to have Patrick as a light and guide in my life. I will love and miss him forever."

Owen Bebie
Patrick's friend, Cleveland

"I could go on and on about how amazing of a person Patrick was. He was unbelievable and words can't describe how he made everyone feel. The first time I met Patty was when we were warming up together for special teams in football and we instantly became friends. He introduced me to Michael Konrad and Michael Finnegan, who are both now two of my closest friends. It was always the four of us, we pretty much did everything together.

A great story was when Coach Massad called a team meeting - the team consisted of Patty, Konrad, and me. The meeting was about the student section. Every game, we would walk out before the rest of the team. Konrad and I would always get right into our warm-up for the second half, but every single time, we would end up having to drag Patty away from the student section. He would be over there warming up right in front of them to get them hyped up instead of in the middle of the field where the special teams would traditionally warm up.

Another fun memory I have of Patrick was our sleepovers. There were so many of them with endless laughs and it was always the same crew.

One day Pat, Finn, Konrad, and I were all hanging out, and Pat asked if we wanted to go to Brian Lowry's because he was having people over. Keep in mind that Pat was a sophomore, I was a freshman in high school, and Brian and all of the people at his house were freshmen in college. I made sure Pat asked Brian if it was okay for me to come and Brian said yes. Pat and I walked into the basement and, I am not kidding; he introduced me to every kid in that basement. He stayed by my side the whole night because he knew I was out of my comfort zone and I didn't know anyone.

If Annabelle or Matilda's kids read this, I just want to let you know that after reading all of these stories, you're going to assume Patrick was an amazing person, and everyone loved him, which is totally right. But if you're talking to me, I personally think Pat was a glimpse of an angel. There is not one bad thing I can think of when it comes to Patrick. He loved his family more than anything and would do anything for them. He was a very rare person, and truly, for me, it was a gift to even call him a friend.

This past football season was a tough one after Pat's accident. The coaches decided to retire his jersey, #13. But Mr. Green, Pat's dad, talked to me and asked me to wear it. It was an honor to wear Patrick's number, the highest honor I will ever be awarded in my life, hands down. I coincidentally won the starting punting job and I ended up making 1st team all-state for punting. You will probably only hear this from me, but I am not a good punter, not even close to where Patty was. I never considered myself a punter up until this past year and I truly believe that the reason my stats were 1st team all-state worthy was because whenever I punted the ball, Pat was right there with me perfecting every little detail. Running out onto the field wearing #13 was truly something amazing. The feeling I got when I threw on the jersey with his number on it was inde-scribable. To me, it felt like anytime I had #13 on, he was right next to me. Pat will forever be missed."

Greta Heider
Patrick's friend, Cleveland
Greta wrote the following poem:

May 20, 2020
It's spring. Summer approaching.
The warm air and sunny rays aren't bringing
me any comfort this year, without you here.
I miss you terribly, Patrick.
I am trying to enjoy the rest of my days for you.
Until I can see your warm and sunny face again.
I love you, Pat.

Adam Burke
Family friend, Melbourne, now Los Angeles

"The dread I felt on that summer 2019 trip from LA to Cleveland was only checked by knowing that what my friends were going through was way worse. When I arrived, I found a devastated, resilient, and welcoming family, hosting a parade of people who wanted to talk about Patrick, morning to late night. I couldn't imagine being anywhere else. All ages and connections to him showed up, revealing that we were mourning a Ferris Bueller-like character. He was one of those rare people who made so many people feel like a close friend. Probably the hardest realization was that the hurt of the loss is equal to the size of what was lost. But later, I've come to see that as an artificial symmetry. A spirit that beautiful may transcend but is never lost, and if you're reading this book, you already know it to be true."

Lincoln Davies
Family friend, Melbourne, now Los Angeles

"Patrick's and my understanding of each other was akin to a 'nudge, nudge, wink, wink' and a touch of the nose. He's a kid I instantly got down to the brass tacks with exclusively around the more enjoyable and brighter, mischievous side of life, cheers to his dad. You couple that with knowing he was without a bad bone in his body and had everyone else's best interest at heart, thanks to his mum, and it was just pure fun. I learned, through Patrick, that when I am more open to strangers, differences, the unknown, and I find myself closer and more present with friends and family, it is in no small part attributable to him. Pat bestowed upon us all his life's positive lessons and I give thanks to every single one and the deeper understanding that comes with them, cheers mate. Our loss of him is a singular language of tears and that will never change."

David Landrigan
Family friend, Melbourne
Dave flew from Melbourne to be at Patrick's funeral

"I had three missed calls from Chris's brother, which was strange, and then I saw my mate calling me, and I knew something was wrong. My heart literally sank as I listened to the news. There was no hesitation at all, I was heading to Cleveland to be there for Chris, Sara, Annabelle, and Matilda, and it was three days I will remember forever.

During my time with them for Patrick's funeral, I came to realize just how special Patrick Green was to every person he crossed paths with. It was fun listening to Chris talk about Patrick's exploits at school, sport, and the bond he had with his sisters and cousins.

The short time I spent with my friends was so hard, just knowing there wasn't much I could do to ease their pain except listen. What made me feel easier about their life going forward was the unbelievable circle of friends that Chris and Sara had in their community.

As I got to know the 'American' Patrick, it hit me that this kid had such an effect on so many people, and age was no barrier. Sara reminded me recently of the same effect Patrick had on my mother. Sara and my mum had an amazing relationship, mother and daughter-like. Sara would bring Patrick over to see my mum when he was a baby and she would just melt at the sight of him. There was just something unique about the love she had for Patrick.

Patrick became himself over time, but there were a lot of his parents that shaped a young man loved by so many."

Christopher Gilbert
Family friend, Melbourne
Chris flew from Melbourne to be at Patrick's funeral

"For as long as I've known Chris (over 30 plus years), the importance of family has shaped his life approach and has been his highest priority. This focus and ethos only solidified as Sara and the kids entered his life, and Chris's own family expanded.

Amongst our friendship group in our twenties, Patrick was one of the first babies to arrive on the scene. Although Chris and Sara were now parents, Patrick's presence didn't slow down our gatherings and celebrations. Patrick must have been a very well-behaved kid because he never gave his parents pause to slow down on their social obligations, particularly Chris. Pub Trust traditions and banter continued unabated following Patrick's arrival, as we squeezed out the last of our misspent youth and navigated our way through early careers. They were halcyon days.

I have fond recollections of my last catch up with Patrick. The extended Green family and old mates had gathered at the Half Moon Hotel the day after Matt Green's wedding to see the family before they jetted out of Melbourne the next day. Patrick had grown (again) and towered over Chris. I enjoyed a laugh with Patrick about his forthcoming high school graduation and what his plans were for a post-school party or getaway; Patrick joining with me to chastise Chris for not funding rite of passage celebrations to mark the occasion. On reflection, it was my first real adult conversation with Patrick, and it dawned on me as we laughed and shared a beer that he was now already a little older than the age I'd met his dad all those years ago. That night at the bar, it was evident Patrick shared his father's dry humor and spirit but was rounded out with his mother's gorgeous charm and demeanor - the perfect complement of them both. It was an all too short encounter but provided a lasting and happy memory.

Given Patrick and the family's popularity and extensive network, I knew Patrick's funeral was going to be a large affair. It was an amazing tribute to see a whole community assemble for the service and then gather back at Chris and Sara's home. It was a great privilege to be with Chris, Sara, the girls, Michael and Rita, and the broader Green clan during such a dark and raw time. We reminisced, laughed, and cried a lot that afternoon after the service and finished late into the night. I know Chris and Sara will always be there for me. It's just the way it is - family and friends first always."

The Bowens
Family friends, Melbourne

"One of the earliest recollections of your gorgeous boy was even before he was born. It was of Sara at our wedding. We remember how radiant Sara looked and how she suited being pregnant. She was glowing.

We were so thrilled and happy to hear the exciting news of Patrick's birth on February 27, 2000. He was the first baby born amongst our close friends; he was beautiful looking with lots of dark hair.

A clear memory I have of Patrick is at an art exhibition Simon Brushfield held at a restaurant in Toorak Road, Melbourne, opposite France-Soir restaurant. I remember being a lot more interested in what gorgeous Patrick was up to rather than looking at the art. He was about four or five months old. He was the cutest little man with those big clear eyes. He was smiling and cooing at all the guests. He was so well behaved and happy.

Johnny has a vivid memory of us at your house watching the Opening Ceremony of the Sydney 2000 Olympics with Patrick sitting on his knee; he was seven months old. I have a memory of this day too. I can see Patrick sitting in a high-chair and you both so adoringly looking after him, there was so much joy and love on your faces. It made us so excited about the impending birth of our first baby. Throughout my pregnancy, I remember Sara and I spending hours chatting about whether we thought it was a boy or a girl. While Chris and Johnny drank beers, we discussed at great length the names we liked and all things about birth, newborns, and family. I was secretly hoping that we'd have a boy too so our babies could be friends. A wish that did come true. Only 14 months after Patrick was born, we welcomed Hamish. Both strong Irish and Scottish names we chose.

Not long after, Annabelle was born and then Will. Life got pretty busy but we made time for playdates and weekend visits so we could get the kids together and catch up. I remember Patrick and Hamish as toddlers sitting eating ice cream on a hot day in Davies

Street, the house we rented in East Malvern. We cherish the photos from this day. Another strong memory is of Patrick wearing his Richmond footy jumper and also his superhero costumes. Little boys doing typical little boy things. Carefree, energetic, and entertaining.

Chris was the doting father. It was clear from early on how proud he was of Patrick; they were going to be the best of mates.

We were sad when you decided to move to Sydney. This was because we simply would not be able to see you as often. From an early age, Patrick had drawn us all in; it was always obvious that he was someone others wanted to be around. He was a leader, but also someone who was easy and fun.

In 2014, we visited you in Cleveland. Our kids were so excited about the trip and connecting again with the Greens. Now teenagers and pre-teens, they did not stop the whole time we were there. We remember Patrick welcoming all of our boys into his world; it was his way. Over five days, with a tribe of Aussies and Americans, Patrick led games of cricket, NFL, basketball, frisbee, Aussie rules football, and baseball … was there a game they did not play?! Patrick loved a bit of 'Tom Foolery.' He tied an electric fence dog collar to Will's ankle. The boys lost it with much laughter over Will trying to leave the boundary of your house and getting zapped every time.

In April 2019, you returned home for Matt's wedding; it was the last time we would see Patrick. The engaging way he spoke with adults, the gentle methods he used to ensure all kids were included, the way he stood so close to his mum, and the biggest, most genuine hug he gave as he said goodbye - these memories remain.

There was something special about Patrick. We are all better for having known him."

Josh Worner
Family friend, Melbourne, now Seattle

"The things that made an impression on me from the time I was in Cleveland for Patrick's funeral were:

- How Patrick was so uniquely loved and loving.

- Even in such tragic circumstances, people smiled and laughed when they talked about him - he clearly brought great joy to everyone around him.

- Annabelle and Matilda recognizing me from Chris and Sara's wedding photos and talking to me as if they have known me all their lives.

- Chris tapping the casket on his way up to give his eulogy. It was like he said to Patrick, 'We've got this - I know you're here and I can do this knowing that.'

- The extended Green family have known me since I was young and having that feeling of being part of the family and maybe making it a little (if that's at all possible) easier made it feel like I was helping."

Ben Dunshea
Family friend, Melbourne

"When I think of Patrick, two things come to mind:

When we went down to your beach house and Chris fired up the BBQ to cook the flathead tails, Patrick (usually wearing a Richmond kit) was always so interested, involved, and present in what we were doing for someone so young. He had a thirst for life.

My favorite funny memory is at Rach's and my engagement party. Patrick came; he was only a few years old. My aunty was following him around taking photos of him on her phone. She said, 'I don't know who this little boy is, and I hope his parents don't mind, but he's just so beautiful.'"

Sophie Duggan
Family friend, Melbourne

"What I loved most about Patrick was seeing what he lit up in my dear friend Sara. Sara was destined to nurture and grow a family.

Becoming a mother was the most natural state in the world for her. I knew that from the first moment I saw her with Patrick. They had a way with each other, bringing each other's light to the fore. Their deep love and admiration for each other was evident. Patrick was indeed special, and I loved that he unlocked Sara and continues to do so, even today."

Rachael Binnie
Family friend, Melbourne

"When Sara and Chris were just newlyweds in Melbourne and living in a cute apartment on Toorak Road, Sara and I had a tradition of getting together on a Friday night and sharing a glass of red wine with our favorite Aussie blue cheese on crackers. One typical night after work, I rocked up to Sara's place with the obligatory wine and cheese. As Sara cooked dinner, I sat in the kitchen, and we chatted about our weeks. At one point she had her hands full so couldn't take the cracker and cheese I passed to her, so I said, 'Here, open your mouth and I'll pop it in.' at which point she put down what she was holding and grabbed my hand before I could shove blue cheese in her face and said, 'I can't eat it, I'm pregnant!'

There was a lot of excitement, laughing and jumping around as somehow a bit of blue cheese got stuck to the ceiling. Only then did I notice a little collection of blue cheese crackers hidden behind the toaster and an untouched glass of red wine.

This lovely story is happily embedded in our history as the most wonderful announcement of Patrick's arrival into our lives. Despite the sadness we all feel for Sara, Chris, Annabelle, Tildy, and the whole family, it's these happy stories that really shine and remind us of the joy that Patrick brought to so many, in so many different ways."

Tim Mueller
Family friend and friend and mentor to Patrick, Cleveland

"Patrick Michael Green will forever be our John F. Kennedy, Jr.

Smart, funny, handsome, and gone from this earth far too early. Like JFK Jr., his true potential and youth will live infinitely as our memories will be tied to an ear-to-ear smile that would light up every room into which he would walk. His future remains stainless, knowing his people skills and positive outlook on life would have carried him far as an adult, family man, friend, and professional.

I first met Patrick at one of his family's infamous parties. Amazing people, incredible food, and a sense of community curated at the Green's home on a regular basis. This particular party was their annual rib cook-off competition, where brave rib aficionados submit their version of BBQ ribs to everyone's taste-testing and voting. With music, libations, and loud conversations all around, I witnessed a young high schooler push aside the food and utensils on a table in the family room and jump on top like the coach of a football team. As I remember it, Patrick clanged two bottles together to command everyone's attention. Almost immediately, you could hear a pin drop. All eyes gazed up at this young 'kid,' who fearlessly proceeded to share the rules of the cook-off voting. He was precise. Crisp. Humorous. And effective. This was Patrick Green. Later, I felt the need to tell him how impactful this simple act was. Who does this? What high schooler gets up in front of dozens of 40-somethings with enough enthusiasm to illuminate all of Northeast Ohio? This young man was special.

Months later, Sara asked if I'd meet with Patrick as he was contemplating his future. Decisions on colleges and a career were coming up. He spent a lot of time speaking about professions with Chris, his father, and role model, but more perspectives were helpful to round out Patrick's plans. When he and Sara came to my office, I could sense hesitation about life after high school. A highly decorated punter for his high school football team, Patrick was being recruited by nationally ranked colleges who envisioned him

184

leading their kicking program. With his infamous Aussie accent, Patrick would talk more about being happy and making the right life choice vs. playing in a Division I NCAA football program. What high school athlete does this? I shared Patrick's perspective with my son, Brady, who was in 8th grade at the time. As a student athlete, he couldn't believe it. But after talking more about the thought that went into such a brave perspective, Brady developed a deep sense of admiration for Patrick's decision-making process.

Recognizing his potential and wanting him to gain some professional experience in the workplace, I hired Patrick as an intern in the summer of his junior year. Patrick slayed his assignments and quickly endeared himself among our staff. He'd pop into our office for a new assignment and quickly turn it around in a timely and professional manner. Patrick was a natural, blending in as though we were his peers at school or family from his homeland.

Always respectful, Patrick would slip humor into various one-on-one discussions about his performance or future growth trajectory. Patrick had a thirst for knowledge and a hunger to prove himself.

In January 2019, ITX moved into its newly renovated offices in the Ohio City neighborhood of Cleveland. Although his family would have been invited to our Open House Celebration as long-time friends, they were there that night as Patrick's guests. They were among Patrick's colleagues and friends, people with whom he'd be working with again following his senior year. I could feel the pride he had at the Open House. He knew he belonged, and he carried himself well beyond the date on his birth certificate.

Once settled into its new offices, ITX made a commitment to feed our West 25th neighbors regularly through Saint Malachi's Backdoor Ministry. Each month, we closed our operations for a half-day to provide food for the homeless and those struggling to make ends meet. As serendipity would have it, Patrick volunteered there multiple times prior to ITX and understood the significance of this ministry. He loved helping people, and it was evident each month we were at Saint Malachi. Patrick embodied the motto: If you can, you must.

The summer following his graduation from high school was filled with great anticipation. Patrick was in our office at ITX on a regular basis, taking assignments shoulder-to-shoulder with three of our college interns. During our regular intern roundtable discussions, Patrick contributed comments and asked questions as though he had already earned his undergraduate diploma and started his career. He totally got it. Patrick understood the underlying strategies of negotiation, a skill I'm certain was learned by listening to conversations at home combined with his natural ability. Most of all, Patrick understood people, and EVERYONE loved him. June 2019 was an important time for Patrick. Graduation parties, special time with friends, and nervous anticipation for starting at the University of Cincinnati. At ITX, Patrick was hitting full stride and gaining even more confidence in a professional environment.

On June 27, he knocked on my glass office door, craned his head in, and humorously said, 'Requesting permission to enter the glass kingdom.' I laughed and said, 'Get your arse in here.' We talked about his current work assignments, and then he asked to leave early so he and his mates could go up to the Lake Erie Islands for the night. Knowing this was his last summer leading into college, I told him to have fun and be safe.

Hours later, Celeste and I got a call from her son telling us of Patrick's tragic death - news that will forever leave an indelible scar on our hearts. Like anyone who loses a loved one far too early, the fact that Patrick is no longer with us in human form continues to be surreal. And like all of the JFK Jr's over time, Patrick's youthful enthusiasm and zest for life will live on infinitely.

In celebration of Patrick, our team at ITX continues to gather monthly at Saint Malachi for 'Green Day,' feeling his smiles as we feed those who struggle to make ends meet. If you can, you must.

Patrick Michael Green will forever be loved, honored, and respected for the impact he had in such a short period of time. For that, we are eternally grateful."

Dr. Keith Jordan
Family friend, chiropractor, holistic physician, and intuitive healer, Cleveland

"I remember a patient visit I had with Patrick. He was experiencing some angst around going to school. Not for any educational reasons, he just didn't like being contained and told what to do, it didn't feel natural to him.

There are some old souls who just can't stay in their bodies for too long. It's not that they don't love being with us all, they just know they can do more good when they are not contained in a small space. Patrick was one of those old souls.

I was blessed to cross Patrick's path during that short time that God had us both in the same classroom. We all were. I am blessed to share the eternal classroom with Patrick now and forever."

Kevin Abrams
Family friend, New York

"My most recent memory about Patrick was the last time I spoke to him in May 2019. We had just drafted a QB with our 1st round pick, and the player we selected was not the consensus pick that the media and fans thought we should take. We took a lot of grief about it in the papers, on TV, and from our fans. The outrage was compounded by the fact that our fans were still seething about us trading Odell to Cleveland two months earlier. Needless to say, that groundswell of fan discontentment and media criticism was about as loud as it could be. Then I got a call from Patrick. He wanted to check in and to see if I was doing OK, given all of the negative coverage and commentary about the state of the Giants. It was really thoughtful and kind. The kind of thing you would never expect from someone his age.

My earliest memory of Patrick was on one occasion when Sara and Chris were in the US from Australia, and I met them in Cleveland. I believe Patrick was three or close to it, and Annabelle about a year old. Sara, Chris, and Annabelle went out to visit someone, and I was on my own with Patrick. This would have been the first time I was ever completely on my own with a three year old, and he ran me ragged. We played every game I could think of, from soccer to tag to hide'n'seek, and he gave me such a workout that I needed another decade and a half to train before I was ready for kids of my own.

Some general recollections:

How polite and well-mannered he was. It's funny the things that stick with us, but I have always remembered how, from an early age, he was comfortable spending time with adults then asking if he could be excused to go do his own thing. I always made a mental note that if I had kids, I was going to make that a point of emphasis and to hold Patrick up as the example to follow.

When the Greens moved to Cleveland and I visited, I always noticed that Patrick had a line of kids following him around like he was the Pied Piper. At the same time, he didn't act like he had to be in charge or boss the other kids around, but they still followed him anyway. I don't know if that was his natural leadership or his kindness, or both. It certainly seemed like he was everyone's big brother.

I loved seeing and hearing about his relationship with his sisters. It seemed to me like he had wonderful respect and deference for Annabelle. I loved hearing stories about Belle's watchfulness over him too. With Tildy, he didn't just find time for her, like most siblings who are that much older would do. I got the sense that he would seek her out as much as she would him, and they had their own world of things they enjoyed doing with each other.

Seeing him at least once a year on the road, I considered him to be a friend of mine as much as he was my friends' son, and the evolution from the latter to the former was amazing. He was the first of my friends' kids to make that transition, so it had never really occurred to me until he was already my peer.

Similarly, watching his relationship with Chris grow from father and son to true peers was remarkable. I've always been so impressed with how Sara and Chris have raised their kids and to witness their relationship evolve into what it has become is a great reminder for a newer parent like myself about what this is all about.

Most of what I know about Sara's relationship with Patrick is what I have gleaned from conversations with Chris. The way Chris has described it over the years has always reminded me of my relationship with my mother when I was growing up. I was far more introverted than Patrick, and I didn't have nearly the relationship with either of my fathers that Patrick had with Chris, so my mother was my go-to person for everything. My sense was that Patrick could go to anyone in the house for anything but for the really emotional topics or difficult times; Sara was his person. He knew that he was safest whenever he could get to his mum. His worst days were never that bad once he had a chance to share what was bothering him with her. She settled whatever it was that could make life chaotic and hard for him.

I only have great memories of Patrick. Memories of being in his presence and memories of hearing about everything that was going on in his life. I love him and I miss him."

The Fogartys
Family friends, Melbourne

"Our first memory of Patrick was of a young beautiful boy with rosy red cheeks, a big smile, wearing his beloved Richmond jumper and beanie with a football under his arm. We remember how well he could kick the footy or hit a cricket ball and how well he spoke; he was so articulate. Memories from Charles St of he and Annabelle in the garden on their swing set and in the blue sand shell as well as Patrick, Jack, and Tom playing footy and cricket together in the backyard.

When Tildy was born I went to visit. Patrick was a very proud big brother when he introduced his new sister, 'Col, this is Matilda,' and if his beautiful mum Sara wasn't in sight, he would ask, 'Where's Mum?'

We have many wonderful memories of Patrick when he, Annabelle, and Sara would come over, or we were visiting them. The first thing Patrick would say at the door was, 'Hi Col, where are Jack and Tom?' Always a big smile on his face and excited to see them, as they were to see him. They spent a lot of time outside playing in the sandpit, jumping on the trampoline, or playing PlayStation games including Lego Star Wars. There was always lots of laughter. When it was time to go, it would be a quick snack, usually rice crackers, and chasing the car down the street while laughing and waving goodbye. We would often go to the park after kinder with the Moors and Patrick would always have a ball with him and head straight to the oval for a kick.

Jack recalls a time when the Greens visited from Sydney. Patrick would have been about 10. 'We were playing FIFA on the PlayStation and singing the Ace of Hearts' theme song together. Patrick got up on the dining room chair while the adults were eating and started singing the song and doing a funny dance. We couldn't stop laughing!'

Tom says, 'For as long as I can remember, Patrick, Jack and I were always very sporty and active outside. One day on the trampoline, the name 'Patrick Green the Jelly-Bean Man' just came out of my mouth. And from then on, that's what I called him as he was always enthused and energetic about everything. And he always knew how to make you laugh.'

Each visit to Melbourne, whether from Sydney or later from the US, Patrick was always smiling and happy, and the laughs would continue, picking up from where they left off. His wonderful sense of humor, kind and loving nature, and the sound of his laughter will stay with us forever. As well as his voice greeting us, 'Hi Col, Hi Mark.'

Our lasting memory of Patrick was the day at the Half Moon in Melbourne, April 2019. Mark loved having a beer with little Patrick, who was all grown up. We spoke about him in the car on the way home saying what an incredible and beautiful young man he had become. Mark says, 'Patrick, I will continue to have a beer every year on February 27, our birthday, that I'm honored to share with you.'

We were blessed to know Patrick and he will forever have a special place in our hearts."

The Moors
Family friends, Melbourne

Simon:
"Patrick was very popular at Hurlingham Kindergarten. Even at a young age, he was the cool kid. He always had a great sense of humor and a good sense of fun. When we visited the Greens in Sydney, I remember a spectacular water fight with my sister and Annabelle. I also remember catching the ferry around Sydney Harbour with Patrick and his family. Even though I didn't see Patrick as often when he moved to Sydney and later America, whenever we caught up, it was very easy to reconnect. When he came to Melbourne, we'd catch up at our place or at the Fogartys, and he would always amuse us with funny stories. We miss you, Pat."

Monique:
"Patrick was always nice to me and very funny. I remember climbing trees in Hurlingham Park with Patrick and Annabelle. We always looked forward to catching up with them in Sydney or when they came back to Melbourne. I can remember jumping on the trampoline with Patrick and Annabelle and getting fish and chips for dinner and eating them on the beach in Sydney. We loved hearing about his life in America. So many happy memories."

Mary:
"When I picture Patrick as a child, I think of him in his Richmond jumper. He was a natural footballer, so skilful at such a young age. He was streets ahead of his kinder mates.

Patrick and Annabelle were frequent playmates for Simon and Monique. Although Patrick was very confident in many ways, he often needed to have his mum at playdates. It was really lovely that he felt comfortable at our house even without Sara. We have photos of him in his Richmond jumper and his Superman costume, two of his favorite outfits at the time.

I remember Patrick at one of the kindergarten Christmas concerts.

He was the Christmas tree. Patrick always seemed so confident, but that night he got stage fright and would not go on and say his lines. Luckily Chris had no such shyness and happily accompanied Patrick on stage to play the part.

When Sara went into labor with Tildy, Patrick and Annabelle came to our house. They were very excited to welcome their baby sister. Patrick's caring nature really shone as a big brother. He was very protective of both his sisters. Seeing him walk around holding Tildy gave me a few heart attacks over those early years, but he was very capable; he just loved to look after her.

The last time I saw Patrick was when he came to Australia for his uncle's wedding in April 2019. We caught up with the Green family at a pub in Brighton the day after the wedding. Patrick was now a tall, handsome young man who happily showed some of the wedding photos to Colleen and me. He chatted away very confidently. He'd gotten over that childhood shyness and was just gorgeous."

Keith:
"I had a long chat with Patrick at the Half Moon in April 2019 and was pleased to see he had grown into a fine young man who was confident enough to converse intelligently with adults across a range of topics. Patrick raved about life in the US and came across to me as a very well adjusted and capable person who was destined to do extremely well at whatever he chose to do."

The Fitzgeralds
Family friends, Melbourne and Sydney

Fiona:
"I remember the day Sara shared the news she was pregnant with Patrick. Eliza was only days old; Sara came in to visit me at the hospital with a gorgeous smile, so happy to meet Eliza but also to tell me she was pregnant. Eight months later, Patrick was born. Sara and I went on to have two more children each, with Annabelle and Sarah only weeks apart, and three years later, Matilda and Declan

very close in age too. In 2007 we moved to Sydney, where the Greens had moved the year before. It was so special to spend those years together with many playdates, dinners, sleepovers, dance parties, and afternoons at the beach. The thing I remember the most was that all six kids were like a little gang. There was never a cross word and there was loads of laughter and energy. Patrick made sure everyone was included, always checking in on the younger ones. The memories and friendship with the Greens were a significant part of our young family's lives, and we were blessed to have shared time living in Melbourne and Sydney."

Eliza:

"So many great memories with Patty. From us being childhood best friends to him being my lifelong brother are the fondest. From playing High School Musical to making up dance routines or roleplays to show our parents, endless games of Sardines and 44 Homes, or just talking for hours. With our two families, we always had the best times. He was the kindest and most genuine soul, loved by so many and a true gem."

The Raltons
Family friends, Sydney

Odile:

"I was lucky enough to meet Patrick when he was a little boy. I distinctly remember two things about meeting him for the first time. The first was that he was the cutest little boy I'd ever seen with the cheekiest of faces, full of freckles and the kindest, warmest eyes and smile. I couldn't believe how cute he was. The second was how chatty he was with me and how he had such advanced thoughts and opinions as a young child, and he was happy to share them with me. I didn't have kids yet and he just blew me away with his cute confidence.

Over the years, he became even 'cuter' (or more handsome, I guess you should say), and his ability to communicate with everyone, young or old, and to engage with people on the level that he did, was exceptional.

I spent a lot of time around Patrick as he was growing up in Sydney into a very special young man. He was close with my two daughters Saskia and Giselle, when they were little and later Millie, who was born only a few weeks before Patrick and the family moved to the US. The girls absolutely adored Patrick and they shared a cousin-like bond with one another. He always made them feel so special by simply giving them his time and attention. We have gorgeous videos of him trying to teach them some crazy cool dance and doing puppet shows with them and Tildy behind the couch. They always used to ask if they could have a big brother 'like Patrick.'

Simon and I always loved being in the Greens company and we miss them dearly in our daily lives. They taught us something really special that we have kept as a tradition - on every birthday we go around the table, and each person says something meaningful about the birthday person. We were often at their home for these occasions and I always remember how beautifully Patrick spoke about his sisters on their birthdays and how his love for them was undeniable from a very young age.

Patrick was truly one in a million, and I do not say that lightly. He was an angel on this earth with a special heart and a gifted soul. He was the person he was because he was the son of Sara and Chris. He had and will always have a special place in our hearts."

Simon:
"Patrick's ability to connect with people of any age was remarkable. He was just as engaging in teaching our girls his shuffle dance as he was talking to me about school, his mates, and his sport. One time when you visited us in Sydney, Patrick was 16 years old. I noticed he had a real curiosity for the differences between his life in the US and in Australia. You afforded him that perspective and he relished it. Sara, you told me that Patrick really enjoyed talking to me on that trip. For whatever reason, he said that it sums up my lasting memory of him as an enthusiastic and thoughtful friend."

Gilly Lechte
Family friend, Melbourne

"As we took off in that massive A380 from Sydney in August 2019, Odile (Oee) and I held hands and sobbed. Tears for our dear friend Sara, tears for Chris, Belle, and Tildy. Tears for Patrick. Part of me wishes I had photographic proof of how Sara looked as Oee and I descended the escalator when we arrived in Cleveland that evening. She was bathed in the most glorious golden shaft of light - seemingly coming from nowhere. We were dumbstruck (hence no photo). It was Patrick. It was a sight I will never forget. If Oee hadn't seen it too, I would have sworn I was dreaming. Sara was tracking our flight. 'Get off your phone,' I called out - she looked towards us and we all started to cry. The hugs followed, in a group and then one-on-one. This would be mirrored when we left just over a week later and daily in between.

I had the pleasure of knowing Patrick as a toddler until he was about six, and then the family moved to Sydney. Looking back, pre-kids for me, I was lucky to babysit Ga and Doll before Sara and I realized we were both pregnant at the same time – me with my first-born, Ella, and Sara with Tildy.

The last time I saw Patrick was April 2019 at a pub catch up in Brighton back here in Melbourne. It was fabulous – loads of old 'hooter' friends and the Green family. It was a gorgeous afternoon. I had not seen Patrick for several years and I will never forget him look at me and that deliberate walk of his as he approached me with the invitation of a bear hug. I didn't think he would even remember my face, 'Of course I remember you, Gilly,' he said. He made everyone in the pub feel special that day, including me. I'll always cherish it.

The trip that Odile and I took to see Sara, Chris, Annabelle, and Tildy in Cleveland after Patrick's accident was incredible. Incredible in their welcoming of us despite their grief, incredible in meeting Sara's Angels and friends who were looking after them, and incredible sensing Patrick's presence the whole time.

The CLE Angel women know who they are. You have taken such divine care of Sara, Chris, and the girls with food, friendship, and love. We were lucky enough to meet you, break bread, drink wine, practice yoga, experience those incredible lake views, take boat tours of CLE and forge new connections that will always be there. Again, I find myself feeling incredibly grateful. A lot of our visit feels intensely private, but we witnessed magical symbols of Patrick's presence constantly: rainbows in the sky where they shouldn't have been; fireflies dancing around us over the family dinner table outside; discovering doors to sacred Patrick places unlocked when they should have been locked at that time. Patrick watched over us during our entire visit. He was everywhere.

The number of times we saw 11:11 during our time in Cleveland was astonishing. Even at the end of the most excruciating moments together, we saw it on the clock of Sara's car, on our phones – almost daily and we'd say 'Patrick!' After a while, a knowing look shared between us was all that was required. We knew he was there.

I feel blessed to have learned so much more about Patrick while on that trip. To see the church where he volunteered with the homeless, to walk the halls at his high school with Tildy and Sara, to see his football field, meet his teachers, see all the references to him there at the school, to visit the rock that had been painted green in his memory after the accident - it was all so special.

There were also beautiful lighter moments. Belle taking me to Patrick's favorite drive-through, Chick-fil-A, for a delicious, all-American, original fried chicken sandwich. Memories of Chris smoking ribs on his grill for us one night and him enjoying watching the Aussie (me) and Pommie (Oee) carnivores chow down. Meeting Patrick's friends and listening to stories from his family and all those in CLE who loved him, which clearly was everyone, was an incredible experience.

I can't imagine the pain and grief that Sara, Chris, Belle, and Tildy survive every day. In his all too short life, Patrick has inspired me to be present more every day with my own family and to try and make a difference. When a butterfly follows me in my garden, I think of Patrick. He helps me stay grateful for all that I have. I am now truly grateful for rainbows.

I cherish that bear hug in April 2019. He had many more people to see that day, but he made me feel special in that short amount of time he shared with me."

Jos Budge
Family friend and the amazing editor of this book, Sydney

"As soon as you told me about gorgeous Patrick, I just knew what utter pain and despair you were all in. Your collective love for Patrick was endless. He was your everything and you four were his. This type of tragedy didn't happen to families such as yours. It was unfathomable. My heartbreak for you all was searing. I worried about how you could ever find a way to move forward, yet you have, which is a credit to each of you. It has been an extraordinary privilege and honor to read this hauntingly beautiful memoir early on while working with you Sara. I truly believe it is the most beautiful tribute that celebrates and commemorates darling Patrick. His very essence radiates through each page. Darling Sara, it's an incredible legacy, a work that will connect with and move people deeply. Importantly, it will help people who are sadly stumbling along a similar path, dealing with loss. I feel the same about how Chris, Annabelle, and Tildy have shared their deep love, loss, and lessons. This really is the ultimate love letter from a mother to her son. Patrick will be beaming with such pride and love, endless love."

Monty Morrison-Budge
Family friend, Sydney

"I really enjoyed the times I hung out with Patrick, Annabelle, and Tildy when we were together in Sydney and in our country place in Exeter, NSW. We had the best time there when we wrote and filmed a murder mystery together. Patrick was the villain and stalked about trying to kill me. It was hilarious and we screamed our heads off.

We also had fun soaking the trampoline with all the bottles of liquid soap we could find, turning on the hose, and jumping about. Somehow we avoided breaking any bones! It was also really cool when we camped in the lounge when the power went out - no-one wanted to go up the dark hall to the bedrooms, especially after dealing with Patrick, the villain that day. It was cold with the central heating off, and we woke up with a jolt when all the lights came on at 3 am. It was also special visiting you all in Cleveland in 2014 when we were over. We got to see where you lived and to just hang out again, like old times. I was so shocked when I heard the news about Patrick. I still am. Patrick will be so missed."

Bob and Isabel Faulds
Neighbors, and family friends, Sydney

"Not a day passes that Patrick isn't in my thoughts. I remember him as a boy. Bob remembers him running barefoot across Canberra St to do an errand for you at the shops while you, Sara, watched him with a glow in your eyes. Patrick came running back with a brighter glow on his face, so pleased that he fulfilled that errand. Bob says that he remembers thinking of that boy turning into a man. He says he will never ever forget Patrick. He was one of the finest young men imaginable.

I remember him in the backyard a few days after you moved in, helping you dig up the garden. I remember him accompanying Annabelle and Matilda when they proudly presented Abby, the cat to me. I don't recall who had the biggest smile, not me for sure. I was taken aback because I wasn't a cat person, until I met Abby. I remember going to a park once to watch Patrick play cricket. He was in white and he strolled over to bat. He went out on the second ball and he was so disappointed leaving the crease until Chris came and put his arms over his shoulders and said, 'Never mind, these things happen.'

On one occasion, I gave Patrick a lift to St. Ignatius. I asked him to 'navigate' me there. He did so in his calm but excited way giggling at my comments all the way up the driveway of the school, proudly pointing out different and interesting things. I gave him 'Sky Flakes' (Filipino crackers) for recess. This was a new experience for him, and his eyes showed how delighted he was. Anyway, that evening, I made it a point to go and see him to ask how he liked the crackers. They come in a packet of three; he proudly said he didn't wait for recess but ate them all as soon as I left him there. This was Patrick to me, an excited boy living his life to the fullest.

Oh, I remember a lot; I miss him. You know how much we loved Patrick, such a special angel."

Kym Hooper
Family friend, Sydney

"Alex is in Europe with a lot of the boys from Riverview and I know they have had several beers in Patrick's memory. Alex has honored Patrick with a little tattoo, 'PG' on his ankle. He considered Patrick his best mate and will miss him deeply. Even though they lived miles apart, their bond was still very strong. Theirs was a special friendship and those memories will be cherished by all of us. Patrick was a kind and generous boy who loved his family and friends. He had a wide range of friends and was well-loved by all who knew him. The Riverview community was deeply saddened by the news. Many will remember him as a great bloke."

The Konrads
Family friends, Cleveland

Therese:
"I think about Patrick every day. So many places, tasks, and feelings are associated with him; he really was a part of our family. It's painful but wonderful to remember him - all at the same time. While some memories are funny, they all tell the tale of friendship, finding the best in people, living life to the fullest, and loving people deeply.

I will forever be thankful that Michael was able to experience a friendship like his and Patrick's. Not many young people, let alone adults, get to experience such a blessing. The two of them just loved to play. Video games, spikeball, basketball (for hours), golf, anything! I also know that Patrick was Michael's true confidante. Michael truly adored him, and I know that Patrick loved Michael deeply too.

We all loved it when Patrick was at our house. He just brought so much life and positive vibes. Maybe it was because he made everyone so happy with his sense of humor and adorable accent. He also made all of us feel special. From the first time Patrick met my mom, she fell in love. I think she really believed he was her boyfriend because Patrick was the world's best flirt. Two summers ago, we had an awesome time when Patrick and Michael Finnegan came up to 'Grandma's Lake.' The three boys played hard. One night, they had a bonfire (of course I found a box of Natty Lite cans the next day) and made Katie smoke a cigar.

I feel like every time I walked out of my bedroom, Patrick (the tall son) would be bounding up the stairs, two at a time. He would go into Michael's room, wake him up, and they'd play video games until I would yell at them both to get moving. Sometimes they would go to breakfast together, or to kick, or sometimes they would just eat here. One day, Michael and Patrick decided to try to make Chick-fil-A sauce. They followed a recipe that they found online, which made a huge vat. It tasted terrible and there was crap all over the kitchen. Now I think it is hysterical.

This past spring 2019, Michael wanted to go golfing on a Sunday. I wanted to get yard work done; however, Michael, Kevin, and Patrick were so excited and set on playing nine holes. In my heart, I knew they should go. Our friend, Terry Hunt, had just died, and I realized that life was short. The three of them had a great time, including seeing Patrick teeing off in his underwear on the ninth hole in front of the clubhouse! I am so glad that Patrick charmed them all into this outing.

Before the football games, I would text Patrick to wish him good luck. Michael thought it was weird that I did this, but Patrick always replied, 'Thanks, Mrs. Konrad.'

I also know how excited Michael was to go to Miami with your family. He truly loves you all and, as a mom, I felt so thankful that he could be a part of another wonderful family experience.

Patrick touched more lives in his too-short life than many others do with a much longer time on earth. I am thankful for the time I was blessed to know him and love him. I am trying to find the best in everyone and live life to the fullest every day - Patrick was so wise."

Katie:

"When I think of Pat and how he made me feel as a friend, every memory I have is truly joyful. He always made me feel welcome, even if he was at *my* house. Not only did he make me feel happy, but he also made my mom and dad feel happy, my grandma, my neighbors, and mostly Michael.

I will always remember Pat as the type of friend that I wanted. Selfishly, I was jealous of what he and Michael had. Their relationship was an unfaltering one, and I don't think Michael ever wanted to be around someone more than he did with Pat. This is all because of the energy and conversation Pat brought to all social situations.

I have many of my own memories with Pat. Most of them involved him slyly convincing me to cook him lunch or make him a snack. He had a way of winning people over, didn't he? The best part of his charm was that it was never bothersome. It was always out of love.

The Skyvenka Club in our basement was a favorite of Pat's and for good reason. My heart would swell when I came home and realized Michael and Pat were hanging out in the Skyvenka. There was never anything more I wanted to do then just be a part of their jokes and shenanigans, even if it was inappropriate and I didn't approve like the classic big sister that I was. Patrick fitted really well into our family; he felt like another brother or cousin just hanging out. The kinds of jokes and banter he sparked with my parents and relatives were so natural and clever. He really did have a part of my heart, and I love him like family.

For me, Pat will always model what it means to be a loving family member, a true friend, and to have a damn good time. I learned a lot from him about how to live your life without regrets. I admire him and the way he treated the people in his life, and how much love he had to give."

Grandma Nancy:
"Whenever I saw Patrick, he always made a special effort to let me know he thought I was very special, and it worked, making me feel very happy. We will always be sad that we can't spend our lives with him on earth. I was among the many who loved Patrick."

Sarah Finnegan
Family friend, Cleveland

"The richest moments are remembered in the most ordinary moments of our lives. Patrick walked through our door on Morewood Parkway hundreds of times and I have so many fond memories of him being here.

I was lucky enough to see Patrick on almost a daily basis when the boys would come here during their lunch period. It would start with Patrick waving to me through the kitchen window with his happy face, followed by him coming into the kitchen to say hello and ask me about my day. Immediately, our house was charged with joy. Patrick could light up a room on even the greyest of winter days.

Michael's graduation party will always be one of my favorite memories that I shared with Patrick. It started with all the talk leading up to it. Patrick was as excited as we were about the party, 'It's going to be a banger, Mrs. Finnegan!' he said. Well, as it turned out, it was. The highlight, aside from all of us being together, was the mother/son beer pong game between Patrick and Sara and Michael and me. I will never forget Patrick making plans for this and how excited and proud he was to have his mom as his teammate. The fact that they won the game was the icing on the cake.

Patrick had a great sense of humor and was never at a loss for words. Bryan's cousin relayed this funny story to me from the grad party. Patrick had just arrived, backpack in tow. When asked what was in the backpack, Patrick replied without hesitation, 'Just puttin' the books on the shelves, sir!' I can still hear him saying it in his Australian accent and see him saying it with a twinkle in his eye. He had an undeniable charm about him. Once you met Patrick, you never forgot him. Patrick was always so quick to smile and ready to laugh. I loved that about him. I always felt proud that he was Michael's best friend.

One last memory I have from Michael's party has to do with my niece, Colleen, who has Asperger's. A few days afterwards, Colleen specifically mentioned Patrick because he was so kind to her. She said to me, 'Aunt Sarah, you know who I talked to for a while and is so nice?' I didn't need to hear the answer; I knew what was coming, 'Michael's friend, Patrick Green.' There had to be at least 50 kids at that party, but to no surprise, Patrick was the one who stood out. He had the extraordinary ability to see people that others consider invisible. (As a side note, a few days after Patrick passed, Colleen was in the middle of interviewing for a job that she really wanted. Interviewing isn't fun for anyone, and it is particularly difficult for Colleen, so I told her to pray to Patrick, and she did. Colleen is now working in her dream job. There is no doubt in my mind that Patrick interceded on her behalf.)

The other thing I will always remember about Patrick's visits to Morewood was his gratitude for the simplest things. If he entered the house and smelled chocolate chip cookies baking, his eyes lit up, and he was like a kid on Christmas morning. The same was true if I happened to buy Coke, I didn't buy it often, but he knew where to look for it. He opened the basement fridge and his eyes lit up. 'Aww, Mrs. Finnegan, you have Coke!' he would say. I knew what he meant because sometimes you just need one.

My other wonderful memories of Patrick came from football. Patrick exuded positive energy and created joy. He was the ultimate teammate, especially to Michael. He was his biggest cheerleader and gave him confidence, and I will be forever grateful for that. Whenever Bryan and I would talk to Patrick about his awesome punts or great plays in a game, he would turn the conversation around and say, 'What about the QB?' It was never about himself. Patrick was unbelievably gifted, but always so modest and humble, never taking himself too seriously. I always admired that so much about him.

I will never forget winning the playoff game. Of course, the first person I looked for right after the game was Michael. After hugging and congratulating him, I immediately wanted to find Patrick, and I think he was looking for us too. I truly felt a special bond with him. Winning that playoff game was the highlight of the season, so of course, we had to celebrate at the Swinging Door. What a night! I'm sure the coaches were thrilled that the football parents were there, along with the younger siblings, but when the punter and QB walked in, they must've died. Leave it to the young guns (as you would say, Chris) to belly up to the bar and order. They earned it! Thank goodness we have a picture to capture the magic that we all felt that night.

I told Patrick once that he was the best thing that ever came out of high school for Michael. I always felt good when the two of them were together. I have countless pictures of Patrick and Michael, but my all-time favorite is the one of the two of them on the sidelines, #10 and #13, side by side, at every football game. A picture paints a thousand words, and to me, that picture says it all. It symbolizes their friendship, their unbreakable bond, and that they always had each other's backs. And I truly feel that Patrick will always have Michael's back.

Patrick's friendship was one of God's greatest blessings to Michael, and in turn, to us. He will forever be in our hearts. It takes two very special people to create such a beautiful boy - thank you, Sara and Chris, for sharing him with us."

The Scotts
Neighbors and family friends, Cleveland

Tim:
"Be More Like Patrick (PG) ...

1. Eat Donuts.

   No matter what time of day and always eat more than one. I love the memory of Patrick running through the front door, sliding on the bench, pushing Mac or Grant to the side to eat donuts on a lazy Saturday morning.

2. Run.

   Not for health reasons, but to get somewhere fast, so you don't miss out on anything. If I close my eyes, I can see him running from our house to his in record time.

3. Go barefoot.

   Shoes slow you down and keep your feet clean; where's the fun in that? Flip flops are acceptable if there is a lot of snow (more than 6").

4. Love your neighbors.

   Patrick loved us and we loved him until he wasn't a neighbor anymore, he was family.

5. Swear.

   Only acceptable in moderation with an Australian accent and only when playing highly competitive group video games. I miss hearing Brady and Patrick's booming voices and the yelling coming from the basement as if they were being attacked and their lives depended on each other.

6. Don't knock.

   Just come in the front door, through the garage or back door and make a big entrance, the louder, the better!

7. Eat meals with friends.

   No invitation necessary as spontaneity is key. Always be very complimentary of the food regardless of whether it was good and show excessive amounts of appreciation for the cook and overall experience.

8. Mediate.

   If you see people not getting along, get involved, and see how you can help to smooth the situation. Patrick was a great referee for the neighbors and the Scott household. He was always great at overseeing and neutralizing the Scott boy disagreements!

9. Never turn down an invitation for a good time.

   Patrick was always up for a party, including a run to get fast food (Chick-fil-A, McDonald's, Circle K, or the Convenience store).

10. Bust balls.

    Patrick was a man's man and was good at razzing his friends. He always enjoyed healthy debates about OBJ (Odell Beckham Jnr) and sports and held fast to his convictions and beliefs.

11. Spread cheer.

    Patrick always exuded positive energy and brought it with him everywhere he went - you really could feel the energy in the room. Always knowing when someone needed a hug, he would be happy to be the guy to give it.

12. Play outside.

Throw the football, play wiffle ball, baseball, punt return, and any game that can be created on the fly that required a lot of made-up rules, and you must keep score. Make sure the activity finishes with someone being a winner and someone feeling that severe gross injustice just occurred.

13. Be joyful.

Joy comes when you make peace with who you are, why you are, and how you are, whereas happiness tends to be externally triggered and is based on other people, things, and thoughts. I believe Patrick was always full of joy, and that is why he had such a positive impact on so many people."

Cindy:
"Patrick was like a member of our family right from the very begin-ning. I remember meeting Chris and Sara for the first time when they had just made an offer on their home. Sara beautifully de-scribed her children and when she mentioned her 12 year old son, she said, 'He likes sport.' I knew from that moment on he would be a great addition to our street, and he would fit in perfectly.

What I didn't know was how Patrick would become much more than just a neighbor, but a fourth son to Tim and me and a brother to Brady, Grant, and Mac.

In the early years, playing wiffle ball in the front yards was their favorite pastime and that game continued for six plus years. We loved watching and hearing Patrick's voice as he tried to be the ref-eree when the Scott boys were fighting over who was safe or out.

Patrick would run back and forth from his house to ours 20 times a day. The memory of his size 15 shoes sitting by the front door will stay in my mind forever. He ran like a gazelle and he liter-ally floated through the front yards. Sometimes he wore shoes, but mostly he just ran over in his bare feet.

The sight of Patrick and Brady reuniting with a running hug after one of them had been away for a few days was one that I will never ever forget.

When I asked Mac for his favorite memory, his response was 'Mom, we have like a hundred.' If he had to narrow it down to one, it would be the time they tied a rope and a sled to the back of Patrick's car and went 'sled riding' at Coffinberry.

Grant truly loved Patrick as a big brother. They had a very special bond that goes back to the day Patrick 'sold' Grant a lighter for $1. They were fun and mischievous, and Grant cherished every minute he spent with him. Patrick didn't make him feel like the younger brother. He was an equal and that was so important to Grant. One of the best days was when Grant asked Patrick to be his Confirmation sponsor while we were driving to Confirmation class on the day the papers were due. Grant had Pat on speaker, and they were trying to answer the questions. What city were you born in? What church were you baptized in? Where did you make your First Communion? Patrick trying to remember and Grant trying to write down the cities and churches in Australia was quite a funny moment.

Brady and Patrick literally shared a million memories, and I'm sure many of them are not shareable. They had their secret inside joke page that Brady now has framed in his room. Memories of Brady and Patrick dressing up like 'super fans' and sitting in the cheap seats for the Cavs games and cheering like lunatics and listening to them yelling and cheering at the tv in the basement at a football/basketball game or a video game is a sound I will never forget. Patrick was the only one who didn't get in trouble for yelling swear words because when they came out of his mouth with his beautiful Australian accent, they didn't sound bad. It was always comforting when Brady was out at night and I would get the text 'I'm home. I'm at Pat's. Don't wait up.'

A piece of our heart is missing, but the memories will be with us forever. We look for signs from Patrick, and we have witnessed a few beautiful ones that we know are from him. There are no coincidences. We know he is looking over us and smiling."

Brady:

"It is difficult to put into words and describe the relationship that Patrick and I had. We were inseparable from the first day we met. I went over to meet Pat and he was shooting hoops in his driveway, and I was happy because basketball was my favorite sport. Up until that day, all the other kids on the street were either girls who were older than me or boys who were younger. We became fast friends. Over the next six years, we were inseparable. We had different friend groups as the years went on, but we always stayed close. If we didn't hang out that day or night, we still met up at the end of the night in his basement or mine to hash out the day.

Our relationship early on was very amusing. He would talk to me about girls and life in Australia, and in return, I introduced him to the new sports he had never played before, such as baseball, basketball, wiffleball, and flag football. I quickly began to consider Pat as more of a role model when just after a year of playing these sports, he was already better than me, and I had been playing them my entire life. Sports came easily to Pat and so did friends. He included everyone and everyone loved him.

In addition to playing sports on the street, Pat and I had many memories that I will remember forever. Playing video games after school, watching YouTube on his iPad, teaching me about Australian slang and food, making a list of inside jokes that we kept hung in his closet, teaching me how to play Australian sports like cricket or AFL, late-night talks in his hot tub where we talked about almost anything you can think of about girls, and lastly our daily bike rides to East Coast Custard where they knew Pat and me by name and gave us free ice cream.

Overall, Pat and I had something special. He grew up thousands of miles away from me, but when he came here, we had a relationship that felt as if we'd been brothers our entire lives. While he only lived here for six years, we made enough memories together to last a lifetime."

Grant, who chose Patrick to be his Confirmation sponsor:
"Patrick was like a brother to me. He moved in when I was 10 years old and we spent almost every day together. He basically lived at my house. He never treated me like I was the younger brother of Brady. He always kept me involved, even at a young age. He was always on my team and by my side. He gave me countless rides, played all kinds of sports and video games with me, and was always down for an adventure. Patrick always stuck up for me and the other younger kids on the street and loved all of us. He brought our street together and made us a family. When it was time for me to choose my Confirmation sponsor, it was a no-brainer. Patrick was my first choice and he enthusiastically agreed. Patrick was with us for six years, but it seemed like most of my life. I keep memories of him in my room and think about him every single day. He'll always be with me."

Mac, who chose Patrick as his Confirmation name:
"Patrick taught me to live life to the fullest. He would never turn down an offer for a good time. He always made time for me and treated me like a brother. I try to live more like Patrick because you never know when your time is going to end."

The McDonalds
Neighbors and family friends, Cleveland

"Never before have I known a 19 year old boy with the charisma and personality of Patrick. He made you feel a certain way, his love of life was contagious, which is why so many people wanted to be around him. Patrick connected deeply with people and he did that by being truly present when he spoke to you.

Emily and Olivia both said they never knew anyone else who would always pick up their phone; it never went to voicemail. He always responded to texts. He was there for his friends. They shared a friendship that was deeper than most neighbors; they had one another's backs. Matthew and Aidan would drop anything to have the chance to hang with Patrick. He rallied the neighborhood boys whether it was wiffle ball, basketball, trips to Circle K (for lots of junk food), Chick-fil-A meals, Xbox marathons, snowball fights, ghost in the graveyard, running bases, the list goes on and on. Patrick was like a big brother to all of them. He was caring, always up for having fun, and filled with energy. His enthusiasm for the moment made even the simplest times fun. Patrick's 'super athleticism' was admired by the gang.

Patrick was never in a bad mood, which is a pretty rare thing. The only times the boys would see him mildly angry was when he would defend Tildy in wiffle ball games; being a protective big brother was his job. It was evident in so many ways that he adored Tildy and Annabelle, and that family was woven through him. He had more friends than anyone I know, but he also demonstrated a deep love and connection for his family. Somehow, he juggled his time and spread his love so he could show up for everyone.

From a grown-up perspective, Harry and I always loved talking with Patrick. He spoke to adults with confidence. He had interesting thoughts and opinions on so many topics and was always happy to share them. He was so comfortable in his skin.

We have talked as a family so much about the void we feel and continue to try to make sense of his loss. We talk about doing our best to live our lives in a way that integrates Patrick's loving, enthusiastic personality, his zest for life, and his willingness to engage with everyone he met. In our six years of knowing him, Pat taught our whole family a lot about living.

Some of our favorite memories with Patrick/Pat/Patty:
Late night talks; trips to Circle K; drives in the Metroparks; running errands; bike rides to East Coast Custard; ghost in the graveyard; kick the can; running bases; wiffle ball; basketball games; biking to Fairview days and watching fireworks; picking out presents for Pat's girlfriends; Uber rides home from Brian Lowry's house; X-box gamin; snowball fights and jumps with snow boards; talks at our kitchen island; family dinners; Memorial Day barbecues at the Marina; scaring

Olivia while she was home alone and Olivia mistakenly calling the police; watching sports; talking sports; dancing through our house at the New Year's Eve Party; celebrating birthdays together; dinner at Hibachi; raiding our snack cabinet' Pat waking up Emily and being so proud that he was one of the only boys ever allowed upstairs in the girls' rooms; bringing his favorite cookies back from Australia; Blossom bus rides and concerts; watching clouds at Blossom; witnessing Emily kiss 'shed boy'; fireworks on our street; rides to school (always running late) and home; smashing the street lamp with a snowball; Halloween celebrations; all the fun times at the Pig Roast; being a great FMP mentor to Aidan; walking us to our classes and making us feel comfortable at school; dirt bike rides; building snow forts in the circle and throwing snowballs at cars; going to Annie's for snacks; teaching us cricket; and giving advice about girls."

Emily:
"People like Patrick are so hard to come by; you'd be lucky to encounter them once in your life - I was blessed to know him for six years. He was more than a neighbor or a friend; he was family. Pat carried himself with such confidence and charisma that he fitted in with every age group, no matter how old or young. One of my favorite traits about Pat was that he always said yes and never turned down an opportunity to hang out, which led to a permanent errand-running buddy, countless late-night back patio hangouts until both of us were too tired to keep talking, fast food runs (because we were both always hungry), long drives through the metro parks, and all other small moments that he made so memorable. He made sure everyone in his life felt loved; no matter how early in the morning I left for college, he got up to give me a hug goodbye and made sure to be free when I came home so that we could go for a drive and update each other on our lives. He was the only friend who donated to my sorority philanthropy event without any hesitation, even when I'm sure he didn't have much money in his bank account at the time. You couldn't help but love Patrick; he had such an infectious personality and an incredible way with words.

One night after a concert, we were in an Uber going home, and Patrick accidentally put in the incorrect address. We were two and a half miles from home, but he was able to persuade the Uber driver to drive us home completely free of charge so that we wouldn't be walking alone at 2 am. People naturally took a liking to him; no one could say no to him. He had the biggest heart of anyone I know. Growing up around him, I gained a greater appreciation for the meaning of our time here on Earth. Patrick loved everyone he encountered. He didn't talk negatively about anyone, he saw the good in everyone, and he didn't take himself too seriously. You couldn't help but be happy around Pat.

When the Green family moved in two doors down from me, I had no idea that the curly-haired boy playing basketball would change my life in so many ways. Thank you, Pat, for teaching me to live life with no regrets, embrace every opportunity with arms wide open, and love unconditionally in the process. You are so loved."

Olivia:
"The day the Green family moved in was the day that, as clichéd as it sounds, my life changed forever. I was wearing my go-to bomber jacket and my hair was in a rat's nest. Little did I know, I was about to be introduced to the biggest cheerleader I would know in my life - Patrick Michael Green.

I met him as a young, insecure girl. Throughout the years, he would change that mold in every way. Patrick was the first boy to call me pretty. I was so confused because I had never seen myself like that, but he did. He always saw everyone in a way that they never saw themselves. For example, I had no idea I had boobs until he told me one day. He was the kind of person who was able to in- still confidence in anyone and he had the uncanny ability to make anyone feel the best that they could possibly feel with no effort at all... it was just because you were around him. Whether it was being the only boy to comment on my Instagram pictures or attending my every sporting event, he was always there for me. He saw things in me I never ever saw in myself.

Growing up with him was a blessing I never realized at the time. I assumed all girls got to have a guy best friend as great as mine. I knew Patrick was special, but I truly had no idea how special he was. With one simple text saying I needed a favor, a simple 'yes' would be granted with no questions asked. I made him dress up in beach clothes and prance around in the lake for hours. I made him star in a short film where he had to spend his afternoon running around the Elmwood woods doing every shot I asked of him. I looked up to him more than he ever knew. I talked him up to all my friends so much, no wonder they all fell in love with him. He was the person in my life I could depend on, no matter what. Anything I needed, anytime I needed help, he was there. He was always there. He put everyone before himself. I truly am so thankful I got to grow up with someone that made me feel so special.

Pat had a way about him where he lit up a room because of his vibrant personality. Everyone wanted to be his friend and it showed when you look at the number of people who were drawn to him. I believe the reason for this was that no matter how many friends he gained, he never forgot about anyone. Pat was one of the most popular kids, but he treated everyone he came in contact with, like they were his best friend. Any person he met wanted to know more about him. The accent helped for sure, and damn did he know it, but after that, it was all his personality and charisma. I know this first-hand because I had to deal with every girl falling in love with him as I introduced him to them.

I learned so much from him. Pat viewed life in a way of constant excitement. He was a smart guy, but he never stressed about things. He went through life with a huge smile. No other person I have met walked into everyone's life and made it better. He truly lifted everyone up. I have never met anyone that has affected such a vast number of people's lives.

I know I met an angel all those years ago and I will have that angel in my heart for years to come. I miss you every day, Patrick, and I would not change the time we had together for the world."

Matt, who wrote his college application essay about Patrick and the following is an excerpt:

"I came home to a silent street, which was enough to tell me something wasn't right. I walked in to find my mother crying, telling me the news that Patrick had passed away. The summer of 2019 was the first time I experienced the loss of someone who I loved more than myself. Patrick was not just my neighbor, but a second brother and role model to me. I was a lost teenager who watched this older charismatic boy enter a room and treat everyone with kindness. Patrick taught me everything about life, including no matter how hard high school was, to find the fun in every single moment. Soon after he died, it became clear to me that the many characteristics that I missed so much about him were not necessarily gone but gifted to me to use and share with others. Pat was, and still is, my life coach who made me the man I am today."

Dillon Bandi

Neighbor, and family friend, Cleveland. Dillon wrote his college application essay about Patrick and the following is an excerpt:

"Patrick was a fun person who never had issues with anyone. I could go on for days talking about the things we did together. June 27, 2019, and the days that followed turned into one of the worst stretches of my life. I got a text from my neighbor that said, 'I'm broken.' I was confused, so I called him. He was hysterical and was only just able to mutter the words, 'Pat died.' I had never felt that amount of hurt and denial in one second. I cried non-stop for two days and was not able to eat or sleep for a week following the news. I simply could not comprehend how God could take someone that young, with such a bright future, and such a great reputation. It did not make sense. I miss my friend every day and that feeling will never go away. Patrick's death brought my neighborhood friends and me closer than we had ever been.

After Patrick's accident, I came across a video of him cheering for me as I played hockey, I had never seen it before. This was fate because I had planned to quit hockey my junior year, but after seeing that video, my heart wouldn't let me quit. I found the love I had for hockey again and ended up having my most successful year in the sport.

I had always wanted to play baseball in college, and following Patrick's passing, my dedication became even stronger for this sport that Patrick and I played in our backyards together. Following Patrick's death, I have found a new passion for everything I have in my life."

(Dillon recently accepted an offer to play baseball at college. I know Patrick would be proud.)

The Kelleys
Family friends, Cleveland

"Patrick 'Patty' Green made our family better, and I suspect had the same impact on many others. Patty arrived from Australia in middle school, with a smile, charm, accent, and athletic ability all above his age.

Patty could engage and develop relationships with a ferocity I had not seen before. Younger children, peers, and parents enjoyed his warmth and sincerity to a point he became a friend, a true friend.

Patty was my son Mickey's peer and ended up my daughter's Senior Prom date. Clare wanted a 'fun date who could get along with everyone.' The choice was clear, 'Patty, he is a friend to all.' What an accomplishment to be everyone's friend. It amplifies and summarizes so many of his warm characteristics. Wendy asked about a flower for his lapel, and Clare said, 'big and fun.' The flower was large, bright, playful, and stylish – it was Patty.

Patty remains a part of our daily lives as we see him with Brady, John, and Mickey in a picture with LeBron. I smile and recall the happiness as I listened to the boys laugh and recount meeting LeBron. The Kelleys sure do love our friend Patty, and every time his name is mentioned, the reply is instant, 'friend to all.'"

Libby de Meyrick
Family friend, Patrick and Annabelle's kindergarten teacher, Sydney

"My first introduction to Patrick was when he was almost six years old. Patrick and his beautiful family had just recently relocated from Melbourne, and I was fortunate enough to be his kindergarten teacher. I remember Patrick's first day of school so vividly. This gorgeous, dark-haired little boy stayed very close to his mum and dad's side while exploring the classroom and meeting his new classmates. When the time arrived to bid the parents farewell, Patrick did not want to see his parents go. With years of experience on her side, the Principal, Sr. Veronica came to my aide and in no time at all Patrick was smiling brightly and enjoying the day's activities. From those early weeks of Patrick's first year at school, I was so lucky to form an amazing friendship with not only Sara but also with Chris and their lovely family. It was an instant connection that just grew from there.

Patrick was a beautiful student. He always showed kindness and consideration to all of his classmates and he displayed a maturity beyond his years. I remember he tried so desperately hard to improve his handwriting, seeking my approval after each handwriting lesson, wanting to get everything right. This determination was evident in so many areas of his schooling. He was so knowledgeable and filled with worldly facts, but one area in which Patrick struggled was public speaking. Completing his morning news in front of his peers was an obstacle, but the biggest challenge of all, was the thought of speaking into the microphone during assembly. I spoke to Chris and Sara about this and we decided that I wouldn't force him to take a microphone role at our upcoming class assembly. I will never forget the day when I was allocating the students' various roles, suddenly Patrick spoke up and said, 'I can speak in the microphone, Miss Thompson. I think I'm ready to do it and I'm actually really excited!' I was so shocked, but at the same time, so immensely proud of Patrick. He had overcome his fear and was determined to prove that he could do it, and he did it so well!

There are so many little moments I remember with Patrick, such as the times when he hurt himself on the playground, and although he rarely got upset at school, he would often just collapse and cry on me until he knew that he would be okay. Or, moments when the class would be playing sport and Patrick would be selected as team captain and he would always choose his team from the least sporty students to the sportiest ones. He didn't care if he won; he was more focused on including everyone in the game.

I remember one afternoon when I drove Patrick and Annabelle home from school and the pure excitement and joy on both of their faces when they got into my car was just beautiful! They were so excited to be in 'Miss Thompson's' car and they both chatted nonstop all the way home. When we were nearing the house, I remember Patrick asking me if they could please call me 'Libby' when we were outside of school and 'Miss Thompson' while at school. Of course, I agreed to this, and they were so happy with themselves.

I used to love dropping by and catching up with Sara after work, and I remember one particular afternoon, I was greeted by Patrick at the door. The first thing he said to me was, 'Libby, is it a wine kind of day or a cup of tea kind of day? Mum thinks it could be a wine kind of day!' I couldn't stop laughing, not only from his question, but the sheer confidence with which he spoke to me. He was about 11 years old at this stage, and after I had given him a cuddle and we walked down the hall together to Sara, who was busy in the kitchen, he spoke up and said 'Mum, I think you're right, white wine it is!' This is the boy I remember. Always polite and beautifully well mannered, but incredibly cheeky with a strong wit to him - he was so much like his dad.

Occasionally I would babysit Patrick, Annabelle, and Matilda. I enjoyed this time with them, as Annabelle used to often confide in me and discuss certain things going on at school, and Patrick would often do the same, but he would usually ask me questions. He always asked about my family, friends, and my travels and why I wanted to become a teacher, and so on. The questions would be endless. He would also often ask me to sit with him until he fell asleep, which I happily did.

Another fond memory I have of Patrick is that he would always greet me with a huge hug. The last time I saw him was in 2016 when the family was visiting Sydney from the US, I was pregnant with Sibella and Sara, Patrick, Annabelle, and Matilda came around for lunch at my place in Paddington. I'll never forget when Patrick basically lifted me off the ground with his embrace. I couldn't believe how much he had grown and what a gorgeous young man he was becoming, but I also loved the fact that he still hugged me, just like he had always done as a young boy. On this particular day, I remember Patrick offering to take Thomas (who was only four years old at the time) down to Trumper Oval to kick the footy around with him. Thomas was so excited to go with Patrick, and of course, Gisele, the admiring little sister, wanted to join the boys too. Annabelle and Matilda kindly took Gisele down to the oval as well. I remember both Sara and me looking over the back terrace watching the children walk down together. Patrick and Thomas hand in hand and the three girls holding hands. It was such a special sight to see and a memory I will always hold very dear to my heart.

I feel blessed and so very fortunate to have known Patrick. His generous, kind, and loving nature, his humor, wit and, charm made Patrick an outstanding boy, and an outstanding young man."

Bob and Mary Vecchione
Family friends, Cleveland

"From our first meeting, Patrick was a genuine soul with an insatiable curiosity for life. Even at a young age, he would be conversant with everyone and anyone, or as we like to say, 'Patrick never met a stranger.'

Another amazing thing about Patrick was his level of respect and courtesy for Mary and me. On every occasion throughout the years, Patrick would go out of his way to seek us out to say hello. If he was with a group of his friends, he would introduce each and every one of them to us.

Patrick was a fabulous human being and we know when we enter the gates of heaven, he will be the first to greet us and introduce us to all of his friends."

Brenda Kirk
Family friend, Cleveland

"Patrick. The joy on the face of his mom is indescribable; she gazes up at this towering teen with adoration and a half-laugh. He's talking about his plans for this evening, with just half the details in an attempt to both appease and entertain her. Most of our encounters are like this; he's a true light that creates a spark in those around him.

That same adoring look can be found in the eyes of two stunning girls, who look up at this towering teen with intense admiration, as only sisters can. The spark here is different, the protector, the friend, the leader.

They're tight, all of them - they have this green twinkle that is hard to describe, but it starts with him. He's a lot like his dad in that way. This father and son transcend all norms; they share so much in common - a love and respect for each other (and sports) above all else. Together, they light up the room with a warmth and welcome that I've never before felt.

He carries the weight of the world and of those less fortunate than he, just like his mom. A caretaker, he's the one who clears the path for his sisters, helping to make the 'brutiful' world a little brighter for them.

The observer, I get to play witness to this family and the dynamics that have been instrumental in building a bond that is truly one of the most amazing things I've ever seen. Each takes on their role, snapping together like a team headed to the championships whenever game time arrives. Mind you, game time could mean the gathering of 100s for the annual pig roast!

He was the captain of this crew, if not by title, then by action. His impact was felt on and off the field, literally and figuratively.

Losing the captain has left a physical space that has been replaced by his beautiful spirit. In his absence, he will be honored by me and many of the hundreds lucky enough to witness what being a beautiful human in action means.

His life in action means caring more about others than himself. It means gathering people together for a common good. It means being a friend, even when it's hard. It means showing up when people need you most. It means protecting the vulnerable. It means working hard for what you believe in. It means family above all else. It means sharing a wink and a smile and saying I've got you, even if you're not exactly sure that you do.

Patrick Green. He is remembered by rainbows, the color purple, #13, the kitchen at St Malachi, the football field at the high school, the rock, family, friends, and countless other physical things. More importantly, he's remembered and honored by the actions we take to keep his legacy very much alive while we can. The world is an incredible place because of you, Patrick Green. I am truly honored to have known and loved you and lucky enough to honor your legacy, #PG13."

Tammy Lyons
Family friend, Cleveland

"Patrick comes into the room and the energy shifts. You can feel his powerful, uplifting presence. A presence that feels like an expansive mountain and a fluid river at the exact same time.

I am speaking in the present tense on purpose because I do still feel his presence often, even when he is physically not here.

I haven't had long conversations with Patrick, but I feel I know him well through Sara and Chris and the way it feels when he is with us. The impact he has on some many lives in a short 19 years is magnificent and reminds me of the power of one kind, empathic, present human heart on all of those it touches.

I see the way he is caring for his family from beyond and the ways he shows up and softens their suffering, and I know for sure that his guidance is always at work. His life here with us was only the beginning of the important work he is meant to do and a blessing to all who know him.

I will sit in wonder alongside my friends Sara and Chris and witness the continued magnitude of Patrick's beautiful presence in our lives. He is always with us reminding us to see one another with kind eyes, to care for one another with compassion, and to always find the many moments of joy this life offers."

Katie Trainor
Family friend, Cleveland

"Sara, I will always remember and cherish when we first met at Inner Bliss Yoga Studio. I felt as if I was on the greatest high; it is one of my most treasured memories. I got to know you, connect with you, and love you deeply. I couldn't believe one of my very best friends and soul mates had been living half-way around the world. You felt like home to me.

Then I got to meet and know Chris, Patrick, Annabelle, and Tildy. What I have always admired and cherished about your family is how connected and loving you were to one another. Yes, I know a lot of families exude love, friendship, respect, and understanding, but yours has always felt different; it goes deeper in a different way. Your family is so unbelievably beautiful.

You and Chris share such admirable respect and love. You are amazing examples as parents and as humans working to give your babies balance and love on every level. Your children truly love one another, not only as siblings but as friends. I have always admired how connected your family is.

When I first met Patrick, he was so darling. He had such a beautiful spirit. He was an exceptionally loving person. He had confidence and showed gentle kindness that was so genuine. I can still hear his charming Australian accent.

Something special that plays over and over again in my mind is when I last saw Patrick. It was just a week or so before his accident and I was leaving the grocery store when from a distance in the parking lot, I heard a voice calling out, 'Hi Katie.' I turned to see it was your sweet Patrick. He was wearing his burgundy River jersey. He walked over to me and gave me a beautiful hug, his right arm just kind of hanging around my shoulders, and we had a lovely exchange of words. I remember this as well as I remember the last great hug I had with my dad.

What I really love about Patrick is his affection for you, Sara. He adored you. I really, really miss that for you. I miss that you don't get to feel his embrace, hear his voice, see his smile, hear his laughter. He deeply loved and respected you, Chris, and the girls. He was the 'Guiding Light'. I love how he and Annabelle hung out together in their circle of friends. He was himself and no one else. He was and still is exactly who God intended him to be - kind, loving, and the most beautiful example of you and Chris."

Kimmie Levinson
Family friend, Cleveland

"As I became a 'regular' at the Inner Bliss Yoga Studio, I was blessed to meet Sara, a beautiful Australian woman who powered through yoga classes like no other and had a smile that could light up the entire studio. One day I mentioned I was looking for a babysitter and Sara suggested her daughter, Annabelle, who was 15 years old at the time. Sara had spoken so highly of her children and family and I knew a little about each of their accomplishments and stories. I knew that Annabelle was like an 'old soul' and very mature for her age so I was happy to have her start working for our family. Fast forward and Annabelle became our babysitter/nanny for over four and a half years, caring for our children Reese (13) and Gray (3), the very best caregiver any mother could ever ask for.

Annabelle quickly became an integral part of our family, and as we became close to Belle (as the kids call her), she spoke of Patrick and her entire family with such love, care, and enthusiasm. Everything she did revolved around Patrick in some way, as many of her close friends were also Patrick's friends. Patrick was Belle's best friend and the stories she described growing up in Australia with their close-knit family and friends always included Patrick and Tildy. The spark Annabelle had in her eye when she introduced me to her older brother was of a proud love that is not easily found between siblings. I remember the first time I met Patrick - a tall, handsome young man whose smile lit up a room - just like his mom, I thought. Patrick met my young son Gray and made an instant connection with him. He sat right down at the little kid's table and immediately started coloring and playing with him. I later found out that this was nothing out of the ordinary for Patrick as he shared a love for children, especially those with special needs.

On Thursday night, June 27, 2019, I received a text from Annabelle saying that she was sorry, but she could not babysit the next night; she'd had some news and wouldn't be available. I replied, saying that that was completely fine but that I hoped she was okay. Not once did it ever cross my mind that Annabelle had lost her best friend, that Tildy had lost her big brother, or that my good friends Sara and Chris had lost their beloved son. The next morning at 7 am, I learned that Patrick had passed away in an ATV accident.

Shock, disbelief, tears, denial, questions as to what happened, 'Oh my gosh Sara, Annabelle, Chris, and Tildy,' more tears. Those reactions were quickly washed away and replaced with how can I help? What can I do? Our community was heartbroken and in shock, but it was time to move into action now.

What I witnessed over the next two weeks, actually months, was purely devastating and astonishing at the same time. Friends, family, acquaintances, and everyone that even remotely knew the Green family began to surround the home. During that time, I would describe all of Sara and Chris's closest friends and family as shining souls, showering the family with love, compassion, sympathy, and assistance in moving through the motions of what needed to be done. There was no leaving their side. These women were some of the most beautiful, compassionate, grounding, and healing 'movers and shakers' I had ever met. They led the way in managing all of the various aspects of arrangements with the Green family, including funeral proceedings, out of town family and friends arriving, each day's events, and just taking care to ensure that Chris, Sara, Annabelle, and Tildy, and even their beloved pets were being taken care of. Everyone who offered to help was given tasks and it was all managed seamlessly in my eyes. It was as if the community was enveloping the Greens in a big plush blanket that would love and protect them. Australian flags adorned the home while stories of Patrick prevailed and astonished everyone, each and every day. Sara, Chris, and the girls were trekking through the unimaginable and I will never know how they came together as one. I remember Chris saying, 'This will not break us.'

Well over a thousand people attended the church service to honor Patrick's life. There was not a dry eye as Chris, on behalf of his family, spoke of Patrick and their strong love and pride for their son and brother. He spoke about Sara, Annabelle, Tildy, and himself and a few joyful stories highlighting each of their relationships with Patrick, and of course, made people laugh with tears in between.

Chris and Sara are amongst the warrior moms and dads that define the words brave and fierce. Not one person, except for those that have experienced a similar loss, will truly understand how hard and difficult it is to wake up each morning, to go to work, to miss Patrick every day, and to simply continue with life. As a mother who has suffered the unthinkable loss of her first child, Sara has turned this tragedy into transformation and her loss into the legacy of helping others in sharing Patrick's story. She teaches all of us to take nothing for granted and to live life to the fullest every day. Sara is present to her suffering, but somehow and in some way, she has not let it impact her beautiful soul and well-being. Sara and Chris are simply astonishing in their ability to believe and maintain courage. I don't know how, but despite their daily pain, the Green family remains strong and perhaps stronger than ever. Annabelle's light has returned in her smile and she continues to share the greatest and funniest stories of her brother and best friend. She now protects her younger sister and family, just as Patrick did. Annabelle is ready to continue her life plans and attend Ohio State University, and our family will miss her greatly. Tears will flow when she leaves for so many reasons. Our family will miss her just being in our home.

Patrick, you are so loved and will be forever missed."

Amy and Colin McNamara
Family friends, who named their son Patrick after our Patrick, Cleveland

"Over the years, we had watched the Greens become family to my parents. We would hear countless stories of the times they spent together - how courageous these three kids were to move across the world. How kind, well respected, and loved they were among their peers and friends in Cleveland. Whenever we would see them, Patrick always stood out to us. We would talk about what a great kid he was - how personable and confident he was, and how protective and kind he always was towards his sisters. We loved hearing stories about him and watching him with Chris always reminded us of my dad and Bobby.

The day of Patrick's funeral was a day Colin and I will never forget. To say that Patrick was loved cannot begin to describe what we felt in the church that day. Sitting in church and listening to everyone speak about him after the funeral, it was very clear Patrick Green was someone who every parent would be proud to have as their son. There was no question in our mind after that; if we had a boy, we would name him Patrick. We believe that one of the first and most lasting impacts we as parents have on our child is their name. Their name connects them with the past - with a person who has come before them who can be a guiding light and someone to emulate. We will tell our sweet Patrick Robert of his namesake, of the wonderful things Patrick Green did in his life and the amazing lives he touched. And if our Patrick can accomplish half of what Patrick Green accomplished and be loved by even a fraction of those that loved him, we will be so proud of our dear boy. He has big shoes to fill, and we will never forget the joy that Patrick brought to so many."

226

The Fritzs
Family friends, Cleveland

"When I think of Patrick, I often find myself feeling lucky. Basically, everyone in our community knows of his very unfortunate and untimely death. But not everyone was as lucky as our family to have called Patrick their friend. He touched each one of our lives in some magical way.

Most of all, he was a cherished friend and classmate to my daughter, Ava. He was always there for her when she needed a trusting friend. I will never forget the time he spent with my youngest son, Gus, who was struggling with baseball, and Patrick took him to the park to practice and sharpen his catching and throwing skills. Then he went one step further and came to a couple of his baseball games to cheer him on. Gus felt like the most special kid on his team when Patrick was cheering for him from the stands. He took his own time and gave it so unselfishly to Gus.

I was fortunate enough to be around him when he would come over with Ava and all of their friends for lunch, and he always went out of his way to come and say hi to me and somehow make me feel as if he was also there as my friend just as much as he was to Ava. Patrick would walk into our house and make everyone in it feel as if we were the most important people in his world. I can honestly say there hasn't been anyone else, especially someone so young, who could make all of us feel so special. It is no secret that we all adored him.

One of my favorite memories is watching him with my youngest daughter, Lila, who is nine years old (going on 19). Whenever he came over, her whole face lit up and she would instantly go running in for her big hug. Patrick's huge embrace and kind words to her would reassure Lila that she was indeed the most important person to him at that very moment. Just days before he passed, Lila was sitting on his lap at a graduation brunch, confirming in her mind that she truly was a part of their gang.

Because of Patrick and his amazing family, our family Is better. To this day, whenever we find ourselves in a situation where we need to pause and think of what the right thing to do is, we find ourselves saying, 'What would Patrick do?' Those words make it easier for us to find our way and take the higher path. We are truly lucky to have known him and we are honored to hold him in our hearts forever."

Matt Gaden and Gavin Buchanan
Patrick's junior football coaches, Sydney

"Patrick's passing has had a profound effect on a lot of us back here who knew him and you all as a family. The similarities in the ages of our kids makes it all very relatable for everyone, and the knowledge that you are all hurting so much just breaks our hearts. It was such a wonderful service you had for him, which we all watched in the small hours of the morning in Australia through tear-filled eyes. Patrick was 100% right about you guys not being able to do a much better job with him than you did. That is also what makes the loss so difficult to comprehend and what also makes it seem so unfair.

Patrick would have been five or six years old when we first met him at Easts. He stood out immediately. He was the only boy who could bounce the ball properly. He could also do it while running, which made him the envy of all the other boys and earned him the label 'freak.' After we saw the ball-bouncing talents, it was hard to miss his raking left boot that also added to the legend of him being called a 'freak.' Seeing him kicking further and higher than anyone else and running around bouncing the ball and having it actually come back to him was certainly a novelty for all who witnessed it. But beyond the obvious physical talents, there were early signs of what type of a person he would become.

One stand-out early memory in this regard was Patrick's care for the other boys. This was no better demonstrated in how he played with a boy on the team who had Down Syndrome. Patrick, unprompted, always went out of his way to make sure in games that his team-mate got the footy and got the opportunity to have a kick.

He never had to be told to do it. It came from a genuine place of caring for others. It was something that was innate within him and it was clearly a character trait that carried on in his life in caring for others who didn't have the gifts he had.

As the winters down at Trumper Park rolled on, we got to know Patrick better. While he was a coach's gift because of his ability, it was the person he was that truly stood out. He was kind-hearted, gentle, and respectful. There was a quiet strength and a quiet leadership that drew the boys to him. This was despite him being a mad Tiger's fan, like his father and family. He would regularly wear his slightly tattered Richmond jersey to training and was happy to put it to all the boys in Swans jerseys (the local team) even though this period was not Richmond's finest hour in terms of on-field success.

We made Patrick the captain of the team in under 12s because we knew he would lead strongly by his words and actions. That season was a glorious year for Patrick and his team. We started well and found our path to goal much easier because we had two or three boys, including Patrick, who could play in the middle then go forward and kick us goals. The arch enemy was Drummoyne, who finished top of the ladder at the end of the year, and we finished second. We went into the semi-final and had a horrible day getting beaten by more than 100 points. We said to the boys that we should write this one off and just move forward. Patrick was one of those who felt deeply about how badly we'd played and was a great inspiration to his teammates in the next fortnight as we fought through to the grand final versus Drummoyne (again!).

On grand final day, we told the boys that if Drummoyne broke away from us, we just needed to keep our nerve and fight on. The game opened with Drummoyne scoring four goals before we could respond. Panic stations, you might think, but at that moment, Patrick took matters into his own hands and singularly lifted us with clearance after clearance from the center. He drove us forward with that long-left foot kick and we were able to regain some lost ground. At the half-time break, Patrick was particularly animated as he tried to motivate his teammates to believe we could win. The second half was a triumph for his positive thinking as we clicked into gear and took the game away from Drummoyne to end up winning by three goals. There's no doubt for us that Patrick was best on ground that day. This was to be his last game of AFL before the family departed to the USA.

We loved Patrick's joy at playing the game he loved, and it turned out to be the best decision we could have made, appointing him to be captain and lead his teammates to victory. His care and compassion for his teammates and his quiet strength of leadership are the things we will remember most about him, and that enormous left boot of course!"

Wade Massad
Patrick's high school football coach and family friend, Cleveland

"My first memory of Pat was when I was introduced to him at football practice mid-season during his freshman year. Coach Wells asked me to check out the freshman punter who may be able to kick for us in the future. I remember the day vividly, one of those beautiful sunny fall afternoons with a strong south breeze. I walked over to the freshman practice and asked the coach if I could work with Pat for a while. I let him know we were going to kick a few. Immediately his enthusiasm was overwhelming and before the first ball was on the tee, he told me how far he could kick and how accurate he was, the usual Patrick confidence. I told him we were not going to aim through the uprights, but we would kick at the end line and try to kick the ball across the field directly at the goalposts in an attempt to hit the goal post or kick it directly over the goalposts to gauge how accurate he was. He lined up on the end line, and I tossed him a bit of an errant pass. Did he miss it? Of course not! He caught it 'Odell' style with one hand while contorting his body. I took notice immediately, making a mental note that this kid was a special athlete.

He was taken back by not kicking at the large goal but aiming directly for the post, he was wild at first, but his strength and power were evident. He thanked me and bounced on down the field back to the team.

Sophomore year I really got to know Pat as I was able to work with him daily, and our relationship grew. He would put a smile on my face every session. His natural ability was evident, and it showed on the field. The bonds that formed that season between Pat, Michael Konrad, Owen Bebie, and me were strong. He was a great asset in keeping Michael loose during his first exposure to football and I think much of the mental success Michael enjoyed was due to Patrick. He executed well on the field despite a few 'lone wolf' plays, which Coach Wells would immediately address with me. Patrick's response was always, 'Coach, I thought.......' I would suggest not to think just to do what was asked. Coach Wells and I would usually laugh about it post-game and shake our heads as his ability would often overcome the tactical error.

Junior year saw the further development of our relationship and with our special kicking crew. Personally, I looked forward to the daily sessions with those kids, with Pat being the outgoing ringleader. We started to use him with various fakes and 2 pt. plays recognizing his raw athleticism. By the end of the year, we would joke that he always seemed to get in the endzone on those plays; he just didn't want to get tackled or hit and was so athletic he could avoid everyone.

Senior year saw more fun and games at practice daily. Konrad had moved on to college. Patrick, Owen, Finny, and I had interesting discussions at practice and on the sidelines. To loosen the guys up during games, they started evaluating the opposing team's cheerleaders or pom squads, always an interesting dialogue.

To keep his focus against opponents, I suggested he use his ability to intimidate the other team and their coaches in warmups. Each team is designated one side of the field during warmups and punters kick one direction and then shift to the other direction to evaluate the wind conditions and ball flight. He loved this exercise, from our end zone bombing balls to their side of the warmups, then in the opposite direction standing right on the 50 yd line encroaching on their space on the field and catching their attention once the bombs started exploding off his foot. The best example of this was during warmups at the Clyde game, when at the 50, I caught half of their coaching staff turning to watch the show. I pulled him aside and let him know, which further fueled his fire. I offered instruction loud enough for them to hear me, kick right, inside the 10, hang, etc. He was on fire and they could not keep their eyes off the show he was putting on. When we flipped sides of the field, their return men were being inundated by his punts from our own end zone.

Around mid-season, we had a talk at practice about his punting future. I know Chris spent lots of time discussing opportunities, traveling to camps, and shagging balls along the way. Patrick conceded that this was probably going to be his final foray in punting; he just wanted to move on. I think this cleared his mind and the little tension in our relationship as I believe he was the most talented kid I had ever coached, and the sky was the limit for him in punting. After that discussion, he went on to have some great games.

In one of the greatest, if not the greatest victory in over 100 years of Pirate football, Pat was, in my opinion, the star of the game vs. Clyde. He was exceptional in every aspect. Free and easy, he flipped the field multiple times, trapping Clyde deep in their territory and providing us with significant field position. All the while keeping the kids loose, especially Finny on the sidelines. It was a special night for him and the program.

I repeat the words that I said at the awards night that year, 'Pat always put a smile on my face and those around him.' His enthusiasm was infectious; he was a beacon for the young kids on the team. They all looked up to him and he treated them all so well as he did everybody. I had a lot of confidence that he would do well in life. People like Patrick find success.

My last memory of Pat was topside at Cleveland Yachting Club. Chris was there, and we were enjoying a beer on a beautiful day. Before he left that day, I mentioned to him privately that things can change, and after a year or so, if he wanted to reconsider playing, I would help.

I miss him. I miss that I didn't have the chance to belly up with him as an adult and have fun with him, not as a coach but as a friend. God Bless #13."

The Pattersons
Family friends, Sydney

"We still remember the day Patrick appeared at Trumper Oval with his raspy voice and a Sherrin under his arm.

He was way beyond his years. He found the kid who went without a kick all season and passed him the ball and the boy at school without a friend. He happily stood up to injustice.

We all had our own relationship with him that we felt was just ours. He joined so many families as that 'other' brother. It has taken him leaving us to realize this feeling spread throughout schools, communities, sport, and countries. We are lost around the world without you.

There is no sense in any of this Paddy Green. We love you to infinity and beyond. We will never ever forget that little boy who walked onto Trumper Oval all those years ago.

Just like the Pirates, we just wanted longer on the field with you, PMG."

Annie Hlad
Neighbor and family friend, Cleveland

"If ever there was someone who could make me smile, it was Patrick. I mean, that guy was a lightning bolt. His eyes lit up; he'd flash his smile, say something funny and brighten everything up. That infectious personality, he just made everything more fun, happier, and better around here.

When outside, he always stopped to chat or yell something out of the car at me. When 'my guys', Patrick and Brady, came over to 'shoot the breeze,' I always knew it was them. They'd keep ringing my door-bell non-stop like maniacs till I answered. I always opened the door with, 'Gee, who could that be?!!' We'd just talk and laugh so darn hard about stuff, baseball, sports, music, politics, the neighborhood, whatever. I liked that Patrick was always interested in my opinion on things. He pitched in whenever I needed help, thanked me over and over, and complimented me often. He made me feel important; he made me feel good inside. Patrick used to say, 'Annie, I haven't stopped by for a while; I didn't want you to think I'd forgotten about you.' Like I'll ever forget him, my friend.

I'm so thankful you all moved here. Be proud that all of you helped shape Patrick into the genuine, loving, and giving person he was, who touched so many in his one-of-a-kind way."

Kristen Kalinowski
Patrick's FMP, Fashion and Design, and Early Childhood Development teacher, Cleveland

"Patrick was a wonderful young man and I truly looked forward to seeing him each day. When Pat was in my classroom, the atmosphere was different. I don't know how to explain it, but he had a calming effect on others. Maybe it was his sense of humor; even on days when I was not having a great day, he found a way to make me smile and laugh. Many of my fondest memories of Pat are from FMP (Freshman Mentoring Program). Having him in the program for two years was very special because he really connected with the freshmen who seemed to need a positive role model in their lives. We had a student who was struggling academically and was not re-sponding to adult interventions, so I asked Pat to step in. I introduced them to each other, and for the rest of the semester, Pat spent every day encouraging this young man. The student was not very social and was very hard to reach, but Pat was never discour-aged by his lack of interaction; in fact, he seemed even more compassionate towards him because of that. It was instances like that where Pat shined. When a student was giving me a hard time, or I was frustrated, Pat had a way of lightening the mood without making anyone feel bad.

It was Patrick's larger than life personality and compassion for others that carried him through life. He made friends everywhere he went. When I think of Patrick, these are the words that come to mind: caring, fun-loving, charming, helpful, humble, funny, calming, mentor, friend, talented, trusting, mature, teammate, charismatic, friendly, positive, fun, the life of the party, and dynamic."

Julie Hill
Family friend, Cleveland

"I always knew upon walking into the Green household, there would be a hug waiting from Patrick. Not just any old hug, but a joyful, 'so happy to see you,' full bear hug. He always took the time to stop what he was doing (basketball, sports, bounding around the house) and make a point to greet me, everyone really. I have a fond memory of him leaving the sideline just before his football game on Senior Night to jog over and greet me with one of those big hugs and thank us for coming. I will never forget seeing him play his last game on a cold, wintry, wet Cleveland night, and sharing the pride that Sara and Chris had for their son. Patrick sought Sara out immediately after the game and embraced her right in the middle of all the football players. An amazing son. A spectacular person. His light and love and joyful presence in this world cannot be overstated. I loved Patrick."

The Robertsons
Family friends, Cleveland

"When I think of Patrick, the following words come to mind: funny, kind, charismatic, adventurous, carefree, handsome, charming, and confident. Simply put, Patrick was one of those rare individuals who possessed what some refer to as the 'It' factor. He was the guy who everyone wanted to be around; the person who exhibited magnetism that made others want to gravitate towards him; everyone wanted to be on his team; he had a self-awareness that affected the way he behaved and treated others; he had superior communication skills, mostly because he could actively listen to others. Although some would argue that people can learn to have behaviors like this, in my opinion, these are traits that you can't teach, you either have them, or you don't.

I had the privilege of getting to know Sarah's friends over the years as they spent a fair amount of time at our house. Kevin and I loved this because it gave us many opportunities to see the kids interact and get to know the friends that our kids have chosen to surround themselves with. Many kids slink in and out of the house, passing us in awkward silence, or a fleeting 'hello/goodbye.' Not Patrick. Patrick was the friend who always greeted us properly, looked us in the eye, and engaged immediately. He always made conversation and acted interested in whatever we had going on. He inevitably put a smile on our faces and made us laugh.

One night we came home from an event and Patrick was over. He came into the kitchen to greet us when we arrived home. He had recently learned from Sarah that our favorite drink was the Moscow Mule. He asked if he could make us each one. Of course, we accepted. I had to teach him exactly how to make it (or rather, how we preferred it), and forever after that, every time he was over, he would ask us if he could make us one. I can't think of another friend of Sarah's who would have taken the time or interest to do something like that. It became a funny bond between us that I will always cherish. To this day, every time Kevin and I have Moscow Mules (and that's pretty often), it makes us think of Patrick and smile.

Aside from the personal interactions I have with Sarah's friends, I feel that the best way I got to know all of them was through Sarah's eyes. She always shared funny stories of Patrick, silly videos, and pictures of him; he endlessly made her laugh and was always able to put a smile on her face. They had a very pure friendship that was genuine and effortless. They looked out for each other, and I know Patrick was one of Sarah's closest male friends who she could turn to for advice or support if she ever needed a male opinion on something. I know Sarah will cherish that friendship forever.

Patrick was truly one of the most charismatic young adults I have ever known. We feel blessed to have had him in our lives for even the short time we knew him. He forever impacted our children and us. I have talked to Nathan about a lot of the amazing attributes that Patrick had as a young man that he should always remember and strive towards. In Nathan's own words, 'Be like Pat'."

The Boettchers
Family friends, Cleveland

"We are so grateful that football brought our families together. What a fun and special season and senior year we all shared.

Patrick's greatest gifts were his extraordinary emotional intelligence, admirable kindness, and exceptional humor. Sara and Chris, the greatest gifts you gave to Patrick were your unconditional love and support. You facilitated and guided Patrick to use his special talents for the betterment of others especially his friends, teammates, people with special needs, and those who do not always find it easy to have a voice and connect with others. Annabelle and Matilda, your greatest gifts to Patrick, were being loving sisters offering guidance, humor, and a candid, sisterly perspective when needed.

When the Green family met with the football team shortly after the accident, you showed Patrick's teammates what it meant to be a good mate and how to support one another with dignity, grace, and class. An important life lesson in the midst of great sadness and tragedy. The funeral service for Patrick was beautiful and inspirational. You taught a community the importance and value of compassion, grace, and forgiveness."

Lisa:
"We were at a football team dinner. The team had not been playing to its potential and they were playing catch-up football. To make a

point, we had a ketchup bottle and were joking with the players as they came through the serving line, asking if they wanted ketchup with their food because they seemed to like playing 'ketchup' football. Patrick immediately made the connection and replied, 'Mrs Boettcher, are you busting on us for our game focus?' When I replied, 'Yes we are,' Patrick just laughed and brought his teammates along with the joke. Fast forward to November and the end of season dinner that the Greens hosted at their home. We were all chatting and somehow, I mentioned that I was behind on grading. Patrick didn't miss a beat and replied, 'Mrs Boettcher, I don't think teachers are supposed to play 'ketchup' grading.' Patrick's humor and quick wit brightened a room. It was always great fun to see Patrick and his teammates on the field, at team dinners, senior dinners, and 5th quarter parties. His kind words, laughter, jokes, camaraderie, determination, and those amazing punts. Whenever I see a well-kicked punt at a football game, I will forever think of Patrick. Patrick's positive attitude, energy, and athletic talent changed this football season, the players, the coaches, the parents, and the fans for the good."

Jeff:
"On the field: I always knew that punting was an athletic endeavor which also took some forethought. What I came to learn and appreciate through the years of watching Patrick play, however, was just how intelligent he was at optimizing his craft, planning, and executing every single play for the best possible outcome for the team. He always had a plan for what he wanted to do, and he would follow that plan to the length that the situation allowed him to. When a variable changed that could derail it, seemingly without panic or effort, he could instantly evolve the play into something completely different, to maximize the outcome. At that point, I came to know that it was something more than just a football play we were all witnessing; it was pure art, and so I never wanted to miss a play when Patrick 'The Artist' was painting a new piece on his canvas!

Off the field: The myriad of times where a simple, 'Hi Patrick' would be met with a bright, 'Hello Mr Boettcher' and a hearty handshake. The exchange was without fail, positive, and uplifting. I realize now that I always sought out Patrick for that greeting for the same reason that everyone else did; he would uplift me even if I wasn't feeling on top of my own game. While I know that God made Patrick Green a most remarkable one-of-a-kind young man, it is my hope that the rest of us can learn from his legacy, and with his memory as a guide, institute those blessings and aptitudes into our own daily lives for the betterment of others, just as Patrick did.

Patrick Green, we are glad we knew you. Patrick, Sara, Chris, Annabelle, and Matilda, because of you, the Boettchers have been changed for the good."

Lisa Kahl
Friend and writer, Cleveland
Lisa wrote the following poem:

Patrick rode a rainbow,
With his bunny by his side,
Into the arms of Christ the King,
In whom he did confide...

"My Lord, My God, My Savior,
Are you sure it's not too soon?
For my mother is not ready,
To face my empty room."

Sweet son you'll see the plans I have,
And the strength your mother carries,
To heal, to love, to nourish,
To write said adversaries.

For now you are her angel,
Whose wings keep her from falling,
As she navigates life's deepest grief,
Sure to lead her to her true calling.

Eliza Wing
Writer and author, Cleveland

"Live like Patrick. I went to a funeral for a young man yesterday. The service was filled to overflowing, music filled the room, and sorrow filled our hearts. The community of grief. The community of loss. I didn't know the boy or even his mother that well. But I knew of her teachings, and her dear friends are women I hold in my heart and admire; they are loving, strong, and heart-filled.

I stood through the service in the back behind several rows of sweet boys in jackets who sat up straight except when they couldn't bear it, and they had to lean forward and pinch at the bridge of their noses to hold the tears. I wanted to soothe and help each one of them.

Here's what I thought in the midst of all the grief - we should all Live like Patrick:

Live inclusively. Relate to the strong, the weak, the shy - notice the person in the corner of the room and befriend them - bring them in. If they can't leave the corner, go to where they are.

Tell it and don't hold back. Be with your family and friends, each one of them. Let them know your best and worst thoughts. Lean on them. Let them lean on you.

Don't take relationships for granted. Take the time to have that lunch with your mom, hang out with your sisters. If you have an impulse to see or talk with someone - follow it. Time goes so quickly, sometimes tragically so.

Love yourself. Take pride in who you are. A lot of work went into the person that you are. If you are young, enjoy the youth, and the strength of your body, the quickness of your feet. If you are older, praise the change, you have lived long enough to see it.

If you have a talent or a gift, develop it but only as far as you can enjoy it. Do not let it become a burden. Use that gift as a transmission of you, of joy. Share it.

Above all, be kind to everyone you encounter whether they are a stranger or friend. Be kind to yourself as well, so that you have the capacity to extend your kindness.

240

This is probably only a tiny fraction of who Patrick was, but it is what I learned from him yesterday. I thank the Greens for a generous, deeply moving ceremony. I speak for myself but more than likely for many in the church yesterday - I could only hope to live Patrick's qualities and perhaps by doing so make the world just a little sweeter."

Maureen Arbeznik
Patrick's 8th grade French teacher, principal, and my friend, Cleveland

"When a teacher is asked to recall a student she has taught, a rush of memories might course through her mind. Can she even remember the student? Where did he sit in class? Who were his friends? What kind of student was he? Were there any memorable interactions with him, good or bad? The more years she has taught, unfortunately, the greater the possibility will be that if the student was somewhat 'vanilla,' the less likely it will be that she will remember anything about him, save his name. There are those students, however, whom, once their name is mentioned, she can not only accurately provide a ready answer to all those questions, but the mere mention of his name can trigger a rush of joy and bring a smile to her face. So, it was with Patrick Green.

What was it about Patrick that made him so unforgettable? One could easily point to his sparkling eyes, his jet-black hair, and his beautiful smile. One might also mention the charm of his Australian accent or the way he took over a room once he entered it. Although all of these things are noteworthy and true, I think Patrick made such an impact on so many people in such a short period of time because of his character and the love he exhibited for his family, which far exceeded his physical attributes.

I met Patrick when he was in his early adolescence, not an easy time of life for a young man, and often not an easy age group for teachers who not only have to teach but also manage a classroom that has in it a charming student with many followers. I was Patrick's French teacher but was also serving my final year as principal during his 8th grade year. During Patrick's high school years, I would occasionally run into him around town. If anything, his charm and his handsomeness had increased as he was always in the company of a pretty young girl. He always greeted me with a huge grin and a big hug - another testament to the character of an extraordinary young man.

As I near the end of my teaching career, I am grateful not only for the hundreds of students and families who I taught but also for the students and families who taught me. Patrick Green and his family are among the top in that category."

Megan O'Bryan
Family friend, Cleveland

"Patrick was such a bright light. When Kevin met Patrick at your house, he walked away impacted by him. That night, Patrick got up and offered sweet and funny remarks before announcing the BBQ winners. We got in the car and Kevin said, 'Wow, what a great kid to engage and talk with everyone and to get up so confidently in front of the room.'"

Mandy Coombs
Family friend, Melbourne

"Even at seven years of age, Patrick was a big enough man to be my son's only friend. Patrick looked well beyond Thibault's autism and quirky ways and only saw a heart, cheekiness, and sense of family and friends that matched his. We love you Patrick."

Symantha Bowen
My friend, Cleveland

"I came to know Patrick through Sara's love as his mother. Each time I saw Patrick, there was a lightness about him, a kindness, and a warmth. The incredible love that you all had and have for one another was very apparent to me. Your home always exuded this love."

Pat Cunningham
Family friend, Melbourne

"It can be so difficult to watch the world keep happening around you when other people's lives continue on as they did before that moment when yours turned inside out. When those close to you get up and go to work like 'normal' when your life is so not normal. Continuing to hold your breath as the next set of waves dumps you. You learn to ride the waves.

There will be people you do want to hear from and don't and others you don't and do. There will be people meaning well and making a hash of it and others doing just the right things in the right moments. It's those who give without expectation that are keepers.

I ran a half marathon recently and when my sad excuses for legs were getting heavy, I took a moment and thought, 'I hope Sara and Chris are putting one foot in front of the other.'

Just keep moving forward team. You're not moving away from Patrick - you never will. You are just slowing picking up the pace while you bring him with you."

John McKenna
Patrick's high school English teacher and family friend, Cleveland

"Music Monday is:
1. A way to ease into 'the Mondays'.
2. A way to get kids talking in spite of themselves.
3. A way to connect kids to poetry - every song is a poem.
4. A low-key backhand way to get kids to appreciate poetry (rhyme, rhythm, point of view, alliteration, etc.)
5. A way for kids to look at the world and society through artists of that time.

Patrick was so into Music Mondays. To be perfectly honest, his reaction week in, week out, was exactly what I hoped for when I started doing this. My selected songs often had a low-key (or high-key) political message and Patrick routinely picked up on that. He would respond with intelligent and respectful insight and dialogue. He liked (and so did his dad) my selection of Midnight Oil's 'Beds are Burning.'

Patrick was such a delight in this and every interaction I ever had with him. I think of him often on Mondays (and all days). I think he would approve of some of my new 'adds' this year."

Joanne Ritschel
A teacher at the high school, Cleveland

"I want to tell you a sweet little story about how I met Patrick. I never had Patrick in class; I first met him when I substituted for his regular math teacher. As usual, his teacher left work for students to do, and as usual, some students were more interested in socializing than doing their assignment.

It was immediately obvious to me that Patrick was a leader of the socially gifted.

I had to decide on an approach to get the group focused. Without any reprimanding, I simply sat next to Patrick with a ruler and graph paper and started to help him with '$y=mx+b$' and graphing lines. To my pleasant surprise, Patrick cheerfully focused and went to work with me. The other students followed his lead.

I discovered a very special young man that day who taught me more than I taught him: kindness is greater than anger. After that day, he always greeted me with direct eye contact, a smile, and a cheerful, 'Hello, Mrs Ritschel.'

I am a better teacher because of Patrick, and he will continue to enrich and bless those who knew him."

Rick Schuler
Patrick's high school American History teacher, Cleveland

"To say that Patrick was a special person seems inadequate. Although I only taught him for a year, he impressed me in a way that few students have. His personality was larger than life, his charm and positive energy lit up the room, and one always came away from an encounter with Patrick feeling better about themselves and life in general.

It would not be an exaggeration to say that few students are as fun to teach or as kind and considerate to classmates. On more than one occasion, I discussed with colleagues Patrick's remarkable personality and how adept he was at relating to others.

About a year after I had Patrick as a student in my American History class, he went out of his way to stop in my classroom on the afternoon of a home boys basketball game. That evening, an outstanding high school player and University of Dayton recruit was to face the Pirates. Patrick recalled me being a UD alumnus and a very avid fan of Dayton basketball and was thoughtful enough to make sure I was aware. The following day Patrick returned to assess the performance and gather my thoughts on the UD recruit. He made my day, having thought to do that on my behalf.

The world lost a treasure with Patrick's passing, but I thank God for allowing him to cross my path. I would like to think that I am a better person for having known him. I know that I will be more apt to consider doing the little things that may lift others as a result of Patrick's example, and for all that Patrick did in the short time he was with us, I am certain he enjoys a high place in heaven."

The Realis
Family friends, Cleveland

Jenny:
"Patrick was one of Jake's closest friends. He was the life of the party. His outgoing personality lit-up every room he entered. As a

teacher at LCA, I loved seeing him in the halls. He always had a smile on his face and made it a point to say hi to me. Having Patrick at our house was joyful for all of us. Patrick showed kindness to everyone he met."

Mike:
"I would say that our fondest memories of Patrick were his friendly smile and always saying hello to Jenny and me when entering the house. Most of Jake's teenage friends would just head down to the basement, but Patrick was always the one to make a point of saying hello. It always made an impression on both of us. Jake was excited about being roommates with Patrick in college. He still carries a picture of Patrick in his wallet."

Anthony, 7th grade, who wrote the following rap song:
For Pat

It all started in 2019.
A kid that was only 19.
The future shined so bright.
I still can't believe it.
Why did it have to happen to him, to us, and to his family?

I never met a better man, a better person, a better friend.
I never saw a bigger future, a bigger dream, a bigger theme.
A day that seemed so far away happened in the blink of an eye.
So why, so why, did it happen last night?
So why, so why, did it happen at all?

Pat Green rest in peace.
You'll never be forgotten, and you will always be missed.
Why it had to happen is a mystery.
You will always be in my thoughts, my prayers,
and in everybody's memories.
Everybody will remember you as a saint and a person to look up to.

The way you brought a smile to everybody's eyes, including my brother.

I cannot lie, he will cherish you and his memories for his entire life. You might not be here physically, but you will always be in our hearts.

Pat Green rest in peace.
You'll never be forgotten, and you will always be missed.
Why it had to happen is a mystery.
You will always be in my thoughts, my prayers and in everybody's memories.

For years to come, you will always be remembered as the one who, with my brother, ate six waffles each.
Or when you played CYO basketball and people would yell out of the stands, "Give the sharp-shooter the ball."
And for all the other people who you impacted in a way that no-one could ever do.
I don't know anyone who could have been a better friend, a better brother or son.
A better man.
Miss you Pat.

Trisha Brown
Mother of Patrick's friend, Ian Bodell, Cleveland

"Ian always appreciated the way Patrick would make him smile. Enclosed is a check for Patrick's scholarship fund. I want to tell you the story behind the check because it illustrates the ripple effects of goodness and generosity in the world that your son created.

Ian played rugby this spring 2019 for a neighboring club team. In early June, the team went to the state finals and won. A week or so later, Ian got a text asking him if he wanted to buy a championship ring, which of course he did, but it was expensive. I told him I'd pay half, so he ordered the ring.

When Patrick died, and we learned about his volunteering and outreach at St Malachi, Ian asked the person ordering the rings if it was too late to cancel his order so he could donate the money instead to St Malachi in Patrick's honor and memory.

Shortly afterwards, Ian received a group text saying that many of the boys from the team chipped in to buy the ring for Ian so he could have it, but most importantly, so he could donate in his friend's memory.

In my mind, your son's good and generous work enabled a whole group of other young men to step up and be good and generous. I believe ripples keep us all afloat and connected. Patrick's ripples are real and continue to grow."

Lorelle Parsons
Family friend, Sydney

"I first met Patrick when he was around 11 or 12, and he came to the door to pick up Annabelle. As the extraction was always a slow process separating Olivia and Annabelle, we had time to chat and chat we did. I have never before or since then met a more engaging and articulate boy of his age, and I was very impressed. After they left, I called out to my girls, 'I would be very happy for one of you to end up marrying Patrick Green!' Not something I would usually say to them, but I knew in that moment I had just met someone special. I will always think of him as my first son-in-law."

Guy Biasotta
Patrick's volunteer co-ordinator at St Malachi's Back Door Ministry, Cleveland

"As his volunteer work supervisor for the past four years, I have witnessed the exceptional contributions that Patrick has made to our church and ministry community. Not only is he an excellent and hard-working volunteer, but he has dedicated himself to enriching the lives of fellow volunteers and those less fortunate in our community. Patrick is truly special for his compassion and commitment to helping others. Many we serve are battling mental health issues, hunger, lack of seasonal clothing, or even basic medical care. After enduring the challenge of moving to Ohio from Australia in the prime teenage years, Patrick has devoted himself to bringing greater awareness about inner-city issues to his family and classmates, many of who volunteer with us now after Patrick's recruitment. He has grown to have a powerful voice in our community, speaking up for what he believes in and proving himself to be an impassioned and inspiring leader. The other volunteers and I would describe Patrick as an insightful, sensitive, perceptive, and diligent young man. He is a kind, compassionate, intelligent, and strong person who has a clear sense of direction and purpose."

John Tucci
Patrick's baseball coach, Cleveland

"I knew Patrick from his baseball playing days. I was lucky enough to coach him in the Rec Pony League. I don't need to tell you what a good kid he was, on earth and in heaven, but I will relay a short story.

I saw Patrick at a graduation party. He immediately brought up the good times (and championship) we had in that season. He told me I was 'his second favorite baseball coach ever, behind Mr Chamberlin.' That comment from him brought me joy and pride. His ability to lift people up was a true gift."

Marilyn Jones
Patrick's 3rd grade teacher, Sydney

"I often think about the year I had Patrick in my class. His energy, warmth, and enthusiasm were contagious. Patrick's smiling face is locked in my heart."

Matt Sterling
Family friend, Melbourne

"When my son started school, I gave him some 'rules' about introducing himself to teachers and kids. I told him about Patrick Green, and we now have 'the Patrick Green rule,' named in Patrick's honor. The rule is that he, and of course all of us, have to look after the person on the edge of the room. That he is to stick up for all kids and not follow the pack, especially when the pack acts wrongly or cruelly. That Patrick was greatly respected by his friends and everybody because he had the strength of character, the courage if you like, to always look for the kid on the edge of the room. Thank you, Patrick."

After Patrick's accident, we were blessed with hundreds of emails, letters, and cards from people, both here in the United States and Australia. Here are some of the many heartfelt words written about our beautiful boy who we so deeply miss:

- "Patrick is held in the highest regard by everyone who knew him, from teachers to coaches to other parents at the high school. His impact on the community is the rainbow; Patrick was the sunshine."

- "One in a million."

- "Always a great story associated with his name."

- "My memory of little Patrick Green is of his beautiful manners and his twinkling eyes when he smiled and laughed."

- "Patrick's angel wings are wrapped around you."

- "An amazing and beautiful soul who changed the lives of those he touched for the better."

- "I was always impressed by the way he carried himself."

- "We miss Patrick's warm smile."

- "A remarkable young man, so loving, caring and thoughtful."

- "Such a beautiful, confident young man with a charming character."

- "A great work ethic."

- "A blessing to this community."

- "I love the way his mind works. We will remember Patrick forever. His most beautiful soul."

- "Patrick had a friendly, easy-going manner. He encouraged players who struggled, a total team player and a pleasure to have on the team. We truly don't know God's plan for Patrick, but we do know it must be something really big that he requires this sweet young man to be part of his team."

- "We remember his smiling face as a three year old pre-schooler."

- "He touched more lives in his 19 years than most could ever dream to."

- "A beautiful soul who the gates of heaven opened so wide for."

- "Amazing and remarkable traits."

- "He always had a twinkle in his eye and a warm smile."

- "He clearly lived his life with a heart full of kindness and brought joy and comfort to so many."

- "His compassionate spirit and bright light."

- "We will honor Patrick's life by striving to live with gratitude, caring for the less fortunate, and cherishing the love of family and friends."

- "Patrick's words and shining light will follow you everywhere and guide you continuously through each life event, day, hour, and breath."

- "The impression he made on me was immediate and lasting."

- "My son always appreciated the way Patrick could make him smile."

- "A precious angel who so positively impacted the world."

- "He was so wonderful with special needs kids."

- "Your son was a gleaming example of the good."

- "What a remarkable son you created - he will forever be remembered."

- "His uplifting effect on family members, friends, teammates, and even strangers."

- "So many people have spoken so highly as to what a fine man he was."

- "Patrick was such a great kid - so well-liked."

- "Anyone who knew Patrick has only the nicest things to say about him."

- "Patrick was such an exceptional and well-loved young man."

- "The most vibrant of young men."

- "The first baby I ever held and the sweetest little boy."

- "We were so impressed with Patrick's sincere, engaging manner."

- "Patrick was a great teammate. He was always approachable. He had an uplifting attitude and cared about those around him."

- "His enthusiasm had no bounds, the energy he brought to everything could lift anyone up. I remember at a party I didn't know the crowd well, and Patrick immediately came up to me and asked how I'd been, and we had a conversation. His ability to include others was in full swing. I plan to take some pages from Patrick's book and embrace them for the greater good of others."

- "I will always remember asking Annabelle and Patrick to read out loud in my class so I could hear their beautiful Australian accents."

- "Patrick was always so polite and cheerful, such a good boy."

- "The first time I met Patrick, I remember the feeling more than the dialogue. What a darling and kind kid, I thought. Patrick would always say hello to me. Respectful, funny, charismatic, and kind. Values that I admired in a young adult in his high school years."

- "We all loved Patrick dearly and will miss him and his joyful presence in our home. He is an inspiration to us all."

- "Patrick was a wonderful boy, full of love and laughter. He was always respectful and personable - he could have an intelligent conversation with anyone young or old, he was a joy to have around."

- "It takes a special kid for me to take additional notice, and I must tell you that Patrick was one of those few. He would always initiate greetings and conversations with me and was exceptionally nice and respectful. I could tell that his peers liked him and respected him, and having interacted with Patrick, I can see why."

- "As I hear of all the accolades about your son, I am particularly moved that he had a special gift for individuals with disabilities. Raising a child that radiates this kind of compassion exemplifies the values he has been taught at home. It was his rare ability to see through the 'different-ness,' show respect, kindness, and love regardless."

- "No-one ever said anything bad about Patrick; he was good to everyone."

- "Patrick made a joyful and profound impact on those lucky people who got to share in his life. He showed kindness and compassion to those less fortunate, selflessness through mentoring, and an undying devotion and love to family."

- "It was an honor to coach him in Little League, play alongside him in football, or talk to him about his plans for the University of Cincinnati."

- "I remember Patrick talking to one of the special needs kids at a school basketball game, taking care of him, being a friend, and I thought, 'What a good kid.'"

- "The spirit of your son soars on; hundreds of young lives have been inspired by his example."

- "Patrick had a big heart."

- "He was just the nicest kid; he remembered everyone."

- "Patrick and his caring ways, his inclusion of others, his sensitive soul, he made so many people very happy."

- "Our hearts are breaking."

- "Patrick had a welcoming heart, a down-to-earth loving spirit, and a positive energy that was contagious."

- "Patrick was such a kind boy; I will always remember him looking after the younger boys, sitting on a log fishing at our camping trip in Bathurst."

- "Warm, kind, funny, smart, and handsome."

- "We will always remember Patrick as the kindest, most caring, and genuine person. He always put a smile on people's faces, no matter what."

- "Patrick lit up every room and his smile shined."

- "Patrick was such a light."

- "I can honestly say that attending Patrick's funeral was the most heartbreakingly moving experience of my life. He was a special young man adored by all who knew him."

- "He had a heart of gold."

- "May the light of your lives, Patrick, continue to shine down on you all."

- "Patrick was an amazing young man. Watching him interact with everyone was incredible. He was so kind and set such a great example for everyone who looked up to him."

- "Patrick was a beautiful soul. I saw the kindness and leadership he possessed. He was always smiling, and you always knew he was just happy and content with life. He will be missed dearly."

- "I met Patrick when we volunteered at Challenge Days and was so impressed by his kindness, warmth, and ability to relate to both middle school and high school students. He was loved by all and truly a gem. A special young man who touched many hearts."

- "Patrick came right over to my son on his first day of school to make sure he felt comfortable. His happiness was infectious."

- "Patrick was so polite and would always chat. I felt a special connection with him, but you know that was one of his many gifts. He made everyone feel that special connection."

- "Every single interaction and conversation with Patrick was so positive and free of negativity."

- "Our son is a rising freshman on the football team. He said, 'Patrick was so nice to me when I was a ball boy.'"

- "Patrick's presence lit up a room. His outlook on life was optimistic and the work he completed was always diligent."

- "His easy smile, casual personality, and joyful outlook will not be forgotten. Patrick gave us a blueprint for how to get along with all people and how to love unconditionally."

THANK YOU

We would like to thank each and every person who shared their stories, favorite memories, funny moments, and the things they loved about Patrick. We have read every word of your contributions. To be able to collate them as a collection in this chapter of the book has been an enormous gift to us. We now have a record of priceless reflections that will be cherished by our family for generations to come.

"Rather than drown in the darkness of our grief, we focus on our gratitude for the time we had with Patrick. We can learn from his example. This is our way forward."

CHAPTER ELEVEN

PATRICK'S LESSONS

The qualities that defined Patrick, the qualities that we loved about him, are the reasons we miss him beyond words. Losing him has amplified the many lessons he has taught us, and he will continue to guide us very powerfully with his spiritual presence and love. Rather than drown in the darkness of our grief, we focus on our gratitude for the time we had with him. We can learn from his example. This is our way forward.

As a way to accept our loss of Patrick, we take the perspective that he did all he was here to do in just 19 years. Some say angels are called home early because they are needed for work at a much higher level. I believe Patrick is doing this work now. He was made for it because he understands life and people. He is now in a place where he has had all of life's teachings transferred to him. He is our teacher, spiritual guide, and guardian angel.

As you read in the previous chapter, Patrick touched so many lives in so many ways in a short time. We are all left wanting more, but with Patrick, there was never going to be enough time. So, we ask ourselves, what can we learn from being given this gift of knowing and loving him as our son, brother, grandson, nephew, cousin, and friend?

This memoir has gifted me the opportunity to be the conduit for Patrick's messages. My intention for the coming pages is to inspire, motivate, encourage, perhaps shift your mindset, and open your heart.

Patrick wants you all to feel welcome to take what you need from his teachings.

Here are his lessons:

LOVE DEEPLY

Patrick loved us and we loved him, unconditionally. He still does and so do we, very much and forever. Patrick openly extended his love to his great-grandparents, grandparents, aunts, uncles, cousins, and friends. When he was born, he had seven great-grandparents and four grandparents. Minus one great-grandparent, it was almost a full set of two generations. That in itself was quite remarkable. In most branches of the family trees, he was the first-born great-grandchild and the first-born grandchild. He was adored and very fortunate to be surrounded by so much love. It brings us comfort to know that he is with his great-grandparents who are now all in heaven: Erena and Victor Foulds, Florence and Ernest Chambers, Nance and Syd Green, and Maureen and Ralph Sierakowski.

The Green family

As babies and small children, Patrick and Annabelle were especially close with Nance and Syd, Chris's paternal grandparents. If we hadn't been to visit them in a few days, I would receive a phone call from Syd asking when we were coming again. We may have even just been there the day before and I would still get a call, they wanted us there as much as possible, and the feeling was mutual. With Syd, they would "fix" his red car, ask him questions about all his tools in the garage, help him pick his homegrown tomatoes, have horsey rides on his leg, devour his bacon and eggs and wait earnestly for him to offer his treats; Juicy Fruit chewing gum and Lift soft drink. With Nance, they would sit on her lap and read stories, "help" her with her crosswords, chat away about anything and everything, and they loved "Nance's roast potatoes." Then there was her lolly (candy) jar that was always well stocked, a little kid's dream. Again, they would wait in anticipation for her to invite them to go to the pantry and choose a lolly, or three.

Patrick shared a very close bond with his grandmother, Rita, and grandfather, Michael. His aunts and uncles: Rich and Mel (his God-parents), Catherine and Lochie, Matt and Sam, Sarah and Grant, and his cousins: Tom, Josh, Will, Lochie, Frankie and Sid were all a huge part of his life, just as they are with Annabelle, and Matilda. His aunts and uncles doted on him as a baby, played all sorts of games with him over the years, showed a great interest in all he did throughout his life, and had really started to enjoy a beautiful friendship with him as an adult. As a group of nine, all the cousins were very close. Although they have grown up living geographically apart, they have stayed connected, and as soon as they reunited, it was all about fun and laughter. Patrick relished cousin time. There was never a squabble; they only wanted to be together. Something his aunt, Catherine, said to me a few months after we lost Patrick has stayed with me in a profound way. She was reflecting on the magnitude of the loss on our family and our relationship with one another, and she said, "We think of one another's children as if they are our own." I appreciated the way she articulated our collective pain.

Over the years, we have created wonderful Green family traditions. Saturday mornings at the Queen Victoria Market and Don Camillo's café in West Melbourne, where Patrick's favorite thing to eat at the market were the warm jam donuts. We have had many holidays together. In Australia, we made memories in Byron Bay, Magnetic Island, Sydney, and Melbourne. Patrick absolutely loved these vacations and the time spent with all our family. The count-less hours of football and cricket, card games and Cluedo, water skiing, body surfing, swimming, the pool and beach volleyball competitions, and when they were younger, exploring the mangroves pretending they were Bear Grylls, and dancing, singing and acting in the family home movies. The endless banter, laughs, and debates. We all love cooking and enjoying good food and some of our best times have been sitting around the table sharing a meal.

The 2018 Green family Christmas in California (Disneyland, San Diego, and Venice Beach) was known as "Greens on Tour." We had two styles of customized t-shirts printed with logos that we all wore; it was awesome. After this trip, Patrick declared it his "best holiday ever!"

The last time the 21 of us were physically together was for Matt and Sam's wedding in Melbourne in April 2019, just two months before Patrick died. Matt and Sam asked all their nieces and nephews to be in their junior bridal party. These memories are now cherished even more. The friendships that formed between the Green cousins and Sam's nieces and nephews were a joy to see; they started to call one another cousins from the moment they met.

The Chambers family

Patrick also enjoyed making memories with our family on my side, the Chambers. Growing up, he spent a lot of time with his Nanna Bev, Pa Kev, and Auntie Narelle. When he was young, we loved living close by to his great-grandmother, Erena, who our kids called Gigi. We would often visit Gigi and she would give Patrick and Annabelle special treats; they especially loved the apricot delights in the glass jar with the yellow lid in her pantry. They would go straight to the toy box that she kept under the bed in her spare room. We went on many walks with Gigi, trips to the park, car rides, and sometimes she would take Patrick up to the local train station where he loved watching all the trains come and go. Such simple pleasures. As a small boy, he enjoyed going on outings with Nanna Bev and spending time at her house. Pa Kev taught him about fishing and playing the guitar, and when he came to Cleveland a few years ago, he went to one of Patrick's football games. When we visited Melbourne, Patrick was able to see his cousin, Charlotte.

Family was central to Patrick's life. My heart breaks for his grandparents, aunts, uncles, and cousins when I consider the impact losing Patrick has had on them. Their grief and sadness are immeasurable. Thankfully they have countless beautiful memories of being with him that are forever in their hearts, and I know these memories make them smile. The cousins had made future life plans together that included travel and fun. I wish their time together to enjoy these experiences hadn't been cut short. Patrick enjoyed special relationships with each family member, and he cherished them all.

BE A FRIEND TO ALL

Our family friends here in Cleveland, the Kelleys, coined the phrase "Friend to all" to describe Patrick, and we think it's perfect. He made time for everyone and he made every single person feel special. He had friends of all ages, from little kids to his friend's grandma, who referred to him as her "boyfriend." Patrick was a relationship builder. His relationships were very important to him. They were far-reaching and he was able to nurture multiple connections simultaneously.

BE KIND

Patrick had a really kind heart. He cared about others and his genuine kindness left a lasting impression on so many people. Chapter Ten is a true testament to the impressions he made on people.

MAKE THE MOST OF YOUR STRENGTHS

High emotional intelligence and a people person; these were definitely some of Patrick's signature strengths. Signature strengths are qualities that come effortlessly to you, and they are innate characteristics of your personality. They may be attributes and talents that you identify in yourself or traits that others compliment you on. Patrick understood people and this was always going to be his gift moving forward in his life. From a very young age, he had a magnetic personality. He knew how to read a situation and act with compassion. He made others feel seen and heard. He had an ease about him. He was great company and he always found a way to have fun.

LEAD WITH HUMILITY, LET GO OF YOUR EGO

Patrick showed leadership qualities from a young age, but he was not ego-driven. He led with humility. He didn't seek accolades for his achievements.

DON'T BE AFRAID TO SHOW YOUR EMOTIONS

Patrick expressed his emotions freely. He was sensitive. He cried openly, loved wholeheartedly, and he leaned into vulnerability without fear. He wore his heart on his sleeve and I loved that about him.

TRULY SEE PEOPLE, INCLUDE THOSE IN THE CORNER OF THE ROOM

From a young age, this was one of Patrick's most endearing qualities. He saw people on a deeper level beyond the surface. He looked past any physical or emotional barriers, and he treated everyone equally. He made a conscious effort to include the special needs students, new kids at school, or anyone who needed a friend. In 5th grade in Australia, Patrick caught the ferry home from school. A mother told me that he was the only boy who walked to the ferry stop with her son, who would otherwise walk by himself every day. In football, he let the younger kids stretch him out during the warm-ups, which meant a lot to them because they looked up to the older varsity players.

LIFT OTHERS UP, YOUR ENERGY IS CONTAGIOUS

Patrick had the ability to lift others up. To see the positive difference that a magnetic personality like his can have on others is something we can all learn from. When he walked into a room, he lit it up; the energetic vibration rose to another level. People often said that about him. This teaches us that our energy is contagious. Think about what sort of energy you project when you are with people. At any moment, we can choose to be the person who is uplifting.

SEEK JOY AND HAVE FUN, LIVE YOUR LIFE FULLY

Patrick was truly joyful. He spread joy and lived joyfully. He never missed an opportunity to have fun. He lived and loved his life fully.

DON'T FORGET YOUR MANNERS

Chris and I like to believe that all our children have good manners. This was something we instilled in them from a young age. I was always very proud of Patrick's manners. He was polite, looked people in the eye when he spoke to them, shook hands firmly, and was respectful.

HUG FREELY

Patrick really was the greatest hugger. His hugs were genuine, relaxed, comforting, and frequent. He didn't hesitate to show affection; he loved willingly. I was always so grateful that as he got older, he never stopped hugging me. His hugs are one of the things I miss the most, I think of them often, and I wish so much that I could feel them again.

BE A MAN FOR OTHERS

Patrick's innate awareness of others, their feelings, and their situations meant that he was able to see outside himself and be of service to make a difference. He used his strengths to make others smile, laugh, and just generally feel better about themselves.

GENEROSITY IS GOLDEN

Patrick was generous. He didn't place value on material possessions; relationships mattered most to him. He didn't care about money. He would usually spend his money on other people; he rarely spent it on himself. He was also generous with his time and his love.

LISTEN MORE

Patrick was a great listener. He understood when someone needed his undivided attention. He listened with intention and he was present. His sensitivity and gentle, empathetic nature made others feel comfortable to share with him. He was interested in their story and he cared.

DON'T HOLD GRUDGES

Patrick had an incredible ability to let things go, a good lesson in non-attachment for all of us. He rarely held a grudge. He was able to shift his mindset and move on. I always admired his ability to do this. It was so refreshing that it just came naturally to him. He didn't get entangled in things that didn't matter.

BE SELF-AWARE AND UNAPOLOGETICALLY YOU

One of Patrick's defining qualities was that he was equally comfortable with who he was and with who he wasn't. He knew himself well and he accepted himself completely, a rare and admirable trait for a teenager. He wasn't influenced by outside pressures. To this day, the coaches of the high school football team shake their heads because Patrick didn't want to play wide receiver. He was happy where he was positioned as the punter and he didn't need to prove himself. He was modest about his athletic ability. When it came time to decide whether he wanted to pursue a college football career or not, he politely declined the interest from college coaches and was very comfortable with his decision.

FOLLOW YOUR INTUITION

Patrick was highly intuitive. His inner voice was his truth and it spoke very clearly to him. He didn't sway from this to follow the crowd. He often talked about his intuitive nudges and he embraced his awareness. I think it gave him a lot of inner peace, emotional freedom, and the ability to trust himself.

MAKE THE MOST OF OPPORTUNITIES, EVEN WHEN CHANGE IS HARD

Twelve years of age was a sensitive time to move countries. Patrick was well established in his friendships and his sports and accepting such a major change took courage. Chris and I felt strongly that our move would be a very positive experience for us as a family and especially for Patrick, Annabelle, and Matilda. Having the opportunity to immerse yourself in a totally different environment facilitates personal growth, and we believed it would be an enriching challenge for the three of them that we hoped they would view as a gift later in life. Without a doubt, Patrick rose to the challenge and made the most of the opportunities presented to him, creating a lifetime of memories in the short six and a half years he lived in Cleveland.

NOBODY'S PERFECT

Throughout this book, I've highlighted all of Patrick's endearing and lovable qualities. Of course, he wasn't perfect; none of us are. He was a normal teenager who pushed against boundaries. When you lose someone so precious to you, you miss it all, even the things that drove you mad. For example, I miss the sound of his voice yelling (and swearing) at his video game as I was trying to fall asleep at night. I reflect on the challenging parenting moments with Patrick and I embrace them all because we always worked through them together. He greatly respected Chris and me and our family values.

Patrick's approach to life was to lead with love, kindness, inclusivity, humility, equality, and compassion.

- What are you inspired to do more of in your life?
- Which of Patrick's lessons resonate with you?
- How would you like to be remembered?
- Do you make the most of your unique qualities?
- How do you make a difference for others?

If you have lost a loved one, take some time to think about the qualities and strengths that you admire in them. If you feel inspired to, commit to emulating these influential attributes in your own life. Use them as your role models, your guides to a more meaningful existence. If you are facing a challenge, ask yourself, what would they do and adopt this direction as best you can.

"I have learned that there is so much more than just the body. Life continues in a different form; death is not the end. Love is eternal. Connection is possible. There is a whole existence that is unseen and available to us."

CHAPTER TWELVE

PATRICK'S SIGNS

In this chapter, I share details about my communication with Patrick and the signs he has sent me and others since his passing. After reading this insight into my experience, perhaps you will discover meaning in situations or feelings that you have been unable to understand, explain, or put into words. Maybe you will make connections and gain clarity with your own communication with a loved one who has passed. Or, you may feel more confident stepping into a new way of seeing and experiencing life following a loss. Perhaps you are already connected to something more and are happily receiving signs from those who have physically departed. Conversely, what I share could bring up some resistance for you. If you are skeptical, it's okay. If this takes you to your edge of comfort, try to see it as an opportunity to open your mind to something new, knowing that in the end, it's completely up to you as to what you believe and receive.

To continue my deep connection with Patrick, I had to start to learn how to live without him in the physical. The day after the accident, he began to guide me into the spiritual realm with him, where I could feel his undeniable presence and energy. It felt like a gentle and loving coaxing, drawing me towards his soul. It was simply beautiful. I wasn't hesitant or afraid, I was right there with him, and he orchestrated it perfectly. I believe the key to me being able to do this was being open to possibility.

From what I have experienced in life with Patrick after his death, I do not doubt that we can communicate with our loved ones who have passed. It affirms our immortality; that life is unending. As humans, we tend to need the physical body as proof of life. We can see it, touch it, have a conversation with it, and hear a response. It's real, the body is tangible, has form, and it makes sense. I have learned that there is so much more than just the body. So much more. Life continues in a different form; death is not the end. Love is eternal. We live eternally. Connection is possible. There is a whole existence that is unseen and available to us.

Patrick's body was his vessel to be here with us on earth and while his body has now gone, he continues to be the love, light, and guide for so many of us through his energetic spirit. Our departed loved ones are our helpers; they are always with us. Even though they are without their physical form, their souls live on. Their consciousness still exists. Patrick is now a spirit enjoying a spiritual experience.

Don't get me wrong; I still crave Patrick's physical presence, all the time. All I want is for him to walk through the door, to be able to hug him, sit with him, visit him at college, see him get married, and be a dad. He would have been an exceptional husband, father, uncle, and grandfather. I want to know what his profession would have been. I know for sure that he would have continued to change lives for the better just by being him.

I have great faith in what is beyond the physical. I am open to learning as much as I can about the afterlife and the consciousness that continues after our physical body dies. I want to know what life is like now for Patrick. I marvel at his journey as he transitioned to where he is. In his physical life, he was comfortably connected to the spiritual realm, he saw spirits, and he willingly shared his sightings with his friends and me. He spoke of a deep fascination with the afterlife. He knew there was more. Now that he is living on the Other Side, he is showing those who are willing to see that he is still right here; he is surrounding us. His signs are his way of getting our attention. He has given me continuous signs since his passing that affirm his presence. I can feel him, hear him, and I believe in him, and his ability to connect. He also communicates with me through a small selection of my close friends, who he knows I trust. They are vessels that he channels, and he has chosen them wisely.

I can feel Patrick's spirit energy as a palpable vibration. He speaks to me with words of encouragement and he comes to me with messages that he knows I need to hear, especially when I'm meditating. These moments are private; however, I will share one that was amazing. My meditation had just ended, and immediately I started to receive messages from Patrick. I grabbed my journal and a pen and started writing. Five pages later and I was in awe. Sentence after sentence; they just kept coming. He was so clear in his message for me to step fully into writing this book, to give it my all because my voice mattered, to visualize it being a success and that we were in it together. He kept telling me that beyond the physical, "There's so much more."

He sends me signs through specific animals. The meaning of these spirit animals is always centered around family, love, community, presence, strength in adversity, healing, and affirmation that I am on the right path. One day in a yoga class, a spider (which you never usually see in the studio) came out of nowhere and made a beeline straight towards me from across the room. It walked onto my yoga mat, I felt calm, and I just let it be there. It stayed on my mat and stared up at me for a while and I acknowledged it, then it started to make its way back across the room. Other students began to feel uncomfortable; I heard one person say, "I'll just squash it with my yoga block." I was not going to let that happen. I locked eyes with the teacher, Ann, who is a good friend of mine, and she knew exactly what I was thinking, so she gently picked the spider up and placed it outside in the garden.

Patrick and I have a beautiful communication between us, for which I am very grateful. The daily missing him feels unbearable at times and knowing that he is always with me gives me great comfort.

I talk to him out loud every day. I think the out loud part is important because the spoken word is so powerful. Sometimes I ask him to show me a sign that he is with me and then I wait, and it will always appear. It may come as something I hear, read, see, or feel. There is always guidance around us; we just need to be open to it. You may hear it in a song, read it in a book, see it on a license plate or a billboard; it may be something someone says to you, a feeling you get, a familiar smell, a number or a sequence of numbers, a person's name, an animal sighting, or something in nature. There are many avenues that our loved ones use to show us that they are right beside us.

I have been fortunate to receive audible and visual messages from other relatives who have passed. When I was participating in a meditation course many years ago in Sydney, Chris's grandfather, Syd, spoke to me. His voice was as clear as a bell and his message confirmed that he was happy and okay. When I was in labor with Matilda, Chris's grandmother, Maureen, spoke to me very clearly. She was the matriarch of the family. She had raised twelve children and she was right there with me as a beautiful maternal figure to give me the encouragement and strength that I needed. I turned to Chris and told him that she just spoke to me and it was at that moment that we decided to give her name to Matilda as a middle name. A few years back, my grandmother, Florence, appeared to me in the middle of the night. She woke me by tapping my arm and I saw her right there next to the bed. She was her younger self as I remembered her in photos; her skin was like porcelain. As soon as I saw my grandma, I was flooded with feelings of peace and joy. My other grandmother, Erena, passed three months before Patrick. We knew her time to go was close, so I sat up all night meditating, waiting to hear the news from Australia. Nanna passed around 4:30 am and as I lay there with my eyes closed, absorbing the news, all of a sudden, I felt a powerful wave of her spirit come over me. I was being lifted up and I saw her face, she looked youthful, and she was wearing a white flowing gown. Her arms were outstretched to me; she was inviting me to rise up with her. We traveled together in what felt like another realm; there was a definite momentum to it, I was very calm. We got to a point and she signaled to me that I was to stop there and that she would keep going. It was, of course, her time to go, not mine. She released my hand and I watched her continue to rise; it was beautiful. I was left with an overwhelming feeling of peace, knowing that she was okay because I had seen her and felt her sense of serenity.

My heart and mind are open to as many forms of connection with Patrick as I can receive. He and I have developed our own language of communication. He comes to me in my dreams. Known as visitation dreams, this is a common way for spirits to let you know they are with you, to comfort you, and to give you messages. In these dreams, he and I have conversations, and I can feel his touch. We are both very aware of our reality; we both know that he has left the physical plane. We talk about it. Everything feels as it always did. He is him in form and his personality, mannerisms, and the sound of his voice are all the same because it is him. I feel immense reassurance from these experiences because they are real and they are an opportunity to be with him. The hardest part is that I am always left wanting more; I never want them to end. When I wake up, I focus on them staying with me. I hold them in my heart, and I soak up every detail.

I always thank Patrick for all that he is doing. The dream visitations and all his signs and messages mean so much to me. He's doing incredibly well to be able to execute them. I think that's an important point to make; we must always say thank you for all that we receive.

My close friend, Tammy, has been unwavering in her friendship with me since I lost Patrick. She always finds words that lift me up, such as these about my communication with Patrick:

"He will keep showing up. He knows it's helping you. All the work you are doing, from writing to coaching to cooking to yoga, and meditation, you are opening the channels for him to come in."

I loved that phrase, "opening the channels." It really resonated with me. The various practices that connect us to our spiritual self are the same avenues we use to channel our loved ones who have passed. If you are unsure about how to cultivate a language with the other side, identify the rituals that take you inwards, tune you into your heart, your intuition, that place where you feel a sense of peace, deep calm, and love. When you are in your own flow, your senses come alive without distraction, and you are open to receive. What does that look like for you? It could be prayer, meditation, writing, art, music, movement, dancing, dreams, nature, or sitting in stillness, to name a few. Next, notice what comes to you when you are in your spiritual practice. This sacred time is an opportunity to hear, see, and feel more. This is when messages and signs may come forth. In my experience, connection is more likely when I am present and grounded. Distraction tends to block connection.

As another way to be with Patrick, I have been seeing a psychic and medium here in Cleveland; her name is Jane Voneman-DuPerow. I would like to thank Jane for facilitating beautiful communication with Patrick. These experiences are incredibly special and the connection with Patrick is without question. It has given me added confirmation that he is fully aware and present in our lives because he communicates knowledge to me of things that have happened to our family since his passing, he comments on events that are coming up for us in the future, he refers to specific people by their names and how they are coping with his death, he describes our relationship so beautifully, and he tells me ways that he will continue to be with me. He gives me details about what it's like where he is now and how he got there so descriptively. He says I will go on to do meaningful work because of what I have experienced with his passing.

The messages that he consistently gives me are that he is happy, it's very peaceful and beautiful where he is, he wants us to be okay, we have to stay strong, he's always with us, and he's proud of us.

I keep what he specifically says to me in readings with Jane private, but I will share one example. It was just before we flew back to Australia for Christmas, six months after his passing. Patrick told me to look for eagles as a sign of his presence. At the time, I wondered whether I would see any as I had never noticed one before. Well, the sightings came thick and fast! The first happened on the day before we left Cleveland and they continued throughout our trip to Australia with several sightings at very significant times; their timing was incredible. It gave me such joy knowing Patrick was with us. Since then, I have seen many eagles. Sometimes it has been when I was out walking or sitting in his garden on a normal day. Other times it has been on the significant days when we have missed Patrick even more, such as birthdays and Annabelle's graduation; each time an eagle has appeared. When we moved Annabelle to college we were trying to find somewhere to go for lunch and realized we were standing in front of a place called *The Eagle Bar*. As we drove home that day, feeling emotional after leaving Annabelle, two eagles flew above our car. Keep in mind, as I said, I had never noticed eagles before.

Some of Patrick's friends have been to mediums and I'm always grateful when they have shared the details with me. What he said to them was specific and meaningful and confirmed his awareness of what was going on in their lives. He took the opportunity to send messages to me through these other mediums that his friends then passed on, which I always appreciated.

Patrick's friends have also received many signs from him, and I've loved it when they tell me about them. Patrick loved playing Die. Brian shared these two stories with me:

"Before every game, someone rolls the dice, and the other team calls evens or odds to determine who tosses first. The first time we played since Patty passed, we rolled two dice. So, here I was waiting for that call and they called odds, and the two numbers on the table were one and three!"

"There was a chipped dice that we lost and couldn't find anywhere. All the boys were over at the Green's house on the Sunday after the accident, and we were standing on the back patio in the bar area. All of a sudden, Michael Konrad saw the chipped dice under the bar. We now keep it to use on special occasions; we throw the first toss with it."

Over the last year, there have been many other ways that Patrick has signaled his presence. The girls and I were at an appointment and we had just sat down in the waiting room. The lady who was calling people to see the doctor yelled, "Patrick." The three of us just smiled. I have seen license plates with words of significance, cardinals have appeared just when I needed them to, several rainbows and double rainbows have emerged at meaningful times, a photo taken of Annabelle depicted the most distinctive white protective light surrounding her, I've noticed a green orb in photos and videos I've taken and on the day of Matilda's first tennis match of the season, we saw a horizontal rainbow (very rare), and an eagle glided around above the court she was playing on. He has come to us through songs and I have found feathers and coins in random places.

The day I got my tattoo, he gave me three clear signs. One, during the appointment and two on the way home, showing me that he loved that I got the tattoo we always said we were going to get together.

I often have days where I see repeating numbers all day: 10:10, 11:11, 1:11, 2:22, 3:33, etc. These are called Angel Numbers.

My friend Andrea Vecchio says, "If we could see who is walking beside us, we wouldn't live in fear." I love this because I feel Patrick's loving light surrounding me like a protective force field and I know I will be okay.

He is within us, next to us, and all around us.

He is as close as he ever was.

"We will wear this veil of sadness for the rest of our lives and we will learn how to wear it the best we can because it represents immeasurable love."

CHAPTER THIRTEEN

ENDLESSLY LOVING YOU

As time moves on, I am learning how to live with my pain. It is always with me. I now know that grief is relentless. It is exhausting and yet there is also inspiration and beauty in its gifts. It requires perseverance, patience, self-love, self-compassion, an open heart and mind, and courage. It will test you enormously. It can flatten you, yet it builds resilience. It feels as if you are running a marathon, over and over again. Grief is confronting and the sensations that come with it are very uncomfortable. Sometimes you may feel as if you are crawling out of your skin. That's because you are, you are shedding layers, you are evolving. When we lose someone we love, we are called to become a new version of ourselves. That's what loss does. We are no longer who we were; a part of us has died too. I welcome my new self and all of life's teachings before me.

Grief is not something that can be solved, like a puzzle. Healing is not linear. From my experience, I have observed several stages: first, we survive, then we absorb, then we process, then we accept, and then we rise. Healing can start in any of these stages. While my wounds feel as if they will never fully heal, I know that the scars they leave are symbols of great love. With each day that passes, the missing gets harder. Some days the sadness takes a tight grip on me, and other days, the grasp loosens a little, and the intensity softens.

It's during these moments that I can breathe more deeply, and I feel hopeful. This softening is possible for you too.

There is no right or wrong way to grieve. I certainly don't have all the answers, but I hope I have given you a place to start with your own journey. Coping with loss looks and feels different for everyone. The four of us have individually and collectively managed to draw on a deep inner strength plus Patrick has given us the loving guidance we have needed to be able to function for ourselves and as a family. I truly feel as if he always has our backs. Don't be afraid to ask your departed loved one for support. Talk to them and ask them to help you. They want to help you. They really want you to be okay and to find a way to live side by side with your grief.

Many people have said to me, "I can only imagine your pain." It's hard to describe, but it feels as if a part of me was ripped away with him. Something is now missing because it is. It's a pain that reaches right to the very core of my bones, my cells, the very depths of me. I know Chris, the girls, and I are not alone. There have been many parents and siblings who have walked this path before us, and, sadly, there will be many who will take this journey after us.

I have accepted our fate that in this life, our cross to bear, has been losing our beloved first-born child and brother, our dearest Patrick. This is a most unwanted reality, but I know that no matter how much I bargain, plea, or beg (all of which I have done), this is my family's story. We are now members of a club we never chose to join. We will continue on with grace and courage for ourselves and for Patrick. This acceptance of where we are at brings a sense of peace because I have stopped resisting what is. Resistance to reality creates suffering, and if you have lost, you are already suffering enough. This new reality is a part of us now and we give it a place to be with us. I think that's an essential part of starting to recover from loss, accepting your situation, and weaving it into the fabric of your life. If you have experienced loss, I encourage you to be open to the possibility of acceptance, but only when you are ready. This definitely does not mean that I will ever think it's right or okay that Patrick was taken from us because it's not and it never will be. It will never feel fair for any of us who have loved him to have lost him.

We are left wanting more; more time, more love, and more memories. We mourn the physical loss of Patrick and we also mourn the life we had with him before he died that no longer exists. We have to somehow let go of our old life that evaporated in a split second and learn how to live in the new one. I will never forget the feeling of horror that overwhelmed me when I realized that our previous life with Patrick was gone.

Cruel circumstance has steered us onto another path where Patrick is still very much with us. While we have lost him in the physical, we now have him in the spiritual. I choose to pour my love for him into what we still have, remembering that it's all about our love.

I am comforted knowing that Patrick is in a glorious place that is filled with love, peace, beauty, compassion, freedom, expansiveness, and joy, a place that does not know hardship, fear, or pain. A whole new existence has opened up to him, more than we can ever comprehend as humans on earth. When we transition to the afterlife, we are released from all the burdens of life. Patrick is doing important work. He is watching over all of us with great love and care. He's perfect for his new role and he's going to be busy because many people have told me they are praying and talking to him. I smile when I imagine him welcoming new arrivals to heaven, showing them the way; I know he's great at that. Through his death, he is our teacher. We have his lessons as our gifts.

I rejoice in the strong and beautiful spiritual connection I have with Patrick, and I know for sure that our love is eternal. I have had to accept that this energetic connection is enough. I don't say this from an ungrateful perspective; I say it from a place of understanding that there is nothing I can do to bring him back physically. I wish with every part of me that I could, but I have had to surrender my human need for the physical and be content with all that is possible in the spiritual, for which I am immensely thankful. Through the commitment that Patrick and I made to each other the day after he died, when we joined our hearts on a spiritual level, I have come to realize that there is much more to life than what we can see and touch. Life does not end with death. Immortality teaches us to be open to more. Connection with your loved ones who have passed is possible if you are willing to look through another lens.

I have learned that pain has beauty. Pain changes us. It can transform us. We need to let it do its work. Each challenging life experience is our teacher. When you lose someone who you love with your whole being, that type of pain can't be fixed. Others cannot fix it for you, nor should they assume that unattainable expectation. I have come to realize that as much as I want to, I can't spare Chris or our girls their pain. It's my nature to nurture, but all the nurturing in the world isn't going to take their anguish away. What I can do is love them, listen to them, be available to them, model healing for them, validate them, and walk beside them, unconditionally. There is no magic wand to ease the burden of grief. When your world collapses from loss, you just want one thing; to be given back what was taken away from you.

Losing our son and brother has changed us. We are different people from who we were before the evening of June 27, 2019. I like to think that we have emerged from this with a greater understanding of the challenges we face as humans. Our tragedy has gifted that lesson to us.

If you are trying to navigate your way through grief, I hope I have somehow lightened your heavy load. I hope you believe you can do this. I hope you feel less alone in your loss. Maybe you've had a breakthrough that will guide you forward in your days to come. Keep going. You are braver than you think; even in the most difficult moments, you are getting stronger. Take the messages that Patrick and I have shared about love, the gifts, self-care, purpose, and the lessons. Try some of our suggestions or find variations that work best for you. Listen to your inner knowing and let it be your guide.

To my fellow mothers who have lost a child or children, I see you. I feel the gaping hole in your hearts. It's said that the death of a child is one of the most traumatic losses. Here we are, surviving the unthinkable. It's soul-crushing. I believe a mother's love is one of the greatest forces that exists. This love takes on a whole other dimension when we continue to mother our child, who we can no longer hold or touch. Keep mothering them. We can still nurture their spirits. It feels different, but the foundation of everlasting love is always the same. Our children are within us. We feel them in our bones, our blood, and our hearts. We carry them and they carry us.

While the title of this memoir is, *The Gifts from Losing You*, we have not lost Patrick. He is still very much with us and always will be, just in a different form. Death is not goodbye. It is an invitation to open your heart and mind and connect to the more profound wisdom of life. Writing this book has helped me live with my grief and heartbreak. I wish more than anything that I don't have the reason I have to write it, but I am grateful for its therapeutic bene-fits. The experience of putting our story into words has been a source of healing for me and I see the ripple effects of my beginning to heal impacting on Chris, Annabelle, and Matilda. A healing for one is a healing for all.

On the particularly hard days when my pain knocks me down, I have noticed if I can shift my mind to a place of calm, then I will also feel some hope. In the ocean, the calm water always sits below the rough waves that throw you around. If you can try to dive un-der the giant waves of your grief, you may just find the calmer waters; even if it's only for small moments at a time, you may find some relief. This is achieved by using your self-care tools. When you do things that nourish you, soothe you and bring you joy (joy can be a hard one to find when you are grieving, but it is there if you can allow yourself to feel it again), you give yourself the chance to experience healing.

Our lives will always be painted with a stroke of sadness. The struggle is real. We will carry its weight just as Patrick carries us. While this is a part of our life now, we acknowledge that it doesn't have to be all of it. Our pain does not have to permeate every part of our world; there can still be happiness in other areas. Not everything has to be broken.

Grief is complex and ever-changing. It teaches us so much. It's a normal process we must go through when we lose someone we love.

Our experience has shown us deep despair, but it has also given us beautiful gifts. These can co-exist if we allow them to. The gifts that have come to us through our loss have helped us begin to heal.

Our shadow of grief will follow us forever, but we know that every shadow has light behind it. We will try to see the light.

We have learned that we can find meaning in life while living with tragedy. What comes next can still be worthwhile.

When we feel so deeply sad that our future family members won't get the chance to meet Patrick in person, we remind ourselves that we are the bridge that connects him to them. We will speak his name, tell stories about him, show photos, and emulate his lessons. He will always have a very prominent place in their lives and hearts.

We continue on with stunning determination and resilience. I say that because I am proud, so very proud of us. I am proud that we survived this. I am proud that we stay strong together. I am proud that we love, understand, and respect one another, and the different ways that we live with our grief. I know Patrick is proud of us too. Most of all, we are beyond proud to be Patrick's parents and little sisters. We will always be the five of us. Our bond is unbreakable.

We honor our story and all the moments of desperation and sorrow that we have experienced. We will wear this veil of sadness for the rest of our lives and we will learn how to wear it the best we can because it represents immeasurable love. We don't want to have to live without Patrick in the physical, but we must. When missing him brings us to our knees, we will remind ourselves to come back to our love for him and our close family of five. Our love for him will always be more powerful than our pain. We love him so very much.

Patrick showed us that in the end, all that truly matters are our relationships and the people we share our life with. The experiences we have together, the connections we make, the love we feel and give, and the imprints we leave on one another's hearts.

As Chris so eloquently said at Patrick's funeral:

"Patrick's core relationships and loves of his life were with his family.
We're incredibly thankful for his 19 years.
We loved him fiercely and will continue to do so."

My final words here are for our darling Patrick:

Patrick,
Thank you for helping me write our family's love story.
I hope I've made you proud.
We miss you endlessly.
We will spend the rest of our days honoring you until we are to-
gether again.
You are our everything.
Thank you for choosing us.
We love you and will always love you more than any words can ever
say.

ACKNOWLEDGMENTS

I have dreamed of holding this book in my hands so many times, and now it's here. I poured every ounce of myself into these pages. My intention was to share our experience with you from the most authentic and honest place. There were times I felt extremely challenged, but I never doubted that I would finish. The writing experience took me through a full range of emotions: love, comfort, exhaustion, frustration, devastation, gratitude, and pride. It took exactly a year from start to finish.

I have many people to thank.

To Patrick, we did this together. Thank you for giving me the words. I love you to a depth that is beyond description. Endless love. My heart aches for you every minute of every day.

To Chris, Annabelle, and Matilda, we are strong, we are resilient, and we are courageous. We will always stay fierce in our love for one another and our love for Patrick. Thank you for your patience and unending encouragement. You never questioned the countless hours that I needed to spend working on this book. You gave me the space and you cheered me on. I did this for the five of us. I love you so much.

To Jos Budge, my soul sister and the editor of this book. When I decided to write, I knew I needed you by my side. Thank you for all of the hours you lovingly devoted, for your effortless way with words, your deep knowledge of book writing, your sensitivity, your attention to detail, and your empathy. Your personal experience with grief infused an exquisite wisdom into this memoir. We were always on the same page with how we wanted the words to sound and feel, and I am so grateful to you.

To Pete White, my friend and the creator of this stunning book cover. You sent me a text about Patrick and I immediately knew you were the one to design the cover. You understood grief and your words really spoke to me. We talked about how I wanted the book to look and feel, and you listened. I fell in love with your design the second I saw it. It is so captivating and layered with beauty and meaning. It has depth, movement, and texture. It is pure art. Thank you for everything.

You shared these words with me about your inspiration and vision: "The cover image immediately spoke to me the moment I saw it. It's a beautiful image in its own right, but I saw the idea of moving through a challenging path with twists and turns and multiple facets to the journey while offering a glimpse of radiating light or hope as you move through it. The color relates to Patrick's favorite hue, albeit a stronger and richer version, and it reflects the color of the crown chakra, the meeting point between the physical body and the universe, and the idea of enlightenment, spirituality, and understanding. I see a relationship to the womb and the idea of rebirth, a rebirth for Patrick as he moves from this physical plane to the next, and a rebirth for you and the family as you come to a new place in your relationship with him beyond our physical existence. It also represents the heart being ripped open, and the light that penetrates even the darkest experiences of our human existence." bywhite.com

To Dorothy Holtermann and Robert Louis Henry, thank you for helping me bring this book to life. I appreciate your mentoring, expertise, dedication, and support in formatting, publishing, and marketing my book. The technical side of self-publishing a book felt

daunting; however, the two of you made this process a seamless collaboration. I've thoroughly enjoyed working with you both.
Dorothy: birthabook.com
Robert: RightHandPublishing.com

To our family, this book is also for you. We know losing Patrick has had a profound effect on you all, and we feel your pain across the ocean from Cleveland to Australia. We never expected to find ourselves in this heartbreaking reality, but we will stay strong together. We love you.

To my Angels, I'd be lost without you.

To Tim Mueller, thank you for your faith in Patrick from the minute you met him. Chris and I really appreciated you taking him under your wing. With you as his mentor and friend, we knew he would have had incredible opportunities to grow both professionally and personally.

To our friends, Patrick's friends, and our communities both in the United States and Australia, you have carried us from the very beginning. You have traveled this road with us, and we are boundlessly blessed to have received your love and care. Thank you for welcoming Patrick into your lives; he saw many of you as family.

Andrea Vecchio's TED Talk: andreavecchio.com

Back cover photography
Sara: shannonahlstrandphoto.com
Patrick: ripchostudio.com

To those who loved Patrick, thank you for being a meaningful part of his 19 years.

ABOUT THE AUTHOR

Sara is a wellness entrepreneur. Her passion for health began during her decade-long career in nursing. She went on to study with the Institute for Integrative Nutrition to become certified as a holistic health coach. Sara's genuine empathy and ability to tune into her clients' unique needs allows her to facilitate the best possible outcomes for those seeking her expertise and guidance.

Sara has given many presentations and workshops and has co-hosted wellness retreats. She has also led group coaching programs. She sees clients one-on-one in her private practice.

With a special interest in women's health, she bases her teachings on the fundamental principles of unconditional self-love, self-compassion, and self-acceptance. She wholeheartedly believes that they are the anchors for finding peace within.

Sara takes an intuitive approach to nutrition, movement, and life. She helps her clients discover their own path to a healthier, happier, and more connected way of living. She goes deeper to uncover the root cause of their health concerns, with an understanding that the mind, body, and spirit are one.

Sara is originally from Melbourne, Australia and currently lives in Cleveland, USA with her husband Chris and daughters, Annabelle and Matilda. Her son Patrick passed away in an accident in 2019, and *The Gifts From Losing You* is a poignant account of their first year grieving his passing.

saragreenhealthcoach.com
Instagram: @saragreenhealthcoach
Facebook.com/saragreenhealthcoach
YouTube Channel: Sara Green Health Coach

Made in the USA
Monee, IL
01 February 2021